THE BEOWULF TRILOGY

THE BEOWULF TRILOGY

BEOWULF, BEYOND BEOWULF, AND YRFA'S TALE

Christopher L. Webber

INTEGRATED MEDIA
NEW YORK

All rights reserved, including without limitation the right to reproduce this book or any portion thereof in any form or by any means, whether electronic or mechanical, now known or hereinafter invented, without the express written permission of the publisher.

These are works of fiction. Names, characters, places, events, and incidents either are the product of the author's imagination or are used fictitiously. Any resemblance to actual persons, living or dead, businesses, companies, events, or locales is entirely coincidental.

Copyright © 2022 by Christopher Webber

ISBN: 978-1-5040-8320-1

This edition published in 2023 by Open Road Integrated Media, Inc.
180 Maiden Lane
New York, NY 10038
www.openroadmedia.com

INTRODUCTION

THE STORY

Beowulf is one of those classic texts that help us understand the human condition. Set in a time as remote from ours as we can imagine, it shows us men and women who have attempted to impose an order, a civilization, on their lives, and who find it disrupted again and again, as all human beings do, by forces of chaos both external to themselves and within. The unknown poet who composed this saga at least 1200 years ago and probably more, did, however, impose his own order on those chaotic events and, as well, on the language with which he tells his story.

The strange thing is that, although the poem ends with forebodings of disaster to come and although there are other foreshadowings throughout the poem, no one in all the centuries since ever seems to have written a sequel. *Beyond Beowulf* was written to supply that need and answer the inevitable question: What happened next? This second poem, we might say, is to *Beowulf* as the *Odyssey* is to the *Iliad*: the journey that takes place when the battle is over. It is filled with references back to *Beowulf* itself but takes its general direction from historical evidence of migration from Scandinavia to the British Isles.

When *Beyond Beowulf* was published, people began asking playfully whether there would now be a sequel to the sequel. That seemed unnecessary; Wiglaf, the central figure, had been duly buried and there was no obvious successor nor any remaining reason to ask, "What happened next?" It is, however, a time-honored practice to retell a story from another perspective—as, for example, John Gardner did in looking at Beowulf's story from the point of view of the monster, Grendel.[1] Logically, therefore, one might also ask, What would this saga of heroes and dragons and monsters look like from a woman's point of view?

As it happened, Wiglaf's wife had been briefly introduced in *Beyond Beowulf*, doing what wives did in Beowulf's day: passing the cups at the parties. What thoughts went through her mind when her husband set off to help Beowulf kill the dragon or when he took leadership in the project of relocating their tribe or as she tried to care for children in the midst of turmoil? Those questions seemed worth exploring and the answer has now been written as *Yrfa's Tale* which, with a new translation of *Beowulf* in the same meter, completes *The Beowulf Trilogy*. Yrfa is not, of course, simply "a woman" or a "typical woman" since there is no such thing. She is a human being living out her life within the particular parameters of a particular age and with the concerns of a wife and mother rather than those of a warrior but nevertheless acting and reacting only as herself, a unique individual living our her life in her own particular way. There is no more intention to suggest that all women are like Yrfa than to suggest that all men are like Wiglaf.

Telling Yrfa's story, as it turned out, could not be a simple retelling of *Beyond Beowulf* but involved a broader focus, telling of Yrfa's life before the dragon came and before her marriage at one end and after Wiglaf's death on the other. Yrfa, it turned out, was more than Wiglaf's wife; she was a person in her own right and had her own tale to tell.

End notes that point up some of the connections between *Beowulf* and the stories of Wiglaf and Yrfa are indicated with an

---

[1] Gardner, John, *Grendel*. New York, Knopf, 1971.

INTRODUCTION

asterisk at the beginning of a line and found by line number in the closing pages. The asterisks also indicate sources and other references.

In constructing these narratives, I have referred as often as possible to *Beowulf* itself but also relied on standard commentaries and histories. I have also turned often to studies of the burials found in England at Sutton Hoo for information about the period and, especially, about the burials that took place there. It does seem that those burials were made by people who had much in common with the people of the *Beowulf* narrative and that Beowulf's people might, indeed, have come to East Anglia at about this time. The double monastery at Whitby, presided over by the Abbess Hilda, with the neighboring communities at Wearmouth and Jarrow, is, of course, well documented. So the narrative I have constructed may be fiction, but many of the places visited are well known while the critical events are historically possible and, in broad terms, even probable.

Although this Trilogy includes three related stories, it should be remembered that the first is by an unknown author who lived well over a thousand years ago while the other two have been written recently. The Beowulf poet assumes a knowledge of and interest in matters that even scholars familiar with the time are not always able to explain. The "Finnsburg Episode" (1068–1159), discussed in an end note, is just one place where a modern reader is entitled to feel a bit lost. The two modern poems, on the other hand, are relatively free of such material since no modern author is much more familiar with the era than anyone else today. Contemporary readers, therefore, might find it easier to begin with *Beyond Beowulf* and *Yrfa's Tale* rather than *Beowulf.*

THE POETRY

The poetry of Anglo-Saxon England was written (as most of to-

INTRODUCTION

day's poetry is not) for the ear, to be read aloud or, probably, sung with instrumental accompaniment. Most of the various translations that have been made, however, try to catch the meaning more than the music. Or, if they do try to make the poetry sing, still very few do it while giving adequate emphasis to the quality that made it sing in its own day, and that is alliteration. We are familiar with poetry that rhymes and poetry that has a rhythmic stress pattern, but hardly anyone writes alliterative poetry anymore. But why not? Alliteration is still important to us, perhaps more important than we realize. We use it often for emphasis: we promise "to have and to hold," we speak of "time and tide," when frustrated we "rant and rave." Alliteration still adds force to our speech. The translations of *Beowulf* that pay no attention to the alliterative poetry of the original, would seem to be ignoring the very quality that has made the poem an enduring classic.

Specifically, *Beowulf* is composed of lines with four stresses of which two must begin with the same consonant (or consonants with the same sound, as *king, cut,* and *quick,* or *know* and *now*) or with any vowel. The line is divided into two segments, often indicated by an asterisk or similar mark. The first stress of the second half line is the key syllable and at least one other syllable (but not the last stress) must alliterate with it.

Ideally a sequel to *Beowulf* would use the same pattern. That I have not done so is a result of my feeling that, however well that pattern may have fit Old English, it fits much less well with the modern form of the language. Old English and Modern English, though they have many words and constructions in common, are very different languages. Critics speak of *Beowulf* as the first great poem in any modern European language, but no modern English-speaker can read *Beowulf* in the original without a great deal of help. Perhaps most significant for anyone attempting to write a sequel to *Beowulf,* the Anglo-Saxon of *Beowulf* is a polysyllabic language and modern English is much more monosyllabic. The "four-letter Anglo-Saxon words" that we refer to so often were not characteristic of the *Beowulf* poet's Anglo-Saxon. He uses only five four-letter words in the first ten lines, while one standard translation into modern English (that of Howell D. Chickering, Jr.) uses thirteen. The *Beowulf* poet, employing a language filled with polysyllabic words (and adding to the problem by using and inventing compound words in almost every line), uses far fewer words per line[2]. At least sixty percent of the lines in *Beowulf* have five words or fewer, while almost eighty percent of the lines in Chickering's excellent translation have seven words or more. No one can capture the meaning and poetry of *Beowulf* in modern English without using more words and, almost inevitably, a longer, looser line. Therefore the *Beowulf* poet could let alliteration dominate the sound pattern with two or three alliterated words or stressed syllables per line. In a modern translation that settles for two or three alliterated stresses in a longer line, the alliteration will play a much less dominant role.

It is worth noting that alliteration was still a dominant pattern in fourteenth century English poetry even though Middle English was more similar to modern English: words were shorter and the lines necessarily longer. William Langland, therefore, in the great epic of that century, *Piers Plowman*, uses a longer line with at least three alliterated stressed syllables per line[3]: "On a May morning on a Malvern hillside ... Charity without chastity shall be chained in hell ... What is readiest to ripen rots soonest."

In constructing a sequel to *Beowulf*, therefore, I have not only followed the example of Langland in using at least three alliterated stresses per line but have also attempted to give the alliteration increased prominence by fitting it within the classic En-

---

2 See Bibliography
3 Line 799 uses only two words, "heardhicgende hildemecgas," and four word lines are common.

glish iambic pentameter (a ten syllable line with the even syllables stressed), so that stress patterns are clear and stressed syllables prominent. Clearly this is not exactly the pattern of the *Beowulf* poet but it is, I believe, a pattern that preserves the feel of the original while, at the same time, providing a format that fits modern English comfortably.

FURTHER NOTES ABOUT ALLITERATION

The experts agree that *Beowulf* is written in lines with four stresses and that the third stress (the first stress of the second half of the line) is the key. One stressed syllable in the first half-line must alliterate with that key stress; the second stressed syllable in the first half-line may also alliterate but the second stressed syllable in the second half-line must not.[4] In *Beowulf*, the stressed syllable is almost always the first syllable of a word since that is where the stress normally falls in Old English. In modern English, on the other hand, the accented syllable of a word is often the second syllable or even the third. It is noticeable that modern translations of *Beowulf* often alliterate on the first letter of a word even when it is not the accented syllable. In effect, they are writing for the eye while the *Beowulf* poet was writing for the ear. *Beyond Beowulf* (the title itself is an example of alliteration for the eye more than the ear) alliterates on stressed syllables whether they are the first, second, or third syllable of a word. The eye may not see this as easily, but the alliteration will become clear when the line is read aloud.

Old English alliteration, it should be noted, treats all vowels as the same so that "It is my own first effort as an usher" would be considered an example of alliteration. The *Beowulf* poet also treats words be-

---

[4] Cf. Alexander, Michael, *Beowulf*, pp. xxv-xxvi, and *Beowulf: A Verse Translation*, pp. 47–48 and Chickering, Howell D. Jr., *Beowulf: A Dual Language Edition*, p. 33.

ginning with "sw" as different from words beginning with "s" alone. I have not continued that distinction, but I have tried to alliterate sounds rather than letters, so "know" and "nine" alliterate as do "one" and "wonder;" "wolf," on the other hand, does not alliterate with "where," nor "ten" with "then," but "who" alliterates with "how." For the same reason, I have not used "one" as an alliterated vowel, but I have felt free to alliterate "s" words whether they are "sw" or "sh."

I should also note that I have not attempted to set the alliteration around the third stressed syllable of the line. I have been concerned not to use so strict a pattern that the alliteration would become too regular and dominating. I have been satisfied if three stressed words (or syllables) alliterate wherever they fall in the line.

THE BEOWULF TRILOGY

BEOWULF

An Alliterative Version in Iambic Pentameter

*5 Attend!
    We Danish people did in former days
    Hear tales they told of how our tribal king
    Had garnered glory, gained great victories;
*   How Scyld, the son of Scef, had strength to seize
    Their drinking benches battling hostile bands.
    Foes feared the foundling who in former days,
    Without a home, and outcast, orphaned, yet
    Had grown to gain great glory, glowing fame,
    Until in every land in all the earth
10   To which the white-flecked ocean whale-roads ran,
    They trembled. Tribal kings with tribute came
    To give Scyld glory; long and good his reign.

    When time went by a boy was born, his heir,
    Who, young in years, was yet a gift of God
    And solace for his subjects, suffering
    So long without a leader. Life's high Lord,
    Who grants all glory, gave him honor great;
    The fame that Beow found reached far and wide;
    And so Scyld's son's fame spread throughout the north.
20   A prince should practice virtue properly
    And give men favors from his father's house
    To garner future help by granting gifts
    Lest foes should find him left alone by friends
    In his old age, without strong arms to help.
    Through deeds well done our destinies are shaped.

Note: Asterisks indicate footnotes which are provided at the end of the text by line number.

Scyld died upon his destined day and went
To greet the God of glory throned above;
They bore his body slowly to the beach;
The leader loved by all, who reigned so long,
30   Was carried by his comrades carefully
To waves and water as he wished to be.

A brightly painted boat rode in the bay,
And waited, ice-clad, eager to sail out;
With loving care they laid in it the lord
Who gave them gold; within the good ship's galley,
They mounded by the mast a mighty hoard,
A fortune fine and fair from far-off lands.
Such noble gifts I never knew before,
With all that armor and array of jewelry,
40   Bright blades and battle axes, body armor,
A gleaming treasure trove to take with him
In floating far away upon the flood.

*   No less they lavished on him, laid out there,
Than others offered him in infancy,
45   Sent forth so friendless on the foaming waves.
They hoisted high above their heads a flag
That shone and shimmered in the sun's bright rays;
In grief they gave him to an ocean grave
So currents cold and waves could carry him
50   While mortals mourned the hero in their minds;
But no one, noble though they be, can know
What human hands have harvested that hoard.

The king who next held court within that castle,
Was Beow; he was loved, and long he led
The folk; his fame grew when his father died
And went forth from this world. It was his son,
The high king, Healfdene, hardened warrior, next
Who led the loyal Scyldings all his life.
Then Healfdene had in his turn children too;
He fathered four, three fearless warriors,
Named Hergar, Hrothgar, Halga called the good,
And Yrs, his only daughter, afterward
The King of Sweden's consort and his queen.
Then Hrothgar held the high throne in his turn.

So great the glory was he gained in war
That others eagerly went after him,
A company of comrades. Then it came
Into his mind to make a mighty hall,
To have a house to hold his warriors,
One higher than those heard of heretofore,
A mead-hall where he might allot to men
The gifts that God on high had given him;
His captives' lands and lives alone he kept.
The word then went throughout the world to find
In every kingdom craftsmen; and they came
To furnish this great folk-hall, finish it,
And soon it stood there, such was Hrothgar's might,
A hall named "Heorot" with gables high.
Such was the power Hrothgar's word could wield;
He boasted of the bounty brought to share
And treasure at his table. Towering high,

    The wooden arches waited wars to come
*   And brightly burning blazes, but not yet
    Was there a reason to arouse that wrath,
    The bitterness of blood-feud and the battle.

    But deep in darkest woods a monster dwelt,
    A terror, torn and troubled by the sounds
    Of harps and happiness from Heorot;
    He dwelt in darkness, daily hearing there
90   The sounds of music, sweetest songs of bards
    Rehearsing how the human race arose.
    They told the tale of how in former times
*   The Lord at first had formed the earth's fair fields
    And set the sun and moon in space above
    And let those lights illuminate the land
    And all the areas of earth adorned
    And garbed with grass, with green leaves, growing flowers,
    And shaped each species that would share this wealth.

    So thus the carefree warriors went their way,
100   Relaxed in easy living till at last
    Rose up from hell, an evil enemy
    Named Grendel; grim and ghost-like was this foe
    Whose fame reached far across the distant fens,
    A wasteland wanderer, a woeful thing,
    Who made his home with monsters on the moors,
    A creature cursed by God and cast away
*   Because of that first crime which Cain had done.
    That rude act roused the Ruler to revenge;
    He drove the doer of the deed away

110 Because he killed his kin in cruel rage.
The origin of Unthings is in that,
Of ogres, elves, and other monsters too,
And giants who rejoiced to joust with God
So long, at last the Lord rewarded them.

This fiend came forward at the fall of night
In hope and hastened up to Heorot
Where Ring-Danes rested after revelry.
All stretched in sleep he saw them lying there,
The soldiers sleeping after supper-time,
120 Not dreaming of their doom. The dreadful foe,
A greedy guest, agog with gluttony
And filled with fury, from the wooden floor
Then seized some thirty soldiers suddenly
And hauled them homeward for his horrid feast,
Their bodies dripping blood behind his back.

When darkness ended and the daylight dawned,
The monster's might was manifest to all;
The feast was followed then by furious tears.
They mourned the men who died; the mighty chief,
130 Beloved leader, grieving for the lost,
Sat still in silence, suffering his loss,
And further when the footprints of the foe
Were found. But soon the strife became too strong,
Too long and loathsome; in a little while
The ruthless raider ravaged them again;
He murdered more and did not mourn at all
For he was fixed on feuds and felony.

And it was easy then to see how others
Now sought their rest in regions hard to reach,
140   Abiding in their beds in far abodes,
For omens now were obvious to all
Of how the hall-lord hated them. Their health
Was found in fleeing further from the foe.
So Grendel ruled and raged against the right,
Alone against them all, he emptied out
The grand house for a great while like a grave.

For twelve long winters' time these troubles came
And high-king Hrothgar had this endless woe.
The tale was told to tribes both near and far,
150   And minstrels' sad songs made them known to mortals.
So Grendel's great hate waged again a war
Of hate and havoc throughout Hrothgar's realm,
And cruel carnage countless seasons long,
An endless outrage without any hope
For all those in the army of the Danes.
He would not put off plundering for pay,
Nor had a hero any hope at all
Of gaining golden gifts from grisly hands.

But meantime then the monster made the hall
160   His own, and lurked alone through long, dark nights.
Out on the moors he moved through silent mists,
A dark and deadly shadow doing harm
To all he ambushed, eating old and young,
Where ghosts may go and glide beyond our sight.

All these offensive acts the foe performed
And did deeds dark and dreadful to be heard,
While Heorot with its hoard became his home.
No gifts were given him, nor could he gain
Emoluments nor know the Maker's mind.
170   Such sorrow did the Scyldings' sovereign know,
Above his mind's ability to bear.
His comrades came and pondered carefully
What brave and bold men might find best to do
Against this enemy and all his onslaughts.
*   It seemed to some that they should sacrifice
And offer idols gifts with ancient prayers
For safety from the Slayer of their souls
And plead their plight as once their practice was.
Their heathen hopes had fixed their thoughts on hell;
180   No tongue had told them of the true Creator
Nor had they heard of how Almighty God
Will weigh our worth nor yet how we should pray
To God, not yet how great their grief who go
Through searing fear and see their soul shoved down
In fire unfathomed and can find no hope
When death's day comes. Far different is the doom
Of all who after death can ask for grace,
And find sure favor in their Father's arms.

Such was the sorrow which King Healfdene's son
190   Endured without an end, nor were there any
Whose wisdom worked to turn this woe away;
Too great the grief that gripped the people's heart
Through all the evil of that envious ghost.

* But distant from these deeds, a doughty Geat,
A good man, got the news of Grendel's deeds;
Of all the human heroes heard of then
In all the earth and any land the best,
The strongest, sturdiest; he straightway sought
A well-made rider of the waves. He willed
200 To seek a sovereign where the swans' roads run,
A noble chieftain needing new support.
That course no captain clear of sight condemned;
They did not dare, though he was dear to them,
But studied omens and then urged him on.

This warrior willed to take away with him
The best and bravest in their boundaries;
Fifteen he found who felt no fear of conflict;
This man with sea-craft skills marched to the shore.

Then time went by, and turning with the tide,
210 The ship sailed smoothly under seaside cliffs.
With eagerness the armed men entered in
As sea-streams swept against the sand. The men
Had brought bright armor to the broad-beamed boat,
Their worthy war-gear; then the warriors
Were one in willing to be on their way
And shoved their ship out from the Geatish shore.

They went across the water blown by winds,
The carved prow cutting through the cold gray waves
Till finally, floating like a bird in flight,
220 At dawn the second day the Danish coast

Was seen, the land for which the sailors sought,
With steep crags and with sea-cliffs shining bright
And hills and headlands high, their journey's end.
So then the sailors and the sturdy soldiers
With armor clanging climbed down from their craft
And made it fast by means of mooring lines.
Then, braced for battle, mail shirts gleaming bright
They bowed to God above who brought them safe
Across the waves. The watchman from the wall,
230 Who kept the coastline carefully in view,
Then saw the soldiers with the gleaming shields
They carried and the question came to him,
Now who are these and how have they come here?
So Hrothgar's servant hurried on his horse
Down to the shore and fiercely shook his spear
And said to those who sailed across the sea,
"We must beware of men who wear such war-gear
And come to Denmark clad in coats of mail
In ships that have been sailed across the sea
240 And come now to our coast with their long keels.
As sentry I have stood beside the sea
Alert for ever lest some foe at last
Should find us with their fleets and forage here.
But never until now has this been known:
Appearing publicly without a passport,
Or king's consent to come. Nor can I say
That I have seen a soldier of more size
Than this; he seems to be no sort of servant,
This warrior with his weapons proved in war
250 Unless his looks belie his character.

Now I must know your nation right away
Before your feet go further on our land
As spies who come to seek and scout our shores,
Sea-faring foreigners who come from far;
And let me leave one last idea with you:
That it will be the best if you obey
And answer all I ask of you at once."

Immediately the eldest of them answered,
The leader of the crew unlocked his lips
And said, "We spring from noble stock, of Geats,
And have King Hygelac to share our hearth;
My father was a famous fighting man
Well known to folk before me, near and far,
Who weathered many winters and then went
To rest in ripe old age, yet readily
Recalled by wise men widely through the world.
We made our way here with a worthy plan
And look now for your leader and your lord,
So give us guidance to your Guardian, please;
We mean our mission for the monarch here
Nor shall we shrink from sharing our intent
Now we are here, for you are well aware,
I think, how true the tales are we were told
Of how some sort of foe has stalked your soil,
A deadly demon in the dark of night
Who revels in his wrath, in death and ruin,
In murder and in mayhem. If I may
Have counsel with your king, I come to offer
A way his wealth of wisdom and of years

280	Might down this demon if it can be done
	And ills and agony be overcome
	And care's convulsions can be cooled by time,
	Or else he ever after must endure
	More suffering and sorrow while still stands
	The best of houses, Hrothgar's feasting hall.

	The sentry said then, sitting on his horse,
	An able officer who said, "Yes, all
*	With wits and shield are surely well aware
	How different deeds and words are, doubtlessly.
290	You say these soldiers serve the Scylding's lord;
	Then walk on with your weapons and your armor;
	I, too, will go to guide and give command;
	Meanwhile my kin will keep your craft secure,
	Protect your pine-tarred prow upon the sand
	Against all enemies and honor it
	Till on the open ocean once again,
	It bears you back, good friends, to your abode,
	The curved prow carrying your comrades home,
*	The warriors of the Wederas God wills
300	To bring unscathed through all the savage strife."

So then they followed from the floating ship,
The broad-beamed boat left anchored in the bay,
Restrained by ropes. The shining shapes of boars
Were gleaming golden on their helmet guards,
The fierce, fire-hardened face-masks for defense.
With war-lust wakened, on the warriors went
Till finally they found themselves before

        The gabled glory of the gold-decked hall,
        The handsomest of halls beneath the heavens
310   Or land below the sun, where lived Lord Hrothgar;
        Its splendor shone through sundry lands.
        The sentry showed them to the shining palace,
        The home of heroes, lying straight ahead.
        The warrior showed the way to walk to it,
        Then, speaking from his steed, he said,
        "Now I must leave; the Lord of every land,
        Almighty God, in mercy make you all
        Stay safe while on your sojourn here. I shall
        Now go to guard the coast against the foe."

320   Quite straight and paved with stone, the street now led
        The warriors on their way. With war-gear bright
        And hardened, hand-linked, heavy iron rings
        That sang and shimmered as the soldiers strode
        In fearsome fighting gear before the hall
        Until they set their shields down with a sigh
        And braced bright bosses on the buildings side
        And bent in battle-dress to sit on benches.
        Their mail-coats clanged like those of conquerors;
        Their seamen's spears they stacked against the wall,
330   Well-trimmed with ash and tipped in gray; a troop
        Of warriors with their weapons. Then a guard
        Came out to ask the men their origins;
        And where they got those great shields trimmed in gold,
        So many mail-coats, helmet masks, and all
        Those stacks of spears? He said he served as aide
        To Hrothgar and he had not heretofore

Observed so strong and bold a set of strangers,
And therefore thought they thronged there in good will,
And not as exiles, as they asked for Hrothgar.

340   With pride the prince of men replied to him,
The well-known warrior of the Wederas'
With well-made war-gear, "We are Hrothgar's men,
And break bread at his board. I, Beowulf,
Have sailed the seas to seek for Healfdene's son
The famous leader, lord of all our lives;
If your great leader grants, we hope to greet him
And say why we have sought your sovereign out."

*   The Wendel's chieftain, Wulfgar, was the one
Who spoke, a man of merit known to many
350   For spirit and for skill: "Now I will speak
To Hrothgar, leader, lord of loyal Scyldings,
Our royal ruler giving rich rewards,
Of your arrival and of all you ask,
And come back quickly carrying the word
Our good king gives to me, and what he grants."

Then turning to the throne to take this word
And going to the great king, gray with years,
Amid his men, he marched toward the throne;
Acquainted with the customs of the court,
360   He faced his friend and found these words to say:
"These fighters faring from a far-off land
Have come across the curling waves to us;
Their chief, the boldest battler, Beowulf

By name, is now, my noble lord and king,
Here asking opportunity to open
Their work and words to you. Weigh well
How you respond, respecting what they seek;
Their weapons seem to be wrought well and worthy;
Their captain has great courage, he who called
370 These soldiers to our shore." The Scyldings shield
And friend, Lord Hrothgar, answered him in haste:

"Ah, yes, some years ago and in his youth,
I knew him, knew his father, too, by name;
The great Lord Hrethel sent back home with him
His daughter; now to Denmark dares to come
His son, a sought-for, steadfast friend to us.
In fact, seafarers who in former days
Had come to carry gifts of coins to us
Have said it seemed to them his strength was more
380 Than thirty other men might ever own,
Such hands he had. The holy God chose him
In mercy, meaning, so I might now hope,
To save us all from such a savage foe
And guard our land from Grendel's rage. Great gifts
Will we be glad to give to this good man
Of courage. Come and call the others in
To meet our men. Now let us move with haste
To welcome warmly all these warriors
To Denmark. Wulfgar, at the door, then did so
390 And went with word of welcome from within:

"My king commands I call you in and say
He knows your nation and your noble birth
And has reviewed your virtue and your valor
And how you hastened here on heaving seas.
We welcome you to wear your war-gear here;
You will be heard by Hrothgar, even helmed,
But spears and shields must stay outside
And wait the outcome of your audience."

The regal man arose; around him warriors
400 Were moving in, a mighty band, but many
Still watched their war-gear at their leader's word.
They gathered, and were guided on together
To Heorot Hall, their chieftain at their head.
So on they went and entered in until
There, by the blazing hearth-fire, Beowulf,
In shining armor shaped by skillful smiths,
Said "Hail, Lord Hrothgar! I am Hygelac's kin,
His son and servant, seeking since my youth
To do great deeds. The dread of Grendel's work
410 Has clearly come across the seas to me.
Some sailors said to us this sumptuous hall,
The best of buildings for a warrior band,
Is idle and unused when evening comes
And heaven's hallowed light is dark and hidden.
The wisest ones I went to for advice,
Most careful counselors, have counseled me,
Lord Hrothgar, high king of the Danes, that here
I seek you. They had seen my tested strength
When bruised and stained with blood I had come back

420   From former battles. I have boldly bound
          And slain the sons of giants. Serpents, too,
          I slew at sea at night and suffered pains
          In righting wrongs the royal Geats endured;
          They asked assistance and I answered them,
          I grappled grimly with these foes; now Grendel
          I seek that so I should myself resolve
          My feud with this foul fiend. And from yourself,
          The Bright-Danes battle-lord, I beg just this,
          O Scyldings' Shelter, shield of warriors,
430   That I might ask for only this one thing:
          That I alone and all my ardent men,
          This crew with whom I came, may cleanse your hall.
          Now, there are those who think this monster is
          So carefree and so cruel he keeps no weapons;
          I also will abstain from any arms
          And scorn to save myself with sword or shield
          So Hygelac will have the happiness
          To hear I dared defy this dreadful demon
          And faced the fiend, as foe against the foe,
440   While trusting truth to triumph over wrong
          When Grendel grapples with my bare hands' grip.
          The monster, I imagine, means to come
          Into the battle building where the brave
          Danes sleep and feast unfearing as before
          On meat of mortal men. Moreover you
          Will never have a need to hide my head
          For blood will surely blanket all my bones,
          If he in conquest carries off my corpse
          And then, alone, unmourning makes his meal

450   Blood-drenched within his den. So do not think
         About my body's burial or mourn;
         Send home to Hygelac, if I here shall die,
         My best-made battle-garment, breast-defense,
*   And well-wrought armor, Weland's workmanship,
         Which Hrethel handed down. Now I am here;
         Let fate affirm us."

                                        "Beowulf, my friend,"
         Said Hrothgar head of Scyldings, "Here you are
         To fight in our defense and favor us.
         Your father fueled a bitter feud before
*460   When he struck Heatholaf with his own hand,
*   A Wulfing warrior. The Weather-Geats,
         Refused him refuge for they feared revenge,
         And so he sought the shelter of the Scyldings,
         The South-Danes' folk, across the surging seas.
         Just then the Danish crown and kingdom came
         To me, a raw youth ruling this rich realm,
         The native home of heroes. Heorogar,
         The son of Healfdene, had just died, and he
         My brother, but a better man, was buried.
470   So first, I settled that sharp feud with fees
*   And to the Wylfings, over water's waves,
         Sent precious treasures; Ecgtheow promised peace.
         I am assailed by sorrow speaking now
         To anyone of Grendel's evil acts,
         The harm his hate has done in this great hall
         By all his onslaughts. You can see with ease
         My war-band now has waned, quite worn away
         By Grendel's grisly deeds. I know that God

Can cut off quickly Grendel's cruel wrath,
480 But fighting men have firmly vowed before
While deep in cups and drunk with beer, to dare
Abiding, sleeping, in their beer-hall beds
To wait the onslaught only armed with swords,
Then daylight dawned and, dreadful to relate,
The morning found the mead-hall marked with blood,
The benches bloodied brutally with gore
And scenes of slaughter. So a smaller band
Of friends and followers is found here now;
But sit and share our feast and speak in time,
490 Great warrior, as you will of what you wish to do."

The band with Beowulf was brought inside
The beer-hall. Bench space for the men was bared
And men of stout heart strode inside to sit;
Their prowess gave them pride. The steward promptly
Came holding in his hands the horn of ale,
And poured the bright brew in the bowls; a bard
In Heorot lifted high his voice and heroes sang
The great and gallant band thus gathered.

* Then up spoke Unferth, he was Ecglaf's son
500 And sat beside the Scylding ruler's feet,
Unbinding blazing words at Beowulf
Whose brave deeds brought him only bitterness
As he would not admit that any other
Might merit more renown in middle-earth
Or gain a greater glory than himself:

  *   "Are you the Beowulf who battled Breca,
And strove in swimming on the salty sea
And who undaunted dared the ocean deep
And left your lives at risk, and yet no logic
510   Of friend or foe could force you to forsake,
Not either of you, such an awesome venture?
You swam together in the salty sea
And in your arms embraced the ocean's streams;
You seized the sea-roads in your stretched out arms,
And slid down billows as the seas swelled up
 In wintery waves. You in the water's hold
Still strove for seven nights till he out-swam you
With greater strength and skill. At sunrise then
The cold sea cast him up on Norway's coast;
520   And so he sought the sweet land of his birth,
  *   Beloved of those who live in Brondings' land,
A stalwart stronghold where, no stranger, he
Had towers and treasure. Truly Breca did,
The son of Beanstan, bear out all his boast.
So I expect an outcome even worse,
Though so far you have seemed to be successful
In grimly grappling with your foe, if Grendel
Should find you near within the next long night."

Then Ecgtheow's offspring, Beowulf, spoke out:
530   "Now listen! Braced with beer, you talk of Breca,
Friend Unferth, free with all your flowery words,
And tell your tales of tests; but I claim truth:
That swimming in the sea my strength was greatest
And I outdid all others and all hardship;

But being merely boys, we bound ourselves
And boasted, both of us, as boys will do,
That all alone, out in the open ocean
We might dare death, and so, indeed, we did.
We held in hand the hard steel of our swords,
540   And thought to save ourselves from spouting whales
When in the sea we swam. Not separate
From him, I floated on the flooding foam,
Nor could he separate himself at sea,
And so we swam together in the salt.
For five long nights we fought the fierce, dark waves
And cold until the currants carried us
Apart beneath the north wind in the night;
The waves were cruel and, war-sharp, worked against us.
The anger of the ocean beasts was roused;
550   My hardened, hand-linked chain-mail helped me then
And armored me against their every onslaught;
My braided battle-dress lay on my breast
Adorned with gold. They dragged me to the depths
And fathoms deep the fierce foe held me fast
In his grim grip. But I was granted grace
To spit the serpent with my sharpened spear;
In battle-clash my blade destroyed the beast;
I hacked the hateful thing with my own hand.

"Still, after that the angry creatures often
560   Were threatening fiercely, so I thrust them through;
My sweet sword stabbed, and surely that was right.
They had no fill nor fun from their planned feast,
Those dwellers in the deep who sought my death,

To bite their banquet on the deep sea-bed,
But, bleeding from my blade, at break of day
Lay limply on the land, the leeward shore.
My sword had sent them off to sleep; since then
The seamen would be safe in all their sojourns
Upon the long waves. Light at last came back,
570 The beacon bright of God, the billows sank,
And I could spy the sea cliffs and the shore
And windswept walls of rock. The fates serve well
The hero who, undoomed, has strength of heart.
My fate was such that with my sword I slew
Some nine sea-monsters. Never such a night
Have I yet heard of here beneath the heavens,
Nor harder fight nor hero harder pressed,
Yet I escaped from all these enemies
As weary as I was. The waves swept me
580 To Lappland, lifted me along the sea-streams
Upon the heaving waves. I have not heard
Them telling tales of terrors you have faced
With blades and blinding fear. But Broca never
Has done such daring deeds—nor did you either
Show courage such as that with shining swords.
But I will breathe no boasts, for your own brothers,
The very closest of your kin, you killed
And so in hell you shall most surely suffer,
Despite your talents, for I tell you truly,
590 Friend Unferth, Ecglaf's son, that I am certain
That Grendel, grim and cruel, would never grieve
Lord Hrothgar nor in Heorot hurt so many
If you disclosed the courage that you claim,

And if you had had a heart as battle-hard
And fought as fiercely. He has surely found
He need not fear your fury in a fight
Or see the sword-play of the Scyldings' tribe.
He takes his toll and shows no tenderness
To Danish folk, but draws his dreadful pleasure
600 From striking and from slicing with no struggle
* From Spear-Danes. I myself shall let them see
The strength and stubborn spirit of the Geats
In battle soon. So bid the rest go back
To mead and merriment till morning-light
Awakens one and all to welcome dawn
And radiant sunlight shines out from the south."

This gave the gray-haired chief the greatest joy,
The trusted treasure-giver, battle-tried,
Lord Hrothgar, nation's head, as he now heard
610 From Beowulf his bold-laid battle plan.
Throughout the hall the heroes' joy was heard
* And happy words. Then Wealhtheow walked forth too,
The Queen of Hrothgar's court, discrete and kind,
All garbed in gold, she greeted all the guests
And came to give the goblet graciously
And filled brimful, first to the East-Danes' friend
And urged him that he empty out the cup.
Delighted, the beloved leader took
The vessel and the victuals, valiant king.
620 The princess, praised by all, was passing round
And offering all of them, both old and young,
The golden goblets, gracious in her ways

She wore gold rings, wrought well and finely worked,
And brought a brimming cup to Beowulf;
She greeted him and gave her thanks to God
In wisely chosen words that now she would
Have met a man who might be able to
Subdue the demon. Drinking from the cup
That Weahltheow gave him willingly, fierce warrior,
630 And with words chosen well, intent on warfare,
He spoke to them, the strong chief, son of Ecgtheow,
"I thought this through at first and then set out
Across the water with my warrior band,
And I will act entirely as you wish
And do the deeds you ask or die in combat
Within the fierce grip of the foe, I forecast
That I shall do this daring deed or else
Within this mead hall must I meet my death."

The woman liked the words thus spoken well
640 And boastfully by Beowulf. Embellished
In gold, the folk queen found her favored place;
And so with strong words spoken in the hall
There came a clamor from the company
In triumph as a tribe until at last
The son of Healfdene sought to find some sleep,
For now he knew the monster would that night
Have hoped to hold a combat in the hall
Since first the sun's rays shone across the land
And till the evening darkened all the earth
650 And shadowy shapes came sliding slowly in
Beneath the black clouds billows. Then the band

Of men within the mead hall made farewells;
They bid to Beowulf the best of fortune
And Hrothgar hailed him with his heartfelt words:

"Until this time I never would entrust
To any save to you the Spear-Danes' stronghold
Since I was strong enough to shake my shield;
Now have and hold this very best of houses,
And give your mind to glory; gather strength;
660   Be watchful and beware. You will not lack
A dowry if you down the dreadful foe."

Then high king Hrothgar went out from the hall,
The Scyldings shield with all his stalwart band;
The war chief wished to go and seek out Wealhtheow,
His queen and consort. Then the Glory King
Set up a guard against the monster Grendel
Assuring safety in that special place
For high king Hrothgar from the monster's harm.
The Guardian of the Geats was glad to give
670   His might and muscle to his Maker's mercy.
So after that he took his iron shirt off
And helmet from his head; his handsome sword
Of finest iron he gave his faithful friend
And gave him orders that he guard his gear.
But prior to bending back toward his bed,
The brave man Beowulf said words in boast:
"I would not think my war-strength any weaker
Than Grendel's or my gallantry less great,
And so I will not send him off to sleep

	Nor end his life entirely, able though I am.
680	
	He does not know the skills he needs to negate
	The skills I have, or how to strike a shield,
	For all his fame in feats nefarious,
	But now at night our swords shall not be used,
	If he is willing weaponless to war.
	The Lord of wisdom will award the triumph
	And give the glory as seems good to God."
	The bold man bent down to his rest, a bolster
	Upheld the hero's cheek, while in the hall
690	The sturdy seamen settled into sleep
	Although they thought that none of them at all
	Would have much hope of seeing home again
	Or finding friends and towns so far away,
	For they had heard how many men were murdered
	While biding in that blood-drenched banquet-hall
	Of Danish folk. But now the dear Lord did devise
	A web of war-fate for the Wederas
	That sent them swift support and solace
	And overcome their enemy with all
700	Their trust in one. We have been taught the truth
	That God Almighty, in the midst of mortals,
	Will deal out destiny. In darkest night
	The shadow-walker came. The soldiers slept,
	All those who had to hold the horned-house safe
	But one. For each and all had understood
	The demon could not drag to darkness those
	Whose gift of life was guarded still by God.
	There was just one man waiting there in anger,
	Who rested, watching, while his rage arose.

710   Then moving from the moors and misty hills,
Came Grendel walking with God's weight of wrath;
The murderer had meant to take a man,
To snare a sample from the splendid hall;
Beneath the clouds, he walked toward the wine-hall
The great hall of the humans, golden, gleaming,
Now clearly came in sight. The cruel demon
Was hurrying once again to Hrothgar's house,
But never until now had Grendel known
That he might have such hard luck in the hall.
720   So, moving to the mead-hall, came the monster
Deprived of joy; the door was driven down,
Bars forged in fire were snapped. He flung his hands
Against the gates, and grim with rage and death,
He broke the building's mouth and, bursting in,
He placed his feet upon the polished floor
And walked in wrath and rage; his eyes sent rays
Of light unlovely, something like a flame;
There in the mead-hall he saw many men
All gathered in their groups, asleep together,
730   A host of warriors, and his heart was happy.
The monster meant, before the morning came,
To take each member of that troop and tear
Him limb from limb since luck had now provided
This feasting for him. But his fate was not
To make himself more meals of mortal men
Beyond this night. For now he had been noticed
By someone strong who stretched out separately,
The kin of Hygelac, who kept the killer
In sight to see how he would set to work.

740	The monster made no great delay. That moment,
	He snatched a sleeping soldier from the floor
	And biting to the bone imbibed the blood
	Of veins as vast chunks vanished; very soon
	The fiend was done; the dead man disappeared,
	Both hands and feet. The fiend moved forward
	And clutched within his claws the man of courage;
	The evil enemy with open palms
	Now reached to rout him from his place of rest.
	He sat up swiftly and he seized his arm;
750	The author of all outrage soon found out
	No man whom he had met in middle-earth,
	Or anyone in its enormous span,
	Possessed a harder hand-grip. Then his heart
	Grew fearful but no force could set him free;
	His greatest goal was just to get away
	Into the dark where devils make their den.
	No luck like this had met him in his life.
	Then Hygelac's kin recalled his words of courage,
	His utterance that evening, and stood upright,
760	Made fast a firmer grip with fingers bursting,
	Stepped forward while the struggling monster strove
	To make away by any means he might
	And find a place to flee to further off
	Within the fastness of the fens; his fingers,
	Were in a grievous grip. A journey grim indeed
	The murderer had made toward the mead hall.
	The royal hall rang. The Danes, the rest of them,
	The fortress dwellers, fiercest fighters all,

               Were filled with fear. So furious in fight
770   Were both the battlers. All the building echoed;
               It was a wonder that the wine-hall could
               Withstand the fighting and yet fail to fall.
               But finely was it built, and fastened firmly
               On both the inside and without with iron
               Well forged by skillful smiths. But shaken loose
               Were many mead-hall benches, all well made,
               As these two fighters struggled, so they say.
               No sages of the Scyldings had supposed
               That mortal men by ordinary means
780   Might break the beauty of that bone-decked hall
               But for the fury of a raging fire
               That filled it with its flame. Quite faint at first,
               A new sound now came to the North-Danes' ears,
               One horrible to hear, that pierced the hearts
               Of those who waited on the wall: the wail
               Of God's own foe, who groaned a grisly dirge,
               A wail of woe, lamenting for his wounds,
               For he, the hellish captive, now was held
               By that one man, the mightiest of mortals
790   And all who ever lived upon the earth.

               The one who willed the welfare of the Danes
               Was loath to let his lethal captive go
               Since his survival did not seem to serve
               The people's purposes. The partners there
               Of Beowulf were brandishing their blades
               And hoped to help the son of Hygelac then
               And wield their weapons with their well-known chief.

The war-proved warriors were not aware,
As now they entered in the awesome fray,
800 And hoped to hew him down with sword in hand
And send to death the huge assailant's soul,
That none of all the earth's best iron
Nor any war-blades would give him a wound
For he bewitched their war-victorious weapons
And all their edges. So his exodus,
His leaving of his loathsome life that day,
Was woeful, wending to another world
And faring far into the fiend's domain.
But now he found, who frequently before
810 Brought many miseries to mortal minds
Accomplishing his crimes and clashed with God,
His body-dwelling did not do his will;
That man of courage who was called the kin
Of Hygelac held him with his hand. It was
An odious thing for each to know the other
Was still allowed to live. The loathsome monster
Now felt a fearful pain, and from his shoulder
The sinews sprang apart and muscles snapped.
So Beowulf was given glory. Grendel,
820 With fatal wounds, then fled to distant fens
And to his dismal den. He could not doubt
That, after this, his end was on its way:
The day that he would die. But, for the Danes,
The fighting had fulfilled their fondest hopes;
This stranger coming from afar had freed them,
By will and wisdom brought back Hrothgar's wine hall
And rescued it from ruin. Now he rested

From famous feats, for he had well fulfilled,
The oath he swore to all the Eastern Danes,
830   The able leader who had eased their anguish
And soothed the sorrow they had suffered long
And all the dreadful deeds they had endured,
Their time of torment. Now the awful token
The stalwart soldier set beneath the roof,
The arm and hand and shoulder, all of it,
Was Grendel's grip now hanging on the gables.

At dawn next day the Danish warriors
Were gathering together at the gift-hall,
The folk-chiefs faring there from far and near
840   In all the world to witness and to wonder
And find the footprints of the foe. They felt
No guilt or grief that he had gone from life
And now, as they traced down his troubled tracks,
How wearily he walked and went away,
Defeated in the fight, to find the fens
Though doomed and driven off still dripping blood.
The blood was bubbling up in blackish water;
The tossing waves were torn and turbulent,
And seethed with sword-juice and with steaming gore.
850   Thus doomed to death and derelict of joy,
And hiding in his hole, he handed over
His heathen soul, and hell then welcomed him.

The trusted servants turned then toward their homes
And many men came riding from the mere,
Like happy hunters, sitting on their horses,

The soldiers singing songs of Beowulf,
That told his triumph, saying many times,
From sea to sea and north to south as well,
In all the earth there was no other man
860 Beneath the spreading sky of such renown,
The worthiest of all who wield their weapons,
Although they found no fault with their good friend,
Glad Hrothgar, nor forgot so good a guide.

The warriors liked to let their stallions leap
And sometimes run in races as they rode
Along the easy, open, earthen tracks,
The better pathways, but the bard at times,
A man of many words, remembered stories;
He sang old songs long stored up in his mind
870 And made new words for many he remembered,
Entwining them so he could tell new tales
To boast the battle deeds of Beowulf.
He sang with skill a saga he created
With well-selected words. He told as well
*   Things such as had been said before of Sigemund,
The daring deeds and all the diverse wonders,
The wars of Wael's son and the wide-spread journeys
Which other humans hardly would have heard of,
The feuds and fighting, none but Fitela,
880 Who sometimes spoke of matters such as these,
The uncle to the nephew, as in all things
They kept together constantly in conflict.
These two had taken on a tribe of giants
And slain them with their swords. And then for Sigemund

A shining splendor sprang up when he died
Because the daring fighter downed a dragon
Who guarded treasure great. A gray stone was
Above the place; the prince's son pressed in;
It was a fearless feat without Lord Fitela.

890 It came to pass his peerless sword impaled
The dreaded dragon, drove it to the wall
With smashing iron so that the slaughtered serpent
Had perished. Then the prince, as he had pleased
Because he was so brave, could bring with him
The ransacked riches of the ring-gold hoard
And bear bright armor back aboard his ship
And mound it up. The monster melted down.
Among the nations there was no one known
More widely than the son of Wael, the warrior,
900 For deeds of daring done in days of old.
No higher heroism had been seen
Or strength of spirit since King Heremod,

But he was slain when some assailed him falsely
Among the giants. Melancholy moods
Had tortured him until they were a trouble
For each and every one of all the people;
And many men of wisdom often mourned
The fate that then befell a king so fine,
Whose might had made amends for misery
910 In other times. His son they trusted truly
Would take his father's rank and rule them rightly:

Both fort and fortune, famous warriors,
And Scyldings' birthplace. Beowulf would be
A help to humankind, but Heremod
At that same time was eaten up by evil.

The riders raced their horses as they rode
Along the dusty roads at dawn of day.
The retinue arose and rushed to see
What high within the hall they hoped would be
920 A startling sight; and so the king as well,
The ring-hoard's keeper, from the queen's room came;
He trod in triumph with a troop of soldiers
Of special bravery beside his spouse
Who moved toward the mead-hall with her maidens.

When Hrothgar had arrived before the hall
He stood upon the step and saw the steep,
Sloped roof agleam with gold, and Grendel's hand
Still hanging on the hall; then Hrothgar spoke:

"Let grateful thanks be given now to God
That we have seen this sight; I suffered sorely
930 These griefs from Grendel. May the glorious God
Still wield great power, working wonderfully.
I have not had much hope in recent years,
However long my life, of leaving all these woes
Or reaching any remedy when red
Blood stained this splendid house and it stood steeped
In gore. This woe was widespread; all my wisest
Advisors could not counsel me to keep

The nation's finest mead-hall free of foes
Or demon devils. Now a daring man
940 Endowed with might by God has done this deed,
This act that all of us had failed to do
For all our schemes. Now listen! She may say,
Whoever it may be who bore him, if
That lady still is living in our land,
The God of old had given grace to her
To bear this child. So, Beowulf, the best
Of men, I make you now like my own son,
To love as long as ever this life lasts.
So hold this kinship. Henceforth you will have
950 No want of worldly goods, such is my will.
Quite often I, in other days, awarded
A treasure trove to men less true than you
And weaker warriors. You yourself have won
Eternal fame by all your fearless feats,
And it will live. Now let the Lord Almighty
Give you again the gifts he gave you now."

The son of Ecgtheow answered in these words:
"With timely zeal we undertook this task,
And offered eagerly to enter on
960 The struggle with the stranger. Still I wish
That somehow you yourself had seen
The fiend's dead flesh before your banquet hall.
My plan had been to pin him promptly down
And fix him fast upon his fatal bed,
I would have had him held in my own hand
And laboring for life unless he fled.

I could not keep him as my captive long
Against God's will, nor was my grip so good
Upon the evil enemy. Too awful
970 The fiend was in his flight, but still his fist
Is left us like a pledge against his life,
The elbow and the arm; and yet not any
Real respite has the wretched creature reaped
Nor will he longer keep his loathsome life
Still snared in sin, because his savage wound
Has gripped him grimly in its narrow grasp
And baleful bond. He shall abide therein
The coming judgment of that crime-stained creature,
The pure All-Powerful One's punishment.
980   Then Unferth, Ecglaf's son, found fewer words
With which to boast and brag of battle-deeds
Since now the nobles all had noticed how
A hand was hanging high upon the roof,
The fingers of the foe; each from the front
It seemed had steel-like sockets for the claws
That were its hand; the heathen fighter's hardened
And terrifying talons. Then they told
Each other that no aged iron, not even
The hardest made, could hope to hurt the monster
990 Or bring his bloody battle-hand to harm.

The order then went out to ready all
Of Heorot; with help from many hands,
Of workmen and their wives, the wine-house was
Adorned. The guest-hall glowed with golden patterns
In wondrous woven tapestries on walls

For people who are pleased to peer at such.
So badly broken was the brilliant building
That all the inside, iron-bound as it was,
Had ruptured hinges. Roof and rafters only
1000 Remained uninjured when the awful outlaw,
Of grim deeds guilty, got away in flight
In deep despair of living. Death indeed
Is difficult to dodge—let doubters try—
But those with souls, who spring from human stock,
Will all be forced at last by fate to find
The place prepared for people of the earth
Where mortal bodies, bound on beds of death,
Will sleep when feasting ceases.

                                    At this season,
The son of Healfdene hurried to the hall
1010 To sit as king and share the splendid feast.
I never knew a nobler gathering
Who better bore themselves about their king.
Those blessed with fame now bent down to the benches
In revelry and reached out, as was right,
For many cups of mead amidst their kin,
With Hrothgar, Hrothulf too, and all who had
Stout hearts within the hall; all Heorot
Was filled with many friends. The Scylding-folk
* Until that time had not betrayed each other.

1020 A shining standard as a sign of triumph
Was brought to Beowulf, son born of Healfdene,
A battle-shirt, embroidered banner, helmet,

And splendid, ancient sword, in sight of all
Was brought the brave man. Beowulf partook
Then from the flagon on the floor. He felt
No shame at such great gifts before the spearmen.

I had not heard before of men who had
Bestowed such gifts as these, agleam with gold,
To others on the ale-bench out of friendship;
1030 Around the helmet's roof there was a rim
Which had been wound with wire to ward off blows
So sharpened swords might never shatter it
With savage shocks when fighters with their shields
Go forward fearlessly against the foe.

The earl's defender ordered other men
To come across the courtyard bringing with them
Into the hall eight horses, golden-harnessed;
One stood with saddle skillfully enriched
And set with gems, a strong king's battle-seat.
1040 When Healfdene's son was seeking sword-play
In front of all, his fighting never failed
To win the widest fame for war-skills as
The dead were beaten down. They drew forth then
For Beowulf to have and hold for his
Own use, the war steeds and the well-wrought weapons.
In manly fashion from the famous chief,
The heroes hoard-guard paid his debt in horses
And fortune so that none could find a fault
If they should rightly try to tell the truth.
1050 And after that, to each and every one

Who went with Beowulf and braved the brine-path,
He meted out much more upon the mead-bench:
A treasure to each trooper, truly heirlooms,
And gold was given for the man whom Grendel
Had murdered in his malice. Many more
Would soon have suffered; God forestalled that fate
Through this man's courage. So God's kindness kept
The human race and rules it rightly now.
Thus understanding always is the best,
1060 The thoughtful mind; for much love, much hate,
Comes every anxious day to all of us
While we exist within this war-torn world.

Then melody and music mixed together
In front of Healfdene's hardy battle-hero.
They strummed the harp and sang the well-known story
Which Hrothgar's bard embarked on bringing them
To make the mead-bench merry with the tale
* About Finn's offspring:

                                      In the battle's onset
The hero of the Half-Danes, Hnaef the Scylding,
1070 Was doomed to fall upon a Frisian field.
But Hildeburh, it happened, had no need
To give the Jutes great praise for faith; though guiltless
Herself, she lost her loved ones; linden shields
Had battled; son and brother both were wounded;
Their fate to fall; she was unfortunate.
Hoc's daughter did have cause when daylight came
To mourn indeed the dreadful doom which she
Could see now in the shining of the sun:

    Her kindred killed, the ones she cared for most,
1080 And all her worldly joy; for war laid waste
    All Finn's retainers but a feeble few,
    So in that meeting place he might not make
    His clash with Hengest come to a conclusion,
    Nor yet by force uproot the ruined remnant.
    He offered peace terms to the prince's party:
    That he would clear for them a hearth to have
    With half control of both the hall and high seat,
    And Jutish offspring in the other half;
    And Finn should also honor all of those
1090 Of Hengest's band on days when Danes were dealt
    Rich gifts, and also given guarantees
    That they would mete as much to Hengest's men
    Of gold and gleaming gifts as when he sought
    To bolden Frisian battlers in the beer-hall.
    Then each tribe offered to the other one
    A pact of peace. Finn firmly pledged to Hengest
    An oath made earnestly, without exception,
    To aid and honor all the sad survivors
    As wise men would advise by word or deed,
1100 Lest any try to terminate the treaty;
    Nor yet could they by plot or plan complain
    That they were forced to follow one so fierce
    He killed their lord and left them leaderless;
    And if some faithless, foolish Frisian should
    Remember, call to mind, the murderous feud,
    Then by the sword's edge should they settle it.
    The pyre was then prepared and precious gold
    Was brought out from the barrow, and the best
    Of Battle-Scyldings placed upon the pyre.

1110	Quite plainly seen reposing on the pyre
	Were blood-stained battle-shirts and boars on helmets,
	Iron-hard, agleam with gold, and heroes great,
	The fallen fighters, finished by their wounds.
	Then Hildeburh had bade them bring her son,
	To let his bone-house be set there for burning
	And placed with Hnaef upon the funeral pyre,
	Set side by side. And so the woman mourned,
	And sang her sorrow. Soaring with the fire,
	The hero rose in clouds as red flames roared
1120	Toward heaven from the high-banked mound. The heads
	Were melted, battle-wounds were burst and blood
	Gushed out from bodies hate had bitten. Blazing,
	The fire ate all, a greedy guest, that gulped
	Those slain on either side; their splendor gone.

	The warriors went their way without their friends
*	To seek the hearths, the homes, and high-walled fort
	Of Frisia. Hengest, forced to stay with Finn,
	Then spent the long and slaughter-stained dark winter
	In languishing and longing for his land.
1130	He could not set out on the sea to sail
	In his own curve-prowed ship; the sea-storm surged
	And fought the wind while winter locked the waves
	In icy ties until returning spring
	Should come to human courtyards, as occurs
	Today within the order of the seasons,
	With weather wondrous bright. The winter fled;
	The earth was fair again; the exile ached
	To go out from the guest-house. Getting vengeance

        Was more upon his mind than making sail,
1140   And how the clash he wanted could occur
        While he still held in heart the Jutish men.

        He would accept the world-wide way when on
        His lap the son of Hunlaf set the sword,
        The best of blades for battle, shining brightly,
        With edges of which Jutes were all aware.
        The deadly foe then fell on Finn in turn,
        The onslaught of the sharp-edged sword at home.
        With Guthlaf, Oslaf sailed by sea to sob
        The savage story of the fierce assault
1150   And tell their trouble's cause; such turbulence
        No heart could ever hold. The hall itself
        Was stained with blood; and so, too, Finn was slain,
        The king and company; the queen was captured.
        The Scylding spearmen bore back to their ships
        The contents carried from the king's own house,
        Whatever furnishings of Finn's they found,
        And gems and jewelry. Journeying by sea,
        The queen was carried to the Danish court
        And safety in her land.

                                  The song was sung,
1160   The minstrel's story. Mirth once more arose;
        The bench-noise brightened, and the bearers brought them
        The wine from wondrous vessels. Wealhtheow came;
        She wore a golden crown, and walked toward the heroes,
        The uncle and the nephew, each of them,
        Still peaceful with the other. Also Unferth

As spokesman sat below the Scylding lord,
Each counting on his courage, though his kin
Were skeptical. The Scylding's lady spoke:

"This foaming flagon, fairest lord, is yours,
1170   The giver of our gifts; you once were glad
To bring your bounty to us, being gentle
In speech to all the Geats as strong men should.
Be gracious to the Geats, and think again
Of all you own that came from every side;
From henceforth, have they said, and I have heard
You wish this warrior were like your own son.
Now here is Heorot, the shining hall;
Employ its pleasures now, then pass it on
To kin and kingdom when it shall become
1180   Your turn to taste of death. I truly know
Good Hrothulf then will hold in high regard
These youths, since he's a younger man; if you,
The strength and stay of Scyldings, leave this world,
He then, I think, will thoroughly repay
Our offspring if he thinks of any part
Of all the work that we did for his welfare
In childhood, favors formerly performed."

She turned then by the bench, her boys were there;
And there sat Hrethric, Hrothmund, heroes' sons,
1190   The young ones, grouped together, and the good
Man, Beowulf the Geat, there by the brothers.

A flowing cup was furnished him, and friendship
Was pledged in words, and with well-woven gold
They offered, with some other ornaments,
A robe, and rings, and collar richer far
Than any I have heard of here on earth;
And nothing nobler have I known beneath
The sky since Hama from the heroes' hoard
Had brought the bright-jeweled Brosings' necklace to
1200　　The shining city. Shunning Eomenric's
Hot-tempered wrath, he chose eternal triumph.

This hoard-jewel had returned with Hygelac,
The son of Swerting's brother when he sailed
And set a standard up above the spoils
Stripped from the fallen. Fate then silenced him
When in his arrogance he asked for trouble
In fighting Frisians flaunting that fine jewel.
He carried it across the wave-filled cup;
The sturdy sovereign fell beneath his shield;
1210　　The Franks then captured it: the kingly corpse
With both the breast-shield and the brilliant ring.
The weaker warriors went to strip the dead
Geats' bodies; when the bloody battle ended,
The corpses filled the field.

　　　　　　　　　　　　　　Applause broke forth.
Then Wealhtheow spoke to those assembled, saying,
"Be blessed, dear brother Beowulf with this
Gold loop; good luck; and let this robe be yours,
Our people's patrimony; prosper well

	And show yourself by strength; assist these boys
1220	With kindly counsel. That will cause me joy.

        And show yourself by strength; assist these boys
1220   With kindly counsel. That will cause me joy.
        Your deeds are known by now both near and far;
        And people in all places sing your praise,
        In all the space encircled by the sea
        Where wall-cliffs stand and winds go on their way.
        Abundant blessings on your bravery;
        May fortune favor you. Be for my boys
        One gentle in your gestures, having joy!
        Here each is always true to every other,
        With lenient manner, loyal to their liege-lord;
1230   Our realm is resolute; our ranks are ready;
        Well warmed with wine, my wish is their command."

        She sought her seat. A splendid feast was served
        And warriors drank their wine all unaware
        That doom and darkness were ordained to fall
        On many men. So evening came once more
        And Hrothgar homeward to his hall returned,
        The strong to sleep, but still, as usual
        Behind him in the hall a host of men,
        Made bare the benches and about the hall
1240   Spread beds and bolsters; but one beer-drunk man
        Lay down that night predestined soon to die.
        They set above their beds their battle shields,
        The brightly painted boards; upon the bench
        Beside each soldier, easy to be seen,
        Were battle-helmets high, and heavy shirts,
        And strong wood spears. The standard practice was
        That each was always ready everywhere

To fight, on foreign fields or while at home;
And so, at such times as their sovereign lord
1250 Had need, no finer fighters could be found;
And then they sank in sleep; a sorry price
Was asked of one that evening as before
When Grendel gained possession of the gold-hall
And did his evil acts until his end
Would smite him for his sins. Then it was seen,
And very well revealed, that an avenger
Still lived although the loathsome one had left.
A long time Grendel's mother groaned in grief;
The monster woman mulled her miseries,
1260 She who was doomed to dwell in dreadful waters
And icy currents after Cain became
His only brother's butcher with his blade;
He slew his father's son, and stole away,
Now marked by murder, made to flee from men
And dwell in deserts. Coming down from him
Were many monsters and, among them, Grendel,
A hateful outcast who at Heorot
Had found one watchful and awaiting warfare.
The monster meant to maul him there, but then
1270 The man remembered all his mighty strength,
The gracious gift which God had given him;
In trust he gave himself to God's own goodness
In grace and favor to defeat the foe
And lay the demon low. He left in sorrow
And drained of dreams, to seek a place to die,
The mortal foe of men. His mother, still
In grief and greedy for revenge, began
To set out sadly to avenge her son.

　　　　　She reached great Heorot, where Ring-Danes rested,
1280　　　The sleeping soldiers spread throughout the hall,
　　　　　But they were soon upset when, stepping in,
　　　　　Came Grendel's mother; mayhem may be feared
　　　　　The less when female force is found in play
　　　　　And women less in war than weaponed men
　　　　　Are feared when using bright blades forged in fire,
　　　　　When sharp-edged swords still stained with steaming blood,
　　　　　Are biting through the burnished boar's head helmets.

　　　　　Then hands throughout the hall were holding up
　　　　　Their rounded shields and all their sharp-edged swords
1290　　　Above the benches, battle-helmets then
　　　　　And shirts were set aside as terror seized them.

　　　　　She moved with speed to get outside, and sought
　　　　　To flee to save her life before they found her.
　　　　　She seized a single soldier suddenly
　　　　　And firmly, fleeing with him to the fen.
　　　　　This man, the hero Hrothgar had loved best
　　　　　Of all his tested troop between the seas,
　　　　　Was savaged as he slept, this strong combatant
　　　　　And brilliant battler. Beowulf was absent;
1300　　　Another space to sleep had been assigned
　　　　　When gifts were given to the greatest Geat.

　　　　　Then heart-ache came to Heorot; she hauled
　　　　　The gory arm down; grief again returned
　　　　　To human homes. How hard the bargain was
　　　　　That battlers bought on both sides of the feud

With corpses of their friends. The care-worn king,
A weary warrior, was filled with woe
When dreadful tidings of his dear friend's death
Taught him his leading thane no longer lived.

1310 They swiftly summoned to the stately room
Unbeaten Beowulf. At break of day
The worthy warrior, well-known champion, went
Accompanied by comrades to the king,
Who waited, wondering if the Ruler would
Contrive a turn from tidings filled with trouble.
The war-proved man walked through the wooden hall
With hand-picked heroes; how the floorboards thundered!
He went with words to greet the worthy king,
The Ingwines's friend, and asked him if he had,
1320 For all his urgent call, enjoyed the evening.
But Hrothgar answered him, the Scyldings helm:

"Ask not of pleasure, now again a new
Ordeal is facing all the Danes, for dead
Is Aeschere, who was elder brother of
Kind Yrmenlaf, my closest comrade, counsel,
And at my flank when fighting was most fierce;
He gave me cover in the clash of combat,
And smashing boar-crests, as a soldier should;
This Aeschere then, most honored, ever good,
1330 Now here in Heorot has been cruelly killed;
That deadly demon did it; I do not
Know where the cruel creature took his corpse,
To fill her feast with joy. She found revenge

For yesternight when Grendel yielded you
His life and grimly grappled in your grip
Because for far too long my loyal land
Was bruised and burdened. He in battle fell,
His freedom forfeit; but another found us,
Another mighty monster, making vengeance
1340 Has forced this angry feud at last too far,
Or thus the thanes are thinking, as it seems.
They greatly grieve the one who gave them gifts;
A heart-ache hard to bear. The hand lies dead
Which worked our will in very many ways.

"My subjects, citizens within this state
And at the hearthside here, have sometimes heard,
That two such solitary shapes were seen,
Two massive marchers guarding distant moors,
Two specters strange. The second one of them,
1350 It seemed to some, so far as they could see,
Was fashioned in the female form; the first
Who walked these wastelands was, they thought, a man
But more in measurement than men might be.
In past time people dwelling in that place
Had named him Grendel; no one knew his father
Or if, in ancient times, he entered life
In some secluded place from secret spirits
Who walk on wolf-worn slopes and windy cliffs
And misty marsh-paths where the mountain streams
1360 Are dropping down to darkness under crags
To flow in floods beneath the earth. Not far
Away as miles are measured, is a mere

Above which heavy, hoar-chilled branches hang,
From towering trees whose tangled roots obscure
A pond where nightly there appears a portent,
A fire within the flood. No human flesh,
However wise, knows well that water's depth.
The hart, though hunted on the heath by hounds,
And seeking safety in the sheltering woods,
1370 Pursued from far, will forfeit first his life
Upon the bank, before he braves that basin
To purchase life; a most unpleasant place.
The surging swells are always swirling up
To black, forbidding clouds when blasts of wind
Are stirring hostile storms and steamy air
And heaven weeps. Our hope for help remains
With you alone. This land you have not learned of,
This dark and dreadful district where you may
Find sin-soaked souls: now seek it if you dare!
1380 If you will wage this war, I will reward you
With ancient treasures, as I earlier did,
And golden garlands if you come again.

Then Beowulf, spoke boldly, born of Ecgtheow,
"No weeping, wise one! It is always well
To make reprisal, not to mourn too much,
For each of us must ever wait the end
Of life at last. So let all those who may
Win fame before they die; for fighters that
Is always best when bodies' breath is gone.
1390 Arise, O ruler of the realm; prrepare
To trace the trail that Grendel's mother's trod.

I swear to you, she shall not shield herself
In folds of earth or far-off hills or forests
Or somewhere in the sea, though she may speed.
Endure, for now at least, this dismal day
With calmness; I am confident you can."

The lordly leader sprang up; "Let us thank
The mighty Lord, for what this man's words mean."
Then Hrothgar had them saddle up his horse,
1400   A mount with braided mane. The mighty prince
Bestrode his steed in state. Foot soldiers marched
With shields on shoulders. They could plainly see
Her traces on the trail through forest trees
And wastelands where she went her way toward
The murky moor; she bore the murdered man,
The soul-less shell of that most splendid thane
Of all who helped Lord Hrothgar guard their homes.
The sons of warriors went along their way
Up steep and stony slopes and straitened paths
1410   And lanes; they left behind the land they knew,
Past wall-like cliffs and water-monsters' warrens.
The king, accompanied by counsellors,
Was leading; looking at the landscape they
Saw suddenly a certain ancient stone,
All green with moss among the mountain trees
Within a woeful wood. The water there
Beneath the bank was boiling up and bloody.
The doughty Danes stood there in deep distress.
The Scyldings' friends were saddened by the sight
1420   And hearts of heroes ached to find the head

Of Aeschere there upon the incline's edge.
The bloody water welled up and the warriors
Stood gazing at the steaming gore; again
The war-horn sang its summons. Sitting down,
They saw all sorts of serpents swimming there
And strange sea-dragons searching through the surf
And monsters likewise, lying on the ledges,
That may on certain morning's sometimes make
Their sojourns spreading sorrow on the sail-road.
1430 The serpents and the sea-beasts scurried off
In burning bitterness to hear the blast
Of war-horn's wailing. With his sharpened arrow
The prince of Geats deprived one beast of power
To struggle still with waves, but struck it with
A well-aimed war-shaft so that in the water
It swam more slowly until seized by death.
They swiftly set upon it with their spears,
And blades with hardened hooks; they hunted it
And roughly wrenched it out upon the rocks,
1440 The wondrous thrasher of the waves. Men wondered
To see the barbarous beast. Then Beowulf,
Unfearing, fitted for the fight in armor
And wearing also his hand-woven war-shirt,
Both broad and brightly-worked, would brave the deep.
His garb was shaped to shield his skeleton
So one might not in warfare wound his heart
Or foes inflict in fury any harm.
A gleaming helm would keep his head from harm
As he was diving downward in the deep
1450 To search through swirling waves; it shone with gold,

A wondrous circle wreathed it; it was wrought
And shaped in former days with special skill
And then embossed with boars so that no blade
Or blow of battle-sword might bite it through.
Then, not the smallest succor to his strength
Was handed him by Hrothgar's spokesman, Unferth,
A noble hilt-sword known by name as Hrunting.
It had no equal in the ancient treasury;
Its blade was iron made hard with battle-blood,
1460 With poisoned patterns streaked and proven true
By all of those who armed themselves with it
And dared make daunting treks to distant lands
Or face the foe at home. Not for the first
Time was it asked to do such daring deeds.

It seems most certain that the son of Ecglaf,
For all his strength, lost sight of what he said
When he was warmed with wine. He lent the weapon
To back a better swordsman, not so brave
Himself to strive beneath the waves or stake
1470 His life on feats performed. His chance to find
Great fame was forfeit. Different far from him
The other of the two when armed for battle.
Then Beowulf, spoke boldly, born of Ecgtheow:

"Consider, stately man, the son of Healfdene,
Who gives us gold, now I am garbed to fight,
The words which once in wisdom you had said:
"If I, on any errand of your own,
Should lose my life, I can rely on you

To fill in future time a father's role.
1480 Keep watch and ward of these young warriors,
These comrades close to me; if my life closes,
The treasures, too, entrusted to my care,
My good friend, Hrothgar, may go home to Hygelac,
And let the lord of Geats from that gold learn
And see, the son of Hrethel, staring at those gifts,
I found a good king, giver of fine gold,
Who gave me kindly comfort while he could.
Let Unferth use the ancient sword which I
Received and wield its wondrous woven pattern
1490 Which has so hard an edge. Now I and Hrunting
Will gain more glory soon or go with death."

So with these words, the Weder-Geatish man,
Unwilling as he was to wait for answers,
Leaped down and dove into the depths; the waves
Embraced the battle-fighter. Time went by
Before he finally found the water's bottom.
She swiftly saw—the one who that flood's sphere
Had held in horrid claws a hundred seasons
With grim and greedy force—a guest had come,
1500 A stranger swimming down to search her home.
She snatched him up and speared that worthy soldier
Upon her fearful fangs, but not so fast
Could she do him much harm whose chain-mail held
Him safe or work her will against his war-dress
Or lance the links of leather with her claws.

The water beast then bore him to the bottom;
She dragged him, dressed in armor, to her dwelling
To balk his hopes, as brave as he might be,
Of wielding weapons. Water-monsters thronged
1510 And scores of sea-beasts swiftly set on him,
Their tusks like sabers stabbed his battle-shirt,
His evil adversaries. Then the earl
Could see himself to be in some strange hall
In which there was no weight of water felt.
The hall's roof somehow held away from him
The flowing flood. And there was firelight too,
A brilliant blaze with bright and shining flames.

    The good man's gaze revealed the gruesome fiend,
The monstrous mere-wife. All his might was placed
1520 Behind his battle-blade, not pulling back
His hard swing from her head; his hungry sword
Sang songs of war. But soon the stranger saw
The battle-flame would not bite through to bone,
Not harming her at all. Its hard edge now
Had failed the fighter; never once before
In hand-clash, when the helm was hacked away
And doomed men's battle-dress could not endure,
Had this fine treasure yet betrayed its trust.
He still was steadfast, never slow in courage;
1530 Now he, the kin of Hygelac, hoping yet
For fame, the furious fighter, flung away,
The patterned, precious sword upon the ground,
The stiff edge made of steel; in his own strength
And mighty grip he'd trust. So must all men
Respond when they in warfare will to win

    Long-lasting fame and lack care for their lives.
    He seized her hair, not sorry for the struggle,
    The great war-Geat engaging Grendel's mother.
    He pushed her hard, a fighter filled with fury;

1540 The deadly foe fell flat upon the floor,
    But bouncing back she brought him her revenge
    And crushed him closely in her cruel grip;
    The worthy warrior stumbled wearily,
    And found, that famous man, that he was falling.
    Then down she sat on him and drew her dagger
    To seek some satisfaction for her son,
    Her only offspring, with its ample blade.
    The links that saved his life were lying on
    His breast; they offered to its edge no entry.
1550 Then Ecgtheow's son would soon have ceased to live,
    The army's leader, buried under earth,
    Unless his battle-shirt had been a bulwark,
    The hard war-harness, and the holy God
    Had worked to win for him, but God all-wise,
    The Ruler of all realms, had chosen rightly
    And easily, so after he stood up
    He saw in storage there a sacred sword
    Of giants' work, and with a well-wrought edge,
    A weapon any warrior would want,
1560 But it was one no other man was able
    To bear in battle being of such size,
    Bejewelled and splendid, shaped by giants' skill;
    The Scylding hero seized the sword's rich hilt,
    And stern and strong-willed, swung the ornate sword;

In rage and wrath he raised the ring-marked sword
So that his thrust bit sharply through her throat
And broke the rings of bone. The blade ran through
The flesh, a fatal wound, and on the floor
She sank. The sword ran blood. The hero sang.

1570 A glimmering light gave out its glow within,
And shed its rays as when sky's candle shines
From heaven high. He hunted through the cave
And went along the wall, his weapon raised,
The hilt gripped hard, the thane of Hygelac, now
In anger, unafraid, its edge not useless
To the fighter for he wished with fervor
That Grendel make amends for many raids
And deeds that he had done to all the Danes
In more than merely one momentous time
1580 When he took hold of Hygelac's battle-friends
And slew them in their sleep, ate while they slept
Those fifteen folk, the finest of the Danes
And others also whom he carried off,
A hateful haul. But he had his reward:
The fighter found his foe's dead body lying
All stiff and battle-broken on a bed,
And lifeless from the limb which he had lost
In conflict at the hall; he cut the corpse asunder
And dealt a deep blow to it, dead already,
1590 A stalwart sword stroke, slicing off its head.

Then suddenly the sober watchers saw,
Those left with Hrothgar, looking at the lake,

A swirl of waves that surged up to the surface
With grisly streaks of gore. The grey-haired elders
Together gave their views about the good man
And said how sure they were they would not see
Him come in joy and conquest from that combat
Once more, their famous master. Many men
Were sure the she-wolf must have slaughtered him.
1600 But now the ninth hour came and from the ness
The sturdy Scyldings set out for their homes;
The giver of their gold as well. Their guests
Still sat there sick of heart and stared into
The lake and longed to see their lord again
Himself; though hopeless, still they hoped for him.
But he now saw the sword itself begin,
A wondrous sight, to melt or waste away
Because of battle-blood, the baleful blade,
Its matter melting more or less as ice does
When God the Father frees us from the frost,
1610 The true Creator, turning times and seasons,
Whose will controls, unwinds the water's rope.

The hero's hands took nothing from that hall,
No more from all that mighty mound of wealth
Than Grendel's head and hilt of her great sword
Enriched with gold. Already ruined was
The blade, all burned up by the boiling blood
Of that foul pest who perished in that place.
He swam up soon; successful in the struggle
Against foes wrath and rage; he rose through waves,
1620 The restless, rolling water in that region,

Now emptied of that alien spirit, who
Had let go now of life, so briefly loaned.

The sailors' leader came at last to land;
He swam with strength, exulting in his spoils,
The baleful burden born up in his hands.
The thanes all thronged to meet him there again
And thanked God, thrilled that he came through the fight
And they might see that he had had no harm.
The hardy hero's helmet and his mail shirt
1630 Were loosened quickly, and the lake still lay
Asleep, with cold blood clotting under clouds.
Then forth they fared again upon the foot-path;
With happy hearts, they hurried toward their homes
Along the routine roads, now royally bold,
And hauled the head down from the high lake-cliff,
An arduous exercise for all of them,
Requiring courage of the four who carried
The spear they stuck it on; they strained to bring
The hulking head of Grendel to the hall.
1640 They presently approached the princely house,
The fiercest of the fighters, fourteen Geats,
Their master marching in the midst of them.
In pride they passed across the mead hall plain
And then the leader of the thanes came there,
His valor valued in their victory,
A hero strong of heart to welcome Hrothgar.
They hauled the head of Grendel by the hair
Out on the mead floor where the men had met;
A wondrous sight it was for men and women,
1650 A startling spectacle at which they stared.

Then Beowulf, the heir of Ecgtheow, opened,
"You see this sea-borne trophy, son of Healfdene,
Which we delight to leave you, Scyldings' lord
The triumph-token toward which you now gaze.
Not lightly did I leave with life still in me
From war beneath the waves, a risky work,
The sternest struggle, which would soon have stopped
Unless our God had given me his guard,
For I could not do anything at all
1660   By hefting Hrunting, handsome though it is,
But God our Governor had granted me
The help to see there, handsome, hanging high,
An ancient, awesome sword. So, very often,
Does God still guide the lost. I got it down
And killed in combat, when the moment came,
The cavern's keeper. Then that keenest sword
With burnished blade burned up as blood burst out,
The heated battle-sweat. The hilt is here;
I fetched it from our foes, their deeds avenged,
1670   The Scyldings' slaughter, as it seemed I should.

"You have my promise, here in Heorot
Your soldiers' troop may slumber without sorrow
And all the leaders of your loyal land,
For now you need fear not for old or young
Or dread the deadly evil, Danish chief,
Or fear a further evil from that source.

He gave the gray-haired man the golden hilt,
The hoary leader held it in his hand,

The ancient art of giants. Ownership
1680 Passed to the Danes' lord when the demon died,
That work of wondrous smiths. So when the world
Gave up the ogre, God's grim enemy,
The murderer, the monster's mother also,
It came then to be cared for by the king,
The strongest sovereign in that sea-girt world,
Who rendered riches in the Danish realm.
    Then Hrothgar spoke, when he had seen the hilt,
The ancient heirloom with its own inscription
Which showed the source of all the ancient strife
1690 When cold waves carried off the giants' kin
In fearful fashion. They, a foreign folk,
Were well rewarded with the waters' rush;
The Lord allotted them their fee at last.
Inscribed in shining gold upon the shank
Was runic writing which was rightly marked,
A statement saying for whom first the sword
Was shaped of strongest iron with spiral hilt,
And worked as well with gold and woven serpents.

When silence fell, the son of Healfdene spoke;
1700 "The one who works to serve the common weal
And truth and right, who tells of former times,
Who guards our homes, may say this hero here
Was born a better man. Yes, Beowulf,
Your fame is now spread forth both far and wide
And over all the earth. You govern steadily
With power and prudence. I for my part promise
To be your friend as formerly; our fortress,

You shall never fail your noble nation
In helping heros. Heremod did not;
1710 In serving sons of Ecgwela, the Scyldings;
He worked not for their welfare but their woe
And dealt out death to all the Danish people.
He felled his feast companions, filled with fury
His close companions, so he was excluded,
The famous prince, from feasts and fellowship
Though God Almighty granted him great gifts
And lifted him alone above his land
And held him high. Yet in his heart increased
Blood-thirsty thoughts. To them he gave no rings
1720 To honor Danes, but dwelt, in deepest gloom,
And in his struggles suffered very sadly,
A long grief to his people. Learn this lesson
Of true integrity; I tell this tale
With many winters' wisdom. Wonderful
Is Mighty God who measures out to mankind
The land and lordship and the learning too
Through strength of spirit. God alone holds sway;
Sometimes in love the Lord allows a soul
To fancy for himself a famous clan
1730 And helps him in his homeland hold earth's joys
And puts a country's castles in his care
And renders regions subject to his rule,
Broad kingdom, so he cannot come to see,
In ignorance, an end of all these things.

          "He rests in riches; nothing reins him in:
Not illness, age, nor anguish of the mind,
No cares of any kind becloud his mind,

Or show him swords in strife. The shining world
Is wending on its way, and nothing worse
1740 Appears until the place of pride within
Is widened and the warder fails to wake,
The shepherd of the soul; his sleep so sound,
Bound up in cares, the killer close at hand
Sets shaft to bow and shoots with sinful skill.
And so his heart is struck behind its shield
By sharpened shafts; he cannot save himself
From crooked counsels of the cursed spirit.
Then all he held so long will look like little;
With avarice and anger eaten up
1750 And pride, he gives no golden rings, forgets,
Forsakes his future state, the share of honor
Which God, the Glory-Ruler, gave to him.
But frail flesh fails; his destined future comes
To him at last: the life-house loaned to him,
As fated, falls; another follows him
Who hands out treasure from the hero's hoard
And has no heed of human hopes and fears.

"Defend yourself against this flaw, my friend,
The best of battlers, choose the better way,
1760 The lasting prize. So put away all pride,
You famous fighter. You are filled with strength
A short time; but, it shall be, all too soon,
That sickness and the sword shall sap your strength
Or fangs of fire or else the surging flood
Or sting of sword or else the spear in flight
Or agonies of age or else the eye,

Now dazzling, dims and darkens, all too soon
Will death, O warrior, work its will with you.

"Thus I, for half a hundred years, had held
1770 The Ring-Danes realm and ruled beneath the sky
All enemies from every tribe on earth
By sword and by the spear, and so at last
I found no foe beneath the firmament.
Then, look, in my own country, conflict came,
And, after gladness, grief, when Grendel rose
As enemy, my ancient adversary,
And all his endless onslaught I endured
And massive mental grief. But praise
The everlasting Lord, that I have lived
1780 To stare myself at that great blood-stained skull
With my own eyes and after awful pains.
Go, find your seat, and share the sumptuous feast
Now, worthy warrior; we shall take the time
To deal out treasures when the daylight dawns."

Then gladly did the great man go at once
To seek the seat the wise king had assigned
And once again, there was for warriors
And fighting men the finest feast prepared
For the occasion. Then night came and covered
1790 The whole assembly; so the soldiers stood;
The senior Scylding now was seeking sleep,
A place for his repose. The peerless Geat
So brave in battle, sought a bed as well.
A hall thane came to help the weary hero,

To guide the guest from such a great way off
And care for all his comfort courteously
And not neglect the needs that such a nobleman
Or seamen such as he might sometimes have.

The hero, great of heart, slept in the hall,
1800 Beneath the gold-decked gables as a guest
Until the black-garbed raven boldly blazoned
The heaven's happiness and sun made haste
To shine through shadows. Soldiers hurried, too,
The heroes hoping to go home again
And eager, anxious, to be on their way
And venture on their voyage; visitors
Prepared. The strong man said to Ecglaf's son
That he should have and hold the sword called Hrunting,
That battle-blade he borrowed; thanking him,
1810 He said it was a worthy friend in war,
And powerful; a proud man, he would put
No blame in battle on that bright sword's edge.
In arms and eager to be on their way,
The warriors were waiting. Worthiest
Of all, the prince approached the throne. His peer,
The battle-hardened hero, Hrothgar, waited.

The battler born of Ecgtheow, Beowulf,
Then said, "Now we who sojourned far by sea
Will say to you that all of us are eager
1820 To seek for Hygelac and our homes. We have
Been welcomed worthily by your good will
And given every gift most graciously.

        If there is anything at all on earth
        That I might ever do to earn your love,
        Aside from what you've seen, then send for me.
        If I should find out, far across the flood,
        That border tribes are bringing threats of battle,
        The sort that fell on you from foes before,
        Then there will I come with a thousand thanes
1830   To help as heroes should. And Hygelac, too,
        Though young in years, I know will yield his help
        And give me good support, his people's guard,
        In words and other ways to work your will
        And strengthen you with shafts of spears
        And mighty forces where you most need men.
        If, Hrothgar, he who is your son, young Hrethric,
        Decides to seek the Geatish court, he shall
        Be sure to find good friends. A foreign land
        Is better sought by someone who is strong."

1840   Then Hrothgar, well-prepared, spoke with these words:
        "The Lord all-wise himself has winged these words
        Into your heart; I have not ever heard
        Such wisdom yet from one so young in years.
        You have a knowing mind and marvelous might
        And with great wisdom speak. I well believe,
        If someday spear or sword-fierce battle-strike
        Or iron, or illness afterward, should take
        Your rightful ruler, Hrethel's royal heir,
        Who leads the loyal folk, and you yet live,
1850   The Sea-Geats could not seek for someone better
        To come to them to be their king and keep

The heroes' hoard, if you agree to hold
Your kinsman's kingdom. As I come to know
You better, Beowulf beloved, the better
It pleases me. You brought our people peace,
The Sons of Sea-Geats and the Spear-Danes, too;
It shall be mutual and so the strife
And enmity of other eras end.
Now, while I rule this realm and all its riches,
1860 They shall be shared across the sea-birds' bath
And greetings shall be given, yes, and gifts
And over surging seas the ring-prowed ships
Shall bring your people presents, proofs of love.
They will stand firm, I know, toward foe and friend,
In every aspect blameless as of old."

Again, the guardian of the warriors gave
The hardy son of Healfdene in the hall
Gifts, twelve of them, and with these treasures told him
To seek his people safely; come back soon.
1870 And then the courteous king, the Scyldings' captain,
Embraced the best of nobles by the neck
And kissed him kindly; tears were coursing down
And streaked his beard. The sovereign's sage advice
Was turned two ways, the stronger of them was
That not again would they be glad to gaze
On such brave counselors. He could not keep
His deepest feelings down; that man was dear
To him, and deep within his heart he held
A lasting longing for that man beloved,
1880 It burned hot in his blood. Then Beowulf,

         The gold-proud gladiator, crossed the grass
         And reveled in his riches. Riding out
         Upon the bay the water-walker waited
         Its owner. As they went toward the water
1885   They praised the parting presents Hrothgar gave them,
         A good and guiltless king till growing age,
         Which wounds so many, worked on him as well.

         They came then to the coast, the dauntless cohort,
         Of youthful warriors wearing woven mail,
1890   Their linked-chain armored shirts. The land-guard looked
         At all the home-bound heroes he had seen
         Before, and from the cliff in friendly fashion
         He greeted them as guests and galloped down
         To tell them Weders would be always welcome
         And bring them brightly armored to their boat.

         Upon the sand the spacious, ring-prowed ship
         Was waiting for them weighted down with war-clothes
         And horses, treasure-piles; the tall mast towered
         On high and over Hrothgar's hoard of gifts.

1900   He gave the guard a sword so wound with gold
         That ever after he was always held
         A man of greater merit at the mead bench
         For that great heirloom. Then they thrust the ship
         Into the deep and drove it out from Denmark.
         Upon the mast a mighty mantle hung,
         The sail, restrained by rope; the sea-beams thundered;
         The breeze upon the billows did not block

        The wave-borne vessel as it went its way,
        The seafoam-walker swimming on the swells,
1910   Its iron-bound keel cut through the icy ocean
        Until they came to Geatish coastal cliffs
        And hove in sight of headlands and the hull
        Was sliding up upon the sandy shore.

        The coast-guard quickly came to say he had
        Been looking long for these beloved men,
        And had been staring steadily to sea-ward.
        They brought the broad-beamed ship up on the beach
        And made it fast and firm with anchors lest the force
        Of waves should break apart the well-wrought wood.
1920   The chief then had him haul the hoard ashore,
        Their journey's gems and gold; then just beyond
        The shore they sought their gift-bestower,
        The son of Hrethel, Hygelac, in his home;
        He kept his court beside the coastal wall.

        The hall was handsome, highly honored in it
        A king of courage sat; his consort, Hygd,
        A wise and well-bred queen, although few winters
        Had Haereth's daughter dwelt in the redoubt.
        They say that she was someone never stingy
1930   In giving out great gifts of wealth to Geats,
*   Both men and women. Modthryth's manner though
        Was different and dreadful deeds were done;
        The courtiers were careful not to cross her.
        Except her lord, saluting her or looking
        At her, whoever did, at any hour

Was well aware that deadly bonds awaited
Which human hands would weave. At once there was
A sword assigned when that man had been seized
To settle subjects with its shapely blade
1940 And deal out death's last trial. To do such deeds
Is always unbecoming in a queen,
The one who should weave peace, with wicked words
To let a well-loved warrior lose his life;
The son of Hemming stopped this practice soon.
Those drinking ale said also it was true
That she had proved less perilous to people,
And acted angry less when it was settled
That she be garbed in gold and then be given
A worthy warrior; so she went away
1950 To Offa's fortress far across the flood
As bidden by her father. But quite soon
She grew to rule her realm in righteousness,
And did the duties for which she was destined
And held the hero's ruler high in love.
Among the multitude he was the most
Remarkable of men it seems to me
From coast to coast because King Offa was
A spear-man brave in bounty and in battle,
And well regarded far and wide, in wisdom
1960 He well and rightly ruled his realm. So Eomer
Was born to him, a help to heroes, kin
To Henning, Garmund's grandson, great in battle.
The hardy hero with his hand-picked men
Then strode along the seashore on the sand,
The broad, flat beach. The world's bright candle beamed:

	The speeding, southern sun. Their sojourn ended,
	They swiftly stepped into the inner stronghold
	Where Ongentheow's assassin, shield of soldiers,
	The good, young war-king was known well to them
1970	For handing heroes rings. So then to Hygelac
	They told the tale of Beowulf's return,
	That here at home the helper of the warriors,
	Shield-comrade, now had come into the court
	Both well and walking with no battle-wounds.

	They quickly cleaned off at the king's command
	The fortress floor for those who came by foot.
	The strife's survivor sat beside the king
	As kin with kin, though first the king had made
	A gracious greeting to his gallant thane
1980	In careful words. Then cups of mead were carried
	Around the hall in Haereth's daughter's hands;
	It gave her joy to give the brimming goblets
	Into the heroes' eager hands. Then Hygelac,
	Was caused by curiosity to question
	His house companion in the high-roofed hall
	To learn the story of the Sea-Geats' sojourn:
	"What fate befell you, Beowulf my friend,
	When you decided suddenly to seek
	A struggle far across the salt-filled sea
1990	At Heorot and go to Hrothgar's help,
	And could you ease in any way the ills
	The famous chieftain bore? I felt great fear,
	A seething sadness and uncertainty,
	Dear Beowulf, and then—not briefly—begged

That you not go to greet that guilty spirit
But let the South-Danes settle for themselves
Their war with Grendel. I will give to God
Great thanks to see you here both safe and sound."

Then Ecgtheow's offspring, Beowulf, spoke up:
2000 "It has not, Hygelac, been hidden now
From many people that a mighty meeting,
A bruising battle bringing Grendel down on me,
Occurred within that country where he caused
Such ceaseless sorrows for the Battle-Scyldings,
Unending agony, but I avenged it
So Grendel's kinsmen have no cause to crow
About that morning's onslaught, any of them,
The longest lived of all that loathsome lot
Encased in crime. I came to that place first
2010 To hail Lord Hrothgar in his hall of rings.
At once the well-known warrior, son of Healfdene,
When he had heard the hopes within my heart,
Assigned to me a seat with his own sons.
The crowd was carefree, and I cannot say
I have beheld beneath the hollow heavens
More merriment in mead. The matchless queen,
The people's pledge of peace, went through the hall,
Aroused the retinue and gave out wreaths
To soldiers, some of them, and sought her seat.
2020 Then Hrothgar's daughter handed to the heroes
No end of foaming flagons filled with ale.
I heard them hail her, people in the hall,
As Frearwaru when she fetched the flagon

And gave it to them, this young, gold-robed girl,
Who is engaged to Ingeld, Froda's heir,
The Scyldings' Friend and Strength has promised so;
The Keeper of the kingdom counts it wise
That with this woman's aid he will end wars
And settle conflicts; seldom is it seen
2030 In any land for long when lords have died
That blades are idle, though the bride be bonny.
The head of Heathobards may be unhappy
And princes of the people be displeased
Were he to walk the hall floor with that woman
While dauntless Danes are dining nobly there,
With all their ancient heirlooms shining on them,
The hand-worked heritage of Heathobards,
And weapons which they wielded once when able
Until at last they lost their lives, both they
2040 And all their comrades, cut down in the conflict.

Then, sitting with his beer, a spearman speaks,
Who sees the treasured swords and thinks of spear-deaths
Of soldiers long ago and sets out sadly—
He has a heavy heart—to let his thoughts
Weigh well the worth of some young warrior
And waken war's worst evils with these words:

"It may be, my young friend, you will remember
That sword your father fought with long before
He went to his last battle with that war-mask,
2050 The dear iron in which Danes then cut him down
And won the field of war where Withergyld

And heroes fell before ferocious Scyldings?
Now here the son of some of those same slayers
Displays himself with pride here in this place,
And boasts of blood and bears the treasured iron,
The prize, appointed properly for you."

He makes the man remember many times
With cutting words until occasion comes
When her unhappy husband, for the deeds
2060 Her father did, is bitten by the blade
And lies in blood; his life is lost; the other
Escapes uncaught, acquainted with the country.
But then on both sides do they break the bonds,
The oaths which earls have sworn; in Ingeld then
Will well up wicked thoughts; his love of wife
Becoming cooler as his cares increase.
I do not hold the Heathobards in high
Regard as firm and faultless friends of Danes
Or take their words as true. But now I turn
2070 Again to Grendel so that you may gain
The truth, my treasure-giver, I can tell
Of combat hand to hand. When heaven's gem
Had slid below the ground, a glowering guest
As dire and dark as night, came down to see
Where we, unharmed, were holding safe the hall.
This dismal fight was fatal first for Hondscio;
His doom was dreadful; soon he lay down dead,
The famous fighter, fitted out for war.
The monster, Grendel, met him with his mouth
2080 And bolted down the brave man bodily.

The red-fanged slayer, still obsessed with slaughter,
Was anxious not to leave with empty arms
And go, all gory, from the gilded hall
For still he stopped to test his strength with me
And grasped with greedy hand. His glove hung down,
A broad, uncanny pouch, secured with clasps,
Which had been worked in weird and wondrous fashion
And done with devilish skill from dragons' skins.
He hoped—this dreadful doer of foul deeds—
2090 To stuff me, sinless, in that dreadful sack
With all the others, but he was unable
When I, in all my anger, stood erect.
To tell the tale would take too long: how I
Repaid the people's foe for evils past.
My noble prince, I paid your people honor
By all my acts, although he did get out
To live his life at ease a little longer.
But in the meantime here his mark remained;
It hangs in Heorot still and he, now humbled
2100 And sad of heart has sunk beneath the surface.
The friend of Scyldings for this fatal gift
Has given me great gifts of plated gold.
When morning came he gave me many more
And sat us down to share a sumptuous feast
With song and sportiveness; a Scylding elder
Was telling tales he knew of former times;
He sometimes strummed the sweet wood of the harp
And sometimes he recited pleasing songs
Both true and tragic, sometimes wondrous tales
2110 Were well recounted by the kindly king;

And sometimes, too, the time-bent sage would start,
The wizened warrior, to bewail past youth
And warrior's strength; his heart would sometimes swell,
His mind remembering so many years.
So we were well employed for one whole day,
Intent on taking pleasure till the night
Came down once more for men; immediately,
To get revenge for grief, came Grendel's mother
Who set out sadly; death had seized her son
In war with Wederas. The monstrous woman,
To seek revenge, then struck a soldier down
In impudence, an instant end of life
For Aeschere, wise and honest old advisor;
Nor might they manage, when the morning came
To all the death-tired, desperate, Danish people,
To place their precious man upon a pyre
For fire to feed on for the enemy
Had carried off the corpse to cold, dark streams
And that, for Hrothgar, was the hardest heartbreak
Of all the sorrows that the sovereign suffered.

"The prince implored me in perplexity
That I display my prowess in the pond
And dare my life to do a warrior's deed
And win renown; he would give rich rewards.
Beneath the water's waves—it's widely known—
I found the grim and ghastly guardian
And held her hard in combat hand to hand;
The billows boiled with blood and I beheaded
The dam of Grendel in that ghastly grotto;

2140 I used an ancient sword. It was not easy
   To bring my body back, as yet not doomed.
   The helper of the heroes, son of Healfdene,
   Again awarded me the greatest gifts;
   The country's king thus kept the proper custom,
   Nor was I willing to refuse reward
   Repaying all my power, precious gifts
   Which have been handed me by Healfdene's son.
   This wealth, O warrior king, I wish to offer
   And gladly give to you; my gladness
2150 Is in your favor, for I have but few
   Close kin, my King, unless I count yourself."

   He bade them then to bring the boar's head flag,
   The high-crowned helmet, handsome battle-sword,
   And strong mail shirt, and then once more he spoke:

  "The wise king, Hrothgar, has enriched me royally
   With war-gear; with his words he ordered me
   That I should tell you all its ancestry.
   He claimed it came from Heorogan, a king
   And long-time leader of the loyal Scyldings.
2160 Reluctantly he left this legacy,
   A breast-shield for his brave, obedient son,
   Named Heoroweard. Now take it; wear it well."

   They told me with this treasure came a team
   Of horses, four of them, all fast, that followed
   Behind, of apple-yellow, and he offered
   More steeds and stores of wealth. So, still, all kin

Should act, and not weave nets for others, nor
Yet draw one's dear companions to their death
With secret skills. King Hygelac had himself
2170 In fiercest fighting found his nephew faithful
And each was careful of the other's interest.
I also heard that he gave to Queen Hygd
The glorious, golden necklace Wealtheow gave him
And stallions, three of them, bright-saddled, sleek.
The princess royal received the radiant ring,
And let the bright jewel beautify her breast.
The son of Ecgtheow showed them thus his spirit,
A man acclaimed in combat, acting kindly,
Not killing comrades caught in drunken revels,
2180 Nor savage-hearted, seeking for esteem.
He guarded well God's gracious gift to him
Of might, much more than other men possessed,
And battle-bravery; but he had been
So meek for many years the Geats' imagined
Him without worth. The lord of Wederas
Thought him no good and gave no gold to him
So well convinced they were he was a weak
And lazy lordling. Later, changes came
And brought him blessings after all these burdens.

2190 The king, the warriors' bulwark, brave in battle,
Then ordered Hrethel's heirloom carried in
All glittering with gold; among the Geats
No one had seen before a sword so splendid.
He laid it in his lap, and gave him land,
Of seven thousand hides, a hall and high seat.

For both of them by birth had been bequeathed
Within that country land by claim of kinship;
To one alone the largest sphere belonged,
The one of higher ranking ruled the realm.

2200 Now, after all of this, events fell out,
When heated clashes caused the king to die
And battle blades had brought about the death
Of his son, too, in spite of sheltering shields,
When savage fighters, Battle-Scylfings, sought
To find their foe while flushed with victory
And hemmed the hunted in with their whole host.
So, as a consequence, the kingdom came
To Beowulf, who bore the burden then
For fifty winters, well he ruled and wisely,
2210 A gray-haired guardian, until one began
To dominate the dark of night, a dragon,
Who held his hoard high up upon the heath.
Beneath a steep and stony barrow stood
A hidden, unknown path. Thus how it happened
Was never known, but someone once went near
The heathen hoard and took up in his hand
A goblet glistening with gems; the guardian
Did not conceal that someone, while he slept,
Conspired to steal it; soon the neighbors knew
2220 And others also what his anger was.
The man had meant to do no mischief,
To do no damage to the dragon's hoard,
But he, a servant, in his sore distress,
A homeless man, I have not heard his name,

In seeking shelter found his way inside,
His soul beset by sin. But when he saw the hoard
All mounded up, this man stood there amazed
And yet however fierce the fear he felt,
The wretched refuge-seeker ran off then
2230 And took the treasure cup. The trove still held
Far more of all that ancient earth-bound treasure,
Concealed by someone who is still unknown,
Who hid there all that huge inheritance,
A costly hoard which came from noble kin,
A deed most wisely done. Grim death took them
In ancient times, but out of all that tribe
The loyal warrior who lived the longest,
A watchman who bewailed his friends, awaited
The same repose; he could but shortly savor
2240 The hoard long held. There, high above the fields,
The barrow waited, waves and water near,
Upon the cliff, secured with skillful care.
The ring-guard quickly carried to the cave
The handsomest of all the heroes' holdings,
The plated gold and priceless pieces, all
The wealth the warriors won, and spoke these words:

* "Hold here, O earth, what heroes may not hold,
The prince's property. In time long past
The warriors won it from you; death in war,
2250 And awful loss of life, has led away
My people; they have perished, passed away;
They knew their hall-joys; none of them can now
Still ply the sword or polish plated flagons

Or costly cups. The cohorts have departed;
The hardened helmets, handsomely adorned,
Shall lose their luster; they shall lie in death
Whose business is to burnish battle-masks;
The coats of war which, close in combat, felt
The bucklers breaking and the bite of iron
2260 Now molder with the men. No more may mail-shirts,
While traveling widely with the warriors, ring,
And hang from heroes shoulders; nor shall harp
Bring joy, nor glee-wood gladden, nor the good
Swift hawk swoop through the hall, no speedy horses
Be stamping in the stable; swept away
By murderous death are many mortal men."

So, sad of heart, he spoke about his sorrow;
As left alone by all, he lingered sadly
Through dark and daylight till the tide of death
2270 Had hit his heart. The hoard's joy then was found
By that black serpent dealing death in darkness
With searing fire and seeking such old barrows,
That smooth assailant soaring through dark skies
Enfolded in his fire. The country folk
Were filled with dreadful fear. He seeks to find
A hoard of heathen gold which he can guard
For endless ages all to no avail.

The people-waster waited three hundred winters
And held the hoard-cave with his hulking strength
2280 Deep under earth until at last his anger
Was called forth by one man. The cup was carried,

Gold-plated, to his lord to plead for pacts
Of peace, and thus the golden pile was plundered,
The ring-hoard's riches robbed, and respite granted
To that unlucky man; his lord then looked
A first time on the fruit of former races.
The serpent then awoke and strife resumed;
The ruthless reptile wriggled over rock
And found a footprint much too far inside.
2290 With quiet cunning he had crept in near
The dragon's head. Thus those undoomed endure
With ease their ills and exile, those the Ruler
Will guard with grace. With greed the hoard-guard hunted,
In hope that he would find that hapless man,
The one who so upset him while he slept.
In rage and wrath, he went around the barrow
And circled, searching, still he found no stranger
In all that wasted land; yet warfare was
His joy; the jolt of battle. So he journeyed
2300 And sought his flagon still, but soon discovered
It was one man who walked off with his gold,
His precious golden prize. Impatiently,
The dragon dawdled until daylight faded,
But by that time the barrow-guard was bursting
With fiery rage and fierce to find again
His darling drinking cup when daylight died
As he had wished. He was not willing longer
To wait upon the wall. He would go out
In flaming fury, frightening in its onset;
2310 For people of that place, and for their prince
It ended afterwards in agony.

The stranger started out to spew his flames
And burn the houses; blazing brightness rose,
Appalling people, for he gave no peace,
That evil thing, to anyone at all.
The serpent's grim assault was widely seen,
The fierceness of the foe, both far and near,
And how he hated Geatish folk and harmed them
And how again he hastened to his hoard
2320 And hall to hide before the sun rose high;
He had enfolded country folk in flames,
A-blaze and burning. In his hidden barrow,
His strength made him feel safe. He was deceived.

They told this terror, too, to Beowulf,
And then he also heard that his own house,
A handsome hall had melted in the heat;
And yet the good man's greatest grief was losing
The high throne of the Geats, that hurt his heart.
The wise man wondered if the Power-Wielder,
2330 The Everlasting Lord, believed his law
Was breached and was embittered. In his breast,
As seldom happened, somber thoughts upsurged.
The serpent's flames had set the forts afire
And flames had leveled lands along the coast
And earthenworks as well. The war-king, then,
The valiant Weder lord, devised revenge;
He bade them build for him, their battle-chief,
An awesome shield, entirely out of iron,
For he was well aware, the warriors' chief,
2340 That wood from all the forests would be worthless,

The linden in the flames. But life is loaned,
And now this proven prince must patiently
Await his journey's end; the worm as well,
Though he had held the hoard-wealth for so long.

The ruler of the rings derided any
Attempt to take a troop against the dragon,
Or use of force; he did not fear the fighting
Nor stand in awe of all the serpent's strength
Or prowess or its power; previously
2350 He had survived adventures, violence,
And heated battle-clash since Hrothgar's hall
Was rid of Grendel's race by that man, rich
In conquest, he who came to grips in combat
With his accursed kin. Not counted least
Is how he fought by hand with Hygelac when
The King of Geats was killed in clash of combat,
The lord and friend of folk in Frisian lands;
The blade imbibed the blood of Hrethel's heir,
The sword had struck him down, but Beowulf
2360 Himself, by his own strength and skill in swimming
Escaped with armor of some thirty earls
Within his arms when he dove in the ocean.
The Hetware battlers would be bold to boast
They faced him ready for a fight on foot
But few of those who faced that fighting man
With shields would safely see their homes again.

The son of Ecgtheow swam across the sea
Alone and low in spirits to his land.

	Here Hygd held out to him a hoard and kingdom,
2370	Both rings and royal throne; she rather thought
	That her son could not hold the homeland throne
	Or fend off foes when Hygelac fell and died.

It soon was clear there was no kind of counsel
The heartsick nobles had that gave them hope
The hero would be head instead of Heardred
Or care to keep the kingdom for himself.
He favored him among his folk with friendship
And kindly counsel till he came of age
To order Weder-Geats. Then exiles entered,
2380 The sons of Ohthere, who sought asylum;
They rose against the ruler of the realm
Of Scylfings, splendid sovereign of the sea
Who spread abroad his store of wealth in Sweden,
Illustrious leader. Then his life was ended;
He was paid back: a mortal wound for welcome;
The sword had struck the son of Hygelac down
And soon the son of Ongentheow went to seek
His home when Heardred had expired in death
And left behind the high throne to be held
2390 By Beowulf. He was a worthy king.

At last he could avenge his leader's loss
And finally become a faithful friend
To Eadgils in his anguish. With his army
He sent across the sea to Othere's son
Both warriors and weapons. Eadgils won
Revenge and coldly cut down King Onela.
And so the son of Echtheow still survived

        In conflict cruel and deeds of courage, too,
        Until the destined day of doom arrived
2400   When he essayed to struggle with the serpent.
        He went as one of twelve, the Geatish warlord
        Aflame with fury, off to find the dragon.
        He heard just how the feuding had begun,
        The malice toward mankind. The costly cup
        The culprit stole had come into his care,
        And that same man, the thirteenth in the throng,
        Because of whom the conflict came to be,
        A captive now, disconsolate, required
        To show the way; unwillingly he went
2410   To show the hidden hall which he had found,
        The secret cave beside the surging sea
        And striving waves; inside the cave was stuffed
        With gems and jewels; the giant guardian,
        A wary warrior kept his watch on it,
        Grown ancient under earth. It was not easy
        For anyone to pay its purchase price.
        The hardy hero sat down on the headland
        And wished his worthy hearth-companions well;
        He gave them gold; but gloom was in his heart,
2420   Which fretted as he faced a fate so near
        That now the gray-haired man must go to greet
        And seek his soul's reward, to cut asunder
        The breath and body; brief henceforth would be
        His fleeting life enfolded in the flesh.
        The battler born of Ecgtheow broke the silence:

"How often I withstood youth's storms and stress
And battle-moments; I remember much;
I was but seven winters when our warlord,
Our folk's befriender, took me from my father.
2430 The king, kind Hrethel, kept and cared for me,
Gave funds and friendship, faithful to our kinship,
Nor was I loved by him the less in life,
A stranger in his stronghold, than his sons,
Than Haethcyn, Herebeald, or my Hygelac.

"His brother brought him to his bed of death,
The eldest; it had been an accident:
When Haethcyn hit him with his horn-tipped shaft,
His lord and friend, the fatal arrow felled him,
It missed its mark and murdered his own kin;
2440 He killed his brother with a blood-stained bolt,
A crime incurable, a costly sin;
It horrified all hearts, but as it happened
The lordling left this life still unavenged.

"Unhappy also is the older man
Who suffers when his son is made to swing
Still green upon the gallows. He must grieve
In songs of sorrow when his son hangs so,
As rations for the ravens; ruing it,
However old he is, he cannot act.
2450 Each morning calls to mind the memory
Of his son's death, nor does he care to dream
Of waiting in his walls for one more son,
A further heir because the first had found

The force of death and fully felt its power;
He sees with sorrow where his son once dwelt,
The wine-hall wasted now, a wind-swept place,
Bereft of joy, where those who rode may rest,
The heroes in their graves, the harps not heard,
No joy within the walls as once there was.

2460 "He seeks his bed still singing songs of grief,
The living for the lost, too large it seems
Are hearths and homes; the head of Wederas
Now had such heartache for his Herebeard that
He suffered ceaselessly, for it was certain
He could not kill the culprit in revenge
Nor show by hostile acts his hate for Heathcyn
Though Heathcyn had no hold upon his heart.
And so, beset by sorrows as he was,
He gave up human gladness for God's glory
2470 And, leaving life here, left to all his heirs
His fields and fortress, like one fortunate.
Then strife resumed between the Swedes and Geats,
A feud they shared across the spreading seas
With hardened hatred after Hrethel died
And Ongentheow's fierce offspring, all of them,
Were fighting fervently; no friendship could
Obtain across the torrent; terrible
And savage slaughter came to Sorrow Hill.

"My closest kinsmen carried out revenge
2480 For feud and falsehood; it is famous now.
The elder of them answered with his life;

A bargain hard it had to be for Haethcyn,
A fatal finish for the Geatish lord.

"When morning came, one kinsman killed the other,
Avenged the slaying with the sword, they say,
When Ongentheow sought Eofor to attack;
His helmet split, the silver-headed Scylfing
Was cut down, colorless; the hand recalled
Such constant quarrels it did not recoil.

2490   "I won in warfare, as I could, the wealth
I had from Hygelac then in heated battle
With shining sword; he gave to me this soil,
My home and heritage; he had no need
To seek among the Swedes or else the Spear-Danes
Or go among the Gifthas folk to gain
A warrior less skillful with his wealth.
In war, it was my way to walk before him;
I liked to be alone and in the lead
And so I shall while this sharp sword remains
2500   Which served and saved me often, soon and late,
And from that moment when, before the forces,
I hewed the Frankish hero down by hand;
He could not carry war-spoils to his king
Or bring the breast adornment back to him,
But he, the banner bearer, fell in battle,
A man of courage, killed but not cut down;
My handgrip crushed his heaving heart within
Its house of bone. But now the biting blade
Must win the hoard by hand and hardened edge."

2510	Then Beowulf spoke boastfully of battle
	And for the final time: "I often fought
	In contests in my youth, and yet I yearn
	As aging folk-trustee to find a fight
	And gain some glory if this grim destroyer
	Comes out in anger from his earthen walls."
	He greeted once again his good companions,
	Each finest fighter for the final time,
	His closest comrades, "Never could I use,"
	He said, "My sword against this serpent seeing
2520	Another means by which to meet this monster
	And grapple, as with Grendel, for the glory;
	But I expect the burning blaze of battle,
	The vapor and the venom, so I venture
	With shield and linked-mail shirt, nor shall
	I ever flee from him one footstep further,
	But we will work out at the wall what fate
	The master of all men may give; my mood
	Is bold, but I forbear to boast for now.
	So wait here at the barrow wearing war-shirts,
2530	In all your armor, till we ascertain
	Who better can abide the battle-wounds
	Between us two. This fight is not a task
	For any mortal's might except for mine,
	To set my strength against the fierce assailant
	And do a warrior's deed by daring this,
	For I shall gain the gold or war's fierce grasp,
	Life's tragic terror, now will take your lord.

The stalwart fighter stood up with his shield,
His sword, and chain-mail shirt; his heart was stirring.
2540 Beneath the stony cliff he stood in strength
And confidence. No coward could so act.
The veteran survivor, virtuous
And good, who came through combat, battle-clash,
And ceaseless strife, now saw a stream come flowing,
And out from underneath the arch of stone
There burst a blazing brook of deadly fire
So hot that he could not approach the hoard
Or long endure the depths of dragon flame
Without the risk of being badly burned.
2550 Then from the Weders' leader went a word:
The fury overflowed that filled his breast
As, strong of heart, he shouted, and the sound
Of it re-echoed from the ancient stone.
The hoard-guard's wrath was roused; he recognized
The human tone; there was no time to talk
Of friendship now, for first there issued forth
Outside the stone the serpent's searing breath,
A scorching battle-smoke that shook the earth.
The battler by the barrow swung his shield,
2560 The Geatish lord, against the ghastly terror.
The coiled-up creature's heart was all inclined
To seek for strife. The sword was drawn already,
The ancient heirloom, edges still undulled.
The stalwart soldier faced the serpent, each
Was fixed on slaughter, fearful of the foe.
Beside his shield and standing stout of heart,
Aware and war-set, while the serpent wound

Itself in coils, the comrade's captain stood.
The serpent slithered from its coils and, scorching,
2570 It sped to meet its fate. The shield was shelter,
Protecting life and limb a lesser time
Than hoped and planned for by the peerless prince
When for the first time on that fatal day
He fought a foe when fate had not decreed
That he should have renown. He raised his hand;
The Geatish leader struck the slimy serpent
But then the ancient heirloom's edge gave way;
The bright blade bit into the creature's bone
But less deep than the leader would have liked;
2580 Embroiled in battle then, the barrow-guard,
In savage mood because the sword had struck,
Spewed out a fatal fire and battle flames
Spread wide. There was no boast of glory won
From him who gave Geats gold. The good blade failed,
Unsheathed in strife, as weapons should not do,
The old, good iron. For Ecgtheow's famous son
It was no easy exodus at all
To put aside his place upon the earth
And, loath though he might be, to live in lodgings
2590 In other realms—as each of us must do—
And leave this loaned-out life. It was not long
Before the fearsome foes met face to face
Again; the guardian took heart; he gasped
Once more. The man who held dominion
Was feeling pain, enfolded in the flames.

No company of close companions came,
No sons of nobles stood beside him now
To brave the battle, bolting to the woods
To save their lives. The sorrow surged up still
2600 In one man's breast; unbreakable the bonds
Of kinship's role for those who reason rightly.
* The son of Weohstan, known as Wiglaf, was
A splendid fighter with the shield, a Scylfing,
A kin of Aelfhere, under armor there
He saw his sovereign suffering from the fire.
Recalling boons that Beowulf had brought,
The wealth and well-loved homes of Waegmundings,
The fiefdom he confirmed to Wiglaf's father,
He could not keep from joining in the clash
2610 But seized his linden shield and drew his sword,
Which all men knew that Eanmund, who was offspring
Of Othere, had passed on, that friendless exile
Whom Weohstan slaughtered with the sharp-edged sword
In battle; later he brought back the bright
And shining helmet, ring-mail shirt, and sword,
The artwork of an older age of giants;
Onela brought these tools of battle back
With metal polished, but he made no mention
Of crossing swords, though he had killed his kin.
2620 He saved this store of wealth for many seasons,
The shining sword and war-shirt, till his son
Might like his father, too, perform great feats.
He gave the gift of garb for battle also,
Of countless kinds, when his turn came to die,
Both wise and full of years. Then, for the first time

          The youthful fighter faced the battle furies;
          He braved the battle by his noble lord;
          His spirit did not shrink back from the struggle,
          Nor did his father's present fail in fight,
2630   As soon the serpent saw in deadly strife.

          With many words of wisdom, Wiglaf spoke;
          He said in saddened spirit to his comrades,
          "I swore our sovereign once a solemn oath
          When in his great hall he was giving gifts:
          We would reward him surely for this war-gear,
          This helmet and this hard-edged sword, if he
          Should be in trouble. From his troops he took us
          According to his will and weighed us worthy
          To go with him, and gave me all these gifts
2640   Because he counted us as capable
          Of bearing helmets boldly in the battle,
          Although our lord had longed to do alone,
          Our country's keeper, this courageous act,
          Since he had gained the greatest glory always
          By daring deeds. But now the day has come
          When he, our lawful lord is lacking strength
          Which good supporters give; so let us go
          To help our battle-hero in this heat,
          This fierce and fiery terror. For, God knows,
2650   I think it better to embrace the blaze
          Together with the one who gave us gold
          Than slink back home with shields upon our shoulders,
          Or so it seems to me, unless the serpent
          Is felled at first and we ourselves defend

Our Wederas' chief's welfare. Well I know
His steps have not been such that he should suffer
And he alone of all the Geats' assembly
Should sink in strife; for us shall sword and helmet,
Mail-shirt and battle-shroud, be shared together."
2660 Then with his war-helm on he waded in
To bring his sovereign his assistance, saying:
"My dearest Beowulf, now do those deeds
That you in youth had said that you would do
As long as you had life, and do not let
Your glory fail. So now in famous feats,
My lion-hearted lord, defend your life
With all your strength and I will give you aid."

When he had made this speech, the savage serpent
Returned again, the grim and angry guest,
2670 In glowing floods of fire, to find his foes,
The hated humans. Heat flowed out in waves,
Consumed the shields down to their central bosses;
His chain-mail shirt assured no shelter
And so the youthful soldier bravely stepped
Beneath the shelter of his sovereign's shield,
Discarding his. The battle-king recalled
His former famous deeds, and by main force
He struck with such impassioned strength
The sword stuck in the skull. And Naegling snapped,
2680 The blade of Beowulf broke off in battle,
So old, engraved in gray. It was not granted
To him to find its edge of iron was able
To help in battle's heat; so strong his hand

That every sword he swung, I surely know,
His stroke would over-strain when borne in strife;
Yes, weapons washed in bloody wounds still failed.

A third time, then, the thrasher of the tribe
Recalled the feud, the fierce and fiery dragon,
2690 And rushed his rival when he found the room
And, battle-grim, he grabbed the good man's neck
In fiendish fangs; there flooded over him
Life-giving blood; the gore was gushing out.
What I have heard is how the hero then
Who kept beside the king disclosed his courage,
The strength and stamina instilled at birth;
He did not heed the head although the hero
Had had his hand burned as he came to help;
He hit the hostile guest beneath the heart,
2700 The armored soldier's sword point sank deep in,
All gleaming gold, and then the fire began
To slacken. Then the king himself, who still
Could wield his wisdom, drew his war-dirk out,
The bitter blade he bore upon his shirt;
The Geatish captain cut the creature's middle.
They felled the foe and, fearless, took its life;
The noble kinsmen killed the cruel serpent;
They stood there side by side as men should do
In time of need. The king would never know
2710 Another hour of triumph of his own
Within the warrior's world. But then the wound
The dragon dealt him earlier that day
Began to sting and swell, and soon he found

That in himself some deadly substance seethed,
Some penetrating poison. So the prince
Then went back to the wall and, thinking wisely,
He sat there on a seat where he could see
The stones the giants set so solidly
To hold the arches of the earth-house up.
2720 And then his thane, so thoroughly kind-hearted,
With his own hand unloosed the battle-helmet
Of Beowulf, his famous friend. He found
Some water with which he could wash his wounds.

His lord then spoke despite the searing pain
The wicked wound was giving; well he knew
The last of his allotted life had come
And human happiness; for him the span
Of days was ending; death was drawing near.

"I would be glad to give these garments now
2730 To my own son if such I had been sent
To be the heir of all that I have owned
And guard my goods. I guided all this land
For fifty winters, while no foreign folk-king
From any of our neighbors anywhere
Was brave enough to bring his troops for battle
Or try to terrify me all that time.
I waited in my world and ruled it well,
I never sought for strife and seldom swore
An unjust oath. And now for all of this
2740 I may be glad, though maimed with mortal wound,
Because the king of all cannot accuse me

When, at the end, my life has left my limbs
Of killing any kin. Now quickly go,
And see the store of wealth beneath the stone;
The deadly dragon, Wiglaf, dearest friend,
Is sleeping, sorely wounded, shorn of wealth;
Go speedily so I may see that store
Of golden goods and gladly gaze upon
The shining, shapely gems and so grieve less,
Because that treasure-trove is here, to take
My leave of life and lordship held so long."

They say the son of Weohstan then went swiftly
When once his wounded lord had said these words,
Obeyed the battle-broken king, and bearing
A battle-shirt embroidered, in the barrow
Beyond the flat ledge, did the fighter find
In triumph that a treasure-trove of jewels
And gleaming gold was lying on the ground.
The dragon, dawn-marauder, in its den
Had hanging tapestries and tarnished tankards,
Great flagons fashioned by a former race,
Their polishers departed, plating stripped,
And rotted, rusting helmets, rings for arms,
All coiled with cunning craft. A treasure cache
Of gold within the ground may make all gasp
No matter who has hidden such a hoard;
And hanging high above the hoard he saw
A golden standard sewn by skillful fingers,
Of matchless merit and emitting light
By which to glimpse the ground within the grotto

And treasure-trove. But yet no trace at all
Was seen there of the serpent. He was slain.
I hear the heaping hoard was rifled then,
The giants' wondrous work, by one lone man
Who bore out in his bosom bowls and plates
Of his own taste. He took the standard too,
That brightest beacon, and the blade which wounded
The ancient ruler with its edge of iron,
The strong protector of the treasure-trove,
2780 Who for so long had fought with fiery terror
And held the hoard with fiercely welling heat
In darkest night till he was doomed to death.
The servant, seeking swiftly to return
With treasure, and intent now to determine
If he would find his lord alert and living,
The Weder leader, where he left him lying,
His strength subsiding, where he saw him last,
Then took the treasure and returned to find
His lord now lying at the end of life
2790 And bleeding; then he bent down there to bathe
His wound with water till a pointed word
Within his breast out burst. The battle-king,
While gazing at the gold began to speak:

"I give the God of glory grateful thanks,
The ever-living Lord, who lets me now
Lay eyes on all this treasure and declare
That I was able at the end of life
To offer all this wealth to everyone;
But I have paid the price for this great pile

2800	With my allotted life. Your lot is now
	To know this nation's need when I am gone.
	Go find strong men when funeral fires burn down
	To shape a shining mound beside the sea
	As my memorial among my people
	And have it tower high on Hronesness
	That so those sailing by may see and call it
	The barrow built for Beowulf; all those
	Who drive their masts through mists upon the main."
	He took the shining circlet from his shoulders,
2810	The hero brave, and handed on his helmet,
	All shining gold, his battle-shirt and circlet,
	And warned the war-like youth to use them well:

"You are the last one left of all our line
Of Waegmundings, for we were swept away
By destiny which doomed us all to death
Though fearless fighters. I must follow them."
This was the final word the warrior spoke,
Words from his heart before he faced the flames,
The pyre, the searing surge of heat; his soul
  2820 Then journeyed out to seek the just man's judgment.
And so the soldier who was still so young,
In sorrow saw stretched out upon the sod
The man most dear of all, now at life's end
And suffering sorely. There the slayer also
Lay down deprived of life, the dreadful dragon
Now routed, ruined; after that, the ring-hoard
Belonged no longer to the loathsome serpent;
The sword with iron edges took him off,

        Its hammer-hardened blade, well honed in battle,
2830   Had stilled the wide-winged flyer with such wounds
        That he fell down and died outside his door,
        No more to mount the midnight air in might
        And turn and glide and glory in his gold
        And flaunt his figure, for he fell to earth,
        The battle-leader's blows had brought him down.

        It is not often in this world that I
        Have heard of heroes who were strong enough,
        However daring were the deeds they did,
        To rush against the rabid ravager
2840   Or lay his hands upon the hidden hoard
        If then the warder were found watching him,
        Abiding in the barrow. Beowulf
        Repaid his portion of the princely hoard.
        They each had come now to the end of all
        The life they had been loaned. It was not long
        Before those late to battle left their lair,
        The ten who timidly had broken trust:
        They shirked the battle with their swords and shields
        And left the lord to whom they should be loyal.
2850   So now in shame they came with shouldered shields,
        War-liveried, to where their leader lay
        And witnessed Wiglaf, weary as he was,
        Foot-soldier sitting there beside his lord
        And washing him with water worthlessly;
        Nor could he on this earth for all his efforts
        Still longer keep his captain clothed with life
        Nor render void the Ruler's resolution,

> For God still gives commands that govern life
> For all of us, and does so even now.".

2860 The fighter found it easy then to fling
Hard words at warriors wanting fortitude;
These words were Wiglaf's, who was son of Weohstan,
Who spoke with sorrow, seeing unloved men:
"To speak the truth, a man may surely say
The lord who lavished lovingly on you
The armor in which you are all arrayed,
Who often on the ale-bench handed out
To those who sat in hall both helm and hauberk,
The chief who gave his chosen choicest gifts,
2870 The finest he could find from far or near:
These war-clothes were thrown uselessly away;
In vain your valiant lord had valued them.
Our country's king would have no cause to boast
Of gallant comrades, yet the gift of God,
The Victory King, was vengeance; he prevailed
To strike with his own sword, himself alone.
I could do little to prolong his life
In that last battle, but above my strength
I yet began to give my gallant kin
2880 My aid; the enemy grew ever weaker,
Less fierce the fire still flowing from his head;
I struck him with my sword, but sparse the helpers
Who crowded round our king when crisis came.
So now shall getting gifts and giving swords
And all the happiness of home and hearth
And claims of land be canceled for your kin

                And every man among your family members
                Must go in exile when the other earls,
                Though far away, shall find out of your flight
    2890   And shameful deeds. I doubt not death is better
                For any soldier than to sit in shame and safety."

                He bade them tell abroad the battle's outcome
                Along the sea-cliff where the soldiers sat
                All morning long and in a mournful mood;
                They sat there with their shields, uncertain whether
                The day of death of someone dear to them
                Had reached him, but the rider on the ridge
                Did not delay to let them learn his news;
                He took great care to tell the story truly:

    2900   "The one who worked the Weders' will so long,
                Our dearest lord is lying down in death,
                Lies still where he was slaughtered by the serpent;
                Beside him stretched out there the one who slew him
                Lies stricken with the dagger since no sword
                Yet made had might to maim the monster
                In any way. There Wiglaf sits and watches
                Beside the dying, smitten son of Weohstan,
                One heartsick hero by the other's head
                Keeps watch now with the ones who died, with both
    2910   The loved and loathed alike. And now it seems
                That warfare will be waged against our land
                When Franks and Frisians learn the king has fallen
                And all become aware. This quarrel came
                Most harshly to the Hugas; Hygelac had

Come faring with his fleet to Frisian land;
The Hetware then had hurled themselves on him
With courage and because their company was strong
They forced the fighting man to fall
And toppled him amid his troops. No treasure
2920 That earl could give his escort. Ever after,
No Merovingian monarch showed us mercy,
Nor should I seek from any Swedish people
Their faith or friendship; people far and wide
Knew Ongentheow had ended earthly life
For Haethcyn, Hrethel's son, at Hrefnawuden
When Geatish people in their pride first pressed
Their siege and struck against the Scylfing tribe;
The sire of Othere made a swift response;
Though old, his craft could fill the foe with fear.
2930 He struck the sea-king down, but saved his wife,
Whose age was great and all whose gold was gone,
But of whom Othere and Onela both
Had come. All those who hated him he harried
Until they scarcely slipped away to safety
And went to Hrefnawuden with no leader.
He sore beset the sword's survivors there
And often in that endless night he vowed
That woeful band so weary with their wounds
Would face his sharp-edged swords when sunrise came
2940 And slaughter; some would swing on gallows-trees
Exposed to beaks of birds. But hope came back
To downcast minds when day again was dawning
And all of them could hear the horn of Hygelac
And trumpet call. And then the king did come

Along the track attended by his troop.
That blood-soaked scene of Swedes and Geats,
The fall of those who fled, was known afar,
And how the folk themselves had fueled the feud.
The good, wise king, though grieving greatly, then,
2950   Earl Ongentheow, so old and overcome
With sadness sought a sanctuary there
Since he had heard of Hygelac's name in war,
That king's great battle-craft, and could not think
His sailors could be sure to stand against
Those sea-born soldiers to protect his treasure,
His kith and kin; and so he took great care
And under earthen walls retired. This offered
The Swedes an opening, and they overran
The refuge fortress flaunting flags of Hygelac's
2960   When Hrethel's cohort came against the camp.

"Then old and honored Ongentheow as well
Was brought to bay behind the flashing blades,
The country's king required to place himself
Before the feet of Eofer for his fate.
Then Wulf's son, Wonred, with his weapon struck
A savage blow and blood came bursting out
And flowed forth from his hair. But fearless still,
The silver-mantled Scylding swiftly answered
That death-blow and he dealt a deadly stroke
2970   When he, the tribal king, then turned back to him;
Nor was the worthy son of Wonred able
To act in answer to the older man,
For he had hacked down through the helmet

So he, half-blind with blood, was forced to bow,
And fell face forward, but it was not fatal;
The warrior rallied from his woeful wounds.
Then Eofer taking up the ancient sword,
The thane of Hygelac, hewed his iron helmet
With his broad blade above the barrier
2980 Of shields, and so the king was subjugated,
The patron of his people perished there.

"Then many quickly came to help his kin
And raise him up when room had been made ready
And they could govern all that gory ground.
So each stripped off the armor of another
And took the iron shirt off of Ongentheow,
The hilted hand sword and his helmet, took
The old king's armor, all of it, to Hygelac.
He took the treasure and he told them gravely
2990 He would reward them, and he kept his word.
The Geats' lord gave to those engaged in battle,
To Eofer and to Wulf, to each he offered
A treasure hoard when he came home at last.
He lavished on them land and linked iron rings,
A hundred thousand worth, which humans hardly
Could grudge to them since they had gained the glory.
He offered Eofer then his only daughter
To grace his home, a good will guarantee.

"It is this feud, this ancient enmity,
3000 This mortal malice, making me believe
The Swedish folk will set upon us soon

When they have learned at last our leader here
Has lost his life, that he who lately fought
To save our hoard and homes from those who hate us
When heroes fell, shield-fighters, fearless, strong,
Supporting people's good and practicing
Brave deeds beside. We must bestir ourselves
And see our sovereign stretched out on the ground
And bear the one who brought such bounty to us
3010 Along his pathway to the pyre. No pittance
Shall melt down with this mighty king, but much
Good treasure, countless gold once grimly gained.
For now, at last, our king has lost his life
To buy these bracelets which the blaze shall eat
And flame enfold. No man in future years
Shall wear this wealth, nor any woman fair
Shall wreathe her neck in all these radiant rings,
But sad of heart and shorn of shining gold shall walk
Not once but always in an alien land.
3020 Our leader now has laid aside all laughter,
High spirits, and all sport. The spear shall be
Clutched often when the cock crows in the cold
And held up in the hand. The harpist's music
Shall rouse no warriors; the raven rather,
Desiring human corpses, croaks its call
To ask the eagle how the eating is
When with the wolf he has laid waste the slain."

Both facts and future doom, with few mistakes,
3030 He spoke of sadly. So the soldiers stood
And entered under Earnaness in gloom

To witness, welling up with tears, this wonder.
There stretched out soulless on the sand they saw,
With death now drawing near, the one in days
Gone by who brought them rings, the bravest man,
The Weders' leader leaving life at last.
The doughty warrior died a wondrous death;
But first they saw an even stranger shape,
The loathsome serpent lying lengthwise there,
3040 Extended flat, the fearful, fiery dragon,
Now flawed by its own flames with fatal marks.
In feet, it measured fully fifty paces
In length while lying there. For long it ruled
The evening air; and underneath the earth
Went down to its own den, but now in death
The end of all his earth-cave joy had come.
Beside him stacks of bowls were seen and flagons,
And piles of plates as well as precious swords,
Rust-eaten, all corroded, as if they
3050 Had been held there all through a thousand winters.
This heirloom store of ancient artistry,
The gold of men long gone, is guarded now
By spells of such a sort that none may touch
That golden garner till the Lord our God,
The Conquest King, our shield and confidence
Enables one to open up that hoard,
A person God may pick as he deems proper.

It then appeared quite plainly that no profit
Was gained by him who hid the glittering gold,
3060 Ill-gotten gains, beneath the wall. The guardian

Had felled one special fighter first. Their feud
Had now been settled. No one knows
Where matchless men shall finally meet the end
Of life, and fate will not allow them longer
To come with kinfolk to the common hall.
So Beowulf went bravely to the barrow
To seek its savage sentry, unaware
What fate might finally take him from this world.
The peerless princes who had placed that hoard
3070 Had cursed it deeply till the day of doom
So any man who made away with much
Would sin, and so be shut in devils' shrines,
Held fast in fetters, tortured fiendishly,
Except a seeker who had first perceived
* That God alone can give us lasting gold.

Them Wiglaf, son of Weohstan, spoke these words:
"The misery of many men is often
The work of one man's will as we have seen.
We could not lend our lord so much beloved,
3080 Our kingdom's keeper, counsel to avoid
Engaging with the guardian of the gold
And leave him lying where he long had been
Within his den until the day of doom.
He held to his high destiny; we see the hoard
He gained at grievous cost. Too grim the fate
Which pushed the people's king to find that place.
I went inside myself and saw it all:
I made my way to see the massive mound.
Unfriendly was the forcing of that fortress

3090 Beneath the earth wall. Quickly I picked up
      As much as might be held, a vast amount
      Of hoarded wealth, and then I hauled it here
      To let my leader see it, still alive.
      He was aware, and we then spoke of much.
      The elder, grieving, asked that I should greet you
      And bid you build for him a barrow high
      Upon the place of pyres, and prominent
      For your beloved lord, of all men living
      The worthiest warrior in the whole wide world
3100 While wealth within his walls still was his joy.

      "But let us now go near another time
      To gaze on all that gleaming heap of gold,
      The glories in the grotto. I will guide you
      So you may now stand near enough to see
      The bracelets, bands of gold. Prepare the barrow
      As quickly as you can so when we come
      Our captain can be carried out again
      Where he, our leader so beloved, must long
      Be kept within the care of God our King."

3110 The battle-brave man who was born of Weohstan
      Gave word of what was wanted to the warriors
      And heads of households, owners of the halls,
      To fetch the faggots for the funeral pyre,
      "For now the flames shall gnaw our noble leader,
      This boldest warrior, as the blaze grows black.
      He often overcame the shower of iron
      When storms of arrows sent out from the strings

           Were shot above the shield-wall and the shaft
           With eager feathers following the flint."

3120   The son of Weohstan, wise in all his ways,
           Assembled seven of the staunchest men
           Of all the earls who followed on the king,
           And he went with the warriors, one of eight,
           Beneath the barrow wall; the one who walked
           In front held up a flaming torch to follow.
           They drew no lots to loot what lay before them
           For all of it was open to them now;
           They saw it resting, rusting in that room,
           And did not take the time to shed a tear,
3130   But quickly carried outward what they could
           Of all that precious pile. They pushed the dragon
           Away and off the cliff where waves would wash
           And flood enfold the treasure trove's defender.
           They weighed the wagon down with woven gold
           Of countless kinds, and then the king was carried,
           The hoary hero, up to Hronesness.
           The Geatish people got together then
           Within that place a pyre not poorly made
           And hung with helmets and with hero's shields
3140   And bright mail battle-shirts as he had bid.
           They sadly set their chieftain in the center;
           The lord they loved was laid there by his thanes.
           They built up on the barrow there the biggest
           Of pyres for warriors, and the wood smoke went
           Up black above the blaze, the blast of flames
           Was woven with the weeping. Swirling winds

Abated till the house of bones was broken
And heat had reached the heart. Unhappy, then,
And mournful, they moaned their lord's demise.
3150 And so a Geatish woman sang her sorrow
For Beowulf; her hair was bound in back;
She gave her grief a voice again, and sang
Her dread of harm to come from hostile hosts,
Of terrorizing troops, captivity
And slaughter. Heaven swallowed up the smoke.

The Weder warriors then all worked to build
A haven on that headland, high and broad,
And widely seen away out on the waves.
In ten days' time, with timber, they set up
3160 Where flames had burned, a battle-hero's beacon,
And with it circling walls, the worthiest
That artful men were able to put up.
They placed within the barrow bracelets, brooches,
And many other things that men had meanwhile
Brought hither from the hoard in hostile mood
So that the earth could hold the heroes' hoard,
The gold within the ground, where still it glows,
As useless as it ever was to all.

Around that rampart rode twelve chosen men,
3170 All brave in battle, born of noble sires,
Who, woeful, wanted to bewail the king,
And make their mournful songs about the man;
They hailed his heroism and his heart,
Repeating praises of his prominence

As any man should laud the lord he loves
And hold him in his heart when he at last
Goes forth, departing from this house of flesh.

Thus did the Weder folk bewail in words
Their famous leader's fall; but all his friends
3180 Asserted he was surely of all sovereigns
The mildest man and gentlest in his manner,
Most kind to kindred and most keen for fame.

BEYOND BEOWULF

* Attend! You sometimes still can hear the sound
Of flames in fury as the funeral pyre
Of Beowulf went blazing up; the bonfire
That caused the corpse to burn had carried with it
The heart-felt hopes of all the hero's folk
Who looked to him to lead them. They had lost
The one who went before them, waged their wars,
Who gave them gold, and helped them guard their homes.
The steadfast warriors stood about and stared
10 As if to find their future in the flames,
And lingered till at last the evening light
Had faded fully from the flaming sky,
Then drifted home to heal their aching hearts
With sleep, the silent cure of ceaseless cares.
Thick darkness then came down around their dwellings;
Around them roamed the beasts unruled by law
Who forage freely in the night for food
And catch and kill the creatures that they seek.

When morning came once more to Middle Earth,
*20 The red sun rose and roused them from their rest,
God's candle cast its light across the world
On fertile fields and forests far away,
And sleepers slowly stirred and sought their friends.
A sense of dread and doom now weighed them down,
Of absence everywhere that all could feel,
The lack of that strong leader they had lost.
With slow and solemn steps they set to work;
They raked the ruined remnants of their houses
To search for something that was not consumed

30   By fire before the serpent's blazing fury,
      The damage that the dragon's wrath had done.
      They brought stout oaken beams to build anew
*   The high feast hall and people's simple homes.

      At last the largest house was laid in order,
      A handsome hall, though less than Heorot,
      Well-braced with boards and bound with hammered iron
      A mead hall meant for mighty warriors
      To celebrate success in war, where bards could sing
      And harpers help them raise the warriors' hearts
40   With tales of triumphs in the times gone by.
      When darkness deepened at the end of day
      The warriors walked into the wooden hall;
      They filled their flagons, foaming ale was passed
      From hand to hand around the feasting house.
      One question came to all: Who will be king
      Since now our guide and guardian is gone?
      Some wondered whether Wiglaf was the one
*   Who might do most to make their foes afraid.
      Undaunted by the dragon, Wiglaf dared
50   To battle in the burning flames with Beowulf
      And wield the weapon left by Weohstan;
      He struck his sword deep in the sky-Lord's throat.
      But others, anxious for an older king,
      A conqueror who had killed his foes in combat,
      Were looking for a leader rather like
      The kings that other countries counted on
      To wage their wars and bring them rich rewards.

Then Sigelac, the strongest champion, stood,
A warrior battle-worn through many winters.
He called for quiet in the clamorous hall
And struck his shield until the tumult ceased.
"The grief we share is great," so he began,
"And all of us are overcome with sorrow;
The leader that we loved, who shared our lives,
Who came to grips with Grendel long ago,
That marvelous man, who made the monster yield,
Was called by Glory's King to come with him
And find the far-off land for men of fame
That no one who is now among us knows.
He sleeps in silence, free of all life's struggles,
And honored even in his death by all of us;
His strength has brought us what we still possess:
The gifts of gold which he so freely gave.
We offer Wiglaf also every honor,
Though young in years, he would not yield to any
But battled bravely there with Beowulf,
And someday, surely, he will strongly lead;
He fears no foe and will win lasting fame;
But meanwhile we must make our plans, take measures,
For truly these are times that threaten tempests;
Dark clouds are coming and we must be careful
As foes in fury come to fall upon us.
They will have heard our hero cannot hinder
Their taking all the treasure that we toiled for.
So let us look then for an able leader
Of strength and stature who can face such storms,
One who can give to us the gifts he garnered,

And such as I have stored away myself:
Bright rings of reddish gold and goblets wrought
90 By seasoned craftsmen using subtle skills,
Sharp biting battle axes and well-burnished shields,
And cups deep cut in curious designs
By elvish artisans in ancient times.
So come, my comrades, let me counsel you,
For everywhere our enemies are arming
And well aware of all our weaknesses.
Today we dare not dally; we must act."

The warriors struck their spears against their shields
Until the rafters rang; they cheered and roared
100 And shouted, 'Sigelac!' A single mind
Held all those in the hall. The warriors hoped
To act, and thus to ease their anxious minds.
They saw in Sigelac a man to suit their mood.
The oldest warrior, Aelric, watched them all
But did not stand or shout. It seemed to him
That he could smell the smoke of smoldering fires
And see the black flames and the buildings burning
And hear the howl of wolves and women wailing,
Lamenting men returning nevermore,
110 But no one noticed that he never moved.
Then cups of mead were carried round; the crowd
Rejoiced and joined their friends in joyous song
Until at last they let the lights go out,
The flaming torches flickered as they failed.
Then men made beds with bolsters on the wooden boards,
And weary soldiers sank down to their sleep.

When bird-song broke out and the daylight broadened
They sent a summons to the sleep-drenched men
From Sigelac to stand with him and swear
Allegiance to their leader, to be loyal
To him their chosen chief and champion.
They gathered round him where the grass was green
And clustered there all clothed as if for combat;
The earls were all well-armed with ashwood spears,
And proud to go campaigning with companions
Whose mettle had been measured many times.
When Sigelac had seen them all he spoke,
A veteran whose voice was vehement,
The son of Selibrod, a seasoned fighter:
"I summoned you to stand with me and strike
Our foes with fear as fighters ought to do,
All those abroad held back by Beowulf
Through soft and kindly seasons. On all sides
Our neighbors knew that they could not attack
Our homes while he, our champion, was here,
But we have gained no gold and won no glory;
Our youths who yearn to fight as young men should
Have never drawn a sword or dealt the death blow
Or seen the steaming blood spurt from the wound.
We lie here far too long like wolves in lairs
Who keep their cubs with care but never go
To forage for their food and fail to teach
Their offspring any of the arts of war.
So peace has poisoned us. Let us prepare
Our swords for slaughter and to slay our foes,
So we shall garner glory for the Geats

And take home treasure to enrich our tribe;
The world shall wonder at the fame we win
And all the trophies that we take in triumph."

150 Then Wiglaf said, "The world may wonder also
What failings of our foes offended us
Enough to cause such killing and such carnage.
The Geats are loyal to leaders; let them hear;
Then we will follow faithfully as friends
And comrades in a common course of action."
The men around him murmured; many thought
It wrong to raise such questions; in a rage
They shook their spears, and shouted, "Sigelac!"
A few, who had not fought before, were fearful,
160 While others, undecided, asked each other
To give them guidance: whether they should go
To far and distant fields in search of fame
Or stay and seek for safety in their homes.
Their eyes turned then to Aelric, oldest of them,
Both gray and gaunt with years, and greatly honored,
One who, at every turn, would tell the truth.
His voice was low, they leaned to him to listen.
So Aelric said in slow and solemn tones,
"I wish I had the wisdom I had once
170 As to the future which the fates have fashioned.
The years have passed, and yet I once was young
And eager to acquire the archers' art;
My sight was sharp then and my hands were steady;
When I had sent my arrow on its way
The shaft could split a distant slender reed,

But then a breeze, a breath, could bend the reed
And override my arrow's careful aim
And so the shot I took could go astray
However good the guidance that I gave.
180 I sought to get myself a sailor's skills
And ventured very far on voyages
Across the cold, black seas to foreign coasts
Where grapes are grown and where the grass is green
In March, and I saw many other marvels,
And I have learned some lessons in my life:
I have been taught you cannot turn the tides
Or steer a ship against a storm-tossed sea.
I learned the human heart can hold much evil
And much good, but what the gods will give us,
190 I think that none can know. How can we name
A force we cannot fathom? We are feathers,
And we are blown about by every breeze."
The ranks were growing restless, ripe for action;
They did not like to listen very long.
The son of Selibrod then called for silence.
"Too many words," he said, "can muddy minds;
Wiglaf has asked a question; I will answer.
* I might remind you of the messenger
Who brought you baleful news of Beowulf
200 And told you tales of terror soon to come.
He said the Swedes would sweep us all away,
The Scylfing spearmen, striving for revenge,
Who think their threats will throw us into flight.
But they have killed our kings; when Hathcyn came
To land they lurked in hiding, launched their spears,

And Ongentheow rushed from unseen ambush
And struck his helmet so he sank and died.
Onela also, honest though he was,
Struck Herdred, son of Hygelac; he hit
210 And broke his bone-cage with a broad axe stroke;
And after that his brother's offspring also
Was slain as slaughter spread and valiant men,
Though brave and true, were beaten down in blood.
Why should we wait and let them work their will?
Let us now venture victory and revenge;
Let those who will keep watch with Wiglaf here
Until the time when we return in triumph.
I call on you to come with me and conquer."

The warriors then went willingly to work
220 To bring aboard the ring-prowed dragon-boats
The gleaming armor they had gladly gathered:
The hardened helmets and the chain-mail hauberks,
The spears and swords and sturdy linden shields.
Above the boat they hoisted colored banners
That shone and glistened in the setting sun.
The heroes then came to the high-roofed hall,
The seasoned fighters sought to celebrate
Their comradeship and courage in the conflict
That they faced. They found their places; food was brought;
230 The mead bowls passed among them; merriment
Increased as warriors cast their cares away.
A bard sang ballads of the bravery
* Of heroes such as Hygelac, whose horn
* Had signaled slaughter of the Swedes

At Ravenswood; their ruler's reign was ended.
He struck his hand upon the harp he held,
His clear voice carrying across the hall,
And sang of Beowulf, who boldly battled
The monster, Grendel's mother, in the mere
240   And dealt a death blow to the fiery dragon
Whose wrath had rained down ruin on them all.
He also told a tale of distant travel,
When Beowulf had brought them strange-shaped bones
Of serpents of a size no one had seen.
He went with other warriors toward the west,
For some had said that there were sun-warmed lands
Where golden stones lie gleaming on the ground,
Where snow and ice are very seldom seen,
And bubbling springs restore the sightless eyes
250   And withered limbs, and wanderers are welcomed
By maids with mead so sweet and marvelous
That all are overcome with ecstasy
And none who tread that soil return to tell
The way. Their chief had chosen champions
And well-made, wide-bowed, wooden ring-necked ships.
They stocked them well with spears and shields
And all the weapons warriors would want
And shoved the sturdy ships away from shore,
The carved prows cutting through the cold gray waves
260   And taking them in time to towering cliffs
Where thick, green glaciers thawed and thundered down
And made great mountains, melting as they floated
Upon the sea, a sight unseen before
By any of the Geats, who watched in awe.

They stared at seals and certain white-winged birds
That skim the waves. Still working further west
They found at last a lifeless, barren land,
A wild and windswept, wintry kind of place.
They did not stay, but steered still further south
270 Until the weather was more mild and warm,
And there they found a fine and fertile land
Where grapes were growing, green on ancient vines.
The natives fled away at first in fear;
They had not seen such helmets, hiding faces,
And burnished bright with gold, prepared for battle,
High-crowned and crafted with great care and skill,
Embellished with the heads of boars and bears,
That gave the Geats a grim and frightening look
And filled the native folk at first with fear.
280 But then they glimpsed their golden rings and bracelets
And saw the wrought iron spear-tips and the swords
And came back creeping very cautiously
To offer beads and broken stones in barter
And certain fruits and finely finished furs,
But Beowulf forbade the men to bargain
Lest one of them be wounded by their weapons.
But when ignored, the natives made a dreadful noise
And set upon the soldiers suddenly,
Who, caught off guard, could barely beat them back,
290 Although they slaughtered some of them with swords.
Then others in the woods let fly their arrows
And wounded Wulfric and two other warriors.
Without their battle bows, the Geats drew back
And sent their ship back out to sea.

They went no further west, but wondered still
How far the ocean flows. They did not find
A land of light and sun. But when at last
They set their sails toward home a monstrous serpent
With hideous fangs and eyes that flashed like fire
300   Bore down on them with dreadful speed and drove
Its head against their hollow boat. In horror
They saw it wrap itself in rings around
The boat with Beowulf on board. It crushed
The oaken beams with ease and all seemed lost.
It gripped one Geat within its gruesome jaws
And diving downward dragged him to the depths
To make his meal. The two remaining boats
Then pulled companions from the pounding waves
And set their sails to flee away in sorrow.
310   But Beowulf forbade them, kept the boats
On watch and waiting in the swirling waves,
Imagining the monster might return
To search for sailors for a second meal.
With twine they tied the ships together tightly
To keep the serpent's coils from crushing them
And, circling slowly in the sullen waves,
They drifted, filled with dread, in dwindling circles,
And wondered whether one of them might well
Be next to know the monster's teeth and nails.
320   Then, suddenly, the serpent struck their boats
From underneath, and all at once came up
With Ferlag's blood still flowing from its fangs
And battered on the boats' stout boards
Till Beowulf could dive and dig his dagger

Into the serpent's scales with all his strength.
The creature coiled around him, carried him
Back down in darkness to its dwelling place,
A coal-black cavern crammed with dead men's bones.
The hero drove his dagger deeper still
330   And hung on tight behind the monster's head
So that it could not catch him in its claws.
It tried; it turned and twisted terribly
And hoped to hold the hero in its claws
Or take him in its terrifying teeth
And break his bone cage. Beowulf held on,
And, slowly sliding forward, stuck his dagger
In brain, beneath the bone, above the neck.
It did not die, but made a desperate lunge
And, hissing horribly, it heaved its back
340   Against a granite wall to grind the champion
To death; but, dropping down, to draw his sword
He quickly struck to cut the creature's head off,
To slice through bone and sinew with his sword.
Although his blade was broken by the bone,
He cut the coiling carcase into pieces.
Meanwhile above, his brothers in the boat
Saw boiling blood and bits of flesh
Come surging up to stain the swollen waves,
But looked in vain and feared their leader lost
350   Until, quite suddenly, they saw him swimming
Toward the boats and holding up the horrid head.
They tied it to the side; they would not take
The scabrous thing inside the ship with them.
Then, hoisting sails, they headed for their homes;

They steered their sea-steed through the stiffening breeze
And wind-blown waves. The weeks away at sea
Had left them longing for the homes they loved.

The champions cheered the song the singer chanted.
The bard sang on of battles, brave deeds done,
360 Of foes defeated, friendships formed, and how
The gods had molded Middle Earth for mortals
With forests, fields, and oceans stretching far.
His clear voice called the names of conquerors
Whose grief and glory are forgotten now.
He sang of love and loss; he sang of loyalty.
They filled the flagons up with foaming ale
And warriors laughed and listened one last time
To tales of tribal triumph and defeat.

When morning came, they met and made their way
370 Toward the boats; the brave men climbed aboard;
The salty spray was splashing over them
As eager men pushed off the beach and out
To deeper water in the waves and wind
While Sigelac himself hauled up the sails
Of wave-birds taking warriors on their way.
The ships grew smaller as they sailed away
And, dim and distant, finally disappeared
As Wiglaf watched them from the water's edge.

For days the weather darkened, clouds came down,
380 And black-clad ravens brooded in the branches;
The howl of wolves was heard at noon; on high

An eagle circled in the sullen sky.
Meanwhile, with many of the men away,
The women went about their daily work
While chimneys smoked and children chased each other;
A time of peace. The people worked and played,
But sometimes brooded, too, about the battle
And wondered if the warriors were well.

At last a lone survivor, limping, blood-stained,
His clothes in tatters, torn by briars and trees,
And worn and weary after weeks of traveling
Appeared, his gaunt and pain-filled face gave proof
Of sorrow and of suffering he had seen.
He almost fell before they fetched a bench
And made him sit. He sank upon it sighing,
"They all are lost, and I alone am left;
They struck us down and Sigelac is slain."
Some women went to him and washed his wounds
While others found some food to set before him,
And as he ate, in eagerness to ask,
They pressed upon him, pleading to be told
About the battle, but he could not speak
So tired was he from travel and from terror.
His name was Wolferth, one of those who went
To fight the Frisians in a deadly feud
When Daeghrefne had died, a dauntless hero,
And Beowulf had brought back battle armor,
By strength and skill across the heaving sea.
At last they led him in and let him rest
On bolsters in the banquet hall; they bade him
To sleep awhile and so regain his strength.

The sun had set before they sought him out
And woke him, wanting any further word;
So he began again to speak and groaned,
"All lost, all dead, and I alone am left;
The sword devoured Sigelac and all
Are gone; our gallant Geats; a grievous day;
They set upon us suddenly. The Swedes
Will come and kill us all; we cannot hope
420   That we can stand against their savage strength;
A massacre; too many more than we;
Too few; too foolish; wolves and ravens food."
But Wiglaf struck him; "Stop and start again,"
He said, "And try to tell us, if you can, the truth:
What happened? Who is dead? And how have you
Escaped? We need to know your news at once.
So tell us all you know of it in order:
You set out on the ship and sailed away;
We have not seen you since, so speak,
430   And tell us all until your safe return.
Speak slowly so we can be sure to hear."
He took a breath and, trembling, told his tale.
He said, "You saw us as we sailed away
In careless confidence that we would conquer,
With shining armor stowed aboard our ship,
God's beacon shining brightly on our banners,
And all of us were eager for the fight;
So we enjoyed our journey, and we joked
About the beating we would bring the Swedes.
440   Our course was close to shore; we did not keep
A watch, or worry; there were often woods

Beside the shore, but once I thought I saw
A horseman high upon an open hill;
I think that they had placed a coastguard there
Who signaled somehow that our ships were coming.
But we were willing just to go our way
Without a thought of any lurking evil.
How could we be so confident and careless?"

His sobs were surging up, and so he stopped
450 To calm himself; he could not keep on talking
Until some time had passed. He took deep breaths
And slowly then went on. "I think that they
Were waiting for us, and so we, unwary,
Were trapped and caught. Their finest troops attacked us
From hiding, hit us; it was horrible;
Our soldiers, suddenly, were falling slain."

Then Wiglaf asked, "But was there no one wise
Enough to know, did none of you remember
* How Ongentheow had acted once to end
460 The life of Hathcyn, Hrethel's son, or how
He lured them to his trap; he let them land
And waited in the woods till like a wolf
He sprang upon our scattered, reckless soldiers
And cut our king down with his cruel blade;
He slaughtered many with the slashing sword
While others fell with arrows in their flesh;
He soaked the Swedish soil with blood of Geats,
And left the bloody bodies all unburied
For carrion crows to come and eat their fill.

| 470 | There was no place to walk not wet with blood.
| * | You can be sure the Scylfings still recall
| | That Weohstan, my father, was the warrior
| | Whose sharpened edge killed Eanmund in his exile.
| | His brother, Eadgils, broods still on that blow
| | And holds the hope forever in his heart
| | To meet with me at last and make me pay
| | For what my father did; a futile feud
| | That only answers death with death unending.
| | But let us hear your story, how it happened
| 480 | That all are lost and you are left alive."
| | They gathered close and he began again
| | But went on in a weak and wavering voice
| | So quietly they could not always catch
| | The sense of what he said, weighed down by sorrow:

| | "Yes, we had heard of Hathcyn's death, and how
| | The Swedes had set on him and slain them all,
| | But we imagined it a matter more
| | Of ballads sung by bards while drinking beer
| | Since those who did those deeds were now long dead;
| 490 | We did not think that they could threaten us
| | With all our armor and our untried swords.
| | We brought our boats to shore and on the beach
| | We saw no sign of life; it seemed most strange
| | That every house was empty; all were gone.
| | The soldiers started looting, setting fires,
| | And taking back their trophies to the boats.
| | Then suddenly, assailed on every side,
| * | The barbs came in above our battle shields,

	The arrows flew at us and fighters fell.
500	Our ancient enemy it was, named Eadgils,
	The Swedish sovereign now, who smote us first;
	His fierce blade fell on us like fangs of wolves
	And bit our bodies till the red blood flowed.
	Our shields were shattered by his smashing blows,
	The linden gave a little less protection,
	We could not ward off well his dreadful war-strokes;
	And then I saw him set on Sigelac
	With all his force, as if to end his days.
	They swung their swords, the clashing iron resounded
510	All through the woods as both men wielded weapons
	Well forged of finest iron and flashing brightly
	As helms and hauberks on both sides were hit.
	Then Sigelac was stunned as Eadgils' sword
	Had hit his head a blow beneath the helmet,
	Blood spurted out, came streaming down his shoulders,
	And blinded him with gore, a ghastly garment.
	He staggered, stunned, and slumped down to the ground,
	Where Eadgils' dagger dealt a deadly blow;
*	He had no breath to boast of battle-deeds.
520	The doomed fell dead; the din of battle rose;
	Then soldiers scattered everywhere and some
	Less firm as fighters looked for ways to flee;
	Their leader being lost, they longed for home,
	But Eadgils followed fiercely felling them
	Along the way; in woods and wilderness
	The Scylfings spears were thudding into shields,
	Their proud spears pierced the soldiers' plaited armor.
	I saw two Swedes attack the son of Modril,

       The mighty Malric in a savage mood;
530   He cut down one of them, whose corpse grew cold;
       The other Scylfing, aiming to do evil,
       Then threw his spear at Malric's shield, which shattered;
       But Malric meted out a mortal wound,
       Sliced through his throat, a deadly, fatal thrust;
       But several Scylfings set on him in turn
       And beat him down with many bitter blows
       Until he toppled on the tawny earth.
       I could not make out more amid the strife,
       The clash and clangor of the raging conflict;
540   I sought to help but was assailed myself
       By other Scylfings, all of them well armed.
       I set upon a Scylfing, swung my sword,
       And hit his helmet; he remained unhurt
       And turned on me, a tall man, twice my size,
       And raised his sword; I stabbed him in the stomach;
       He groaned and hit the ground; I glanced around
       But someone struck me from behind. I saw no more.
       The next I knew, it was already night;
       I lay there, looking for some light to see,
550   And heard the sound of Scylfings celebrating,
       And far away a blazing fire; I feared
*   The worst, but wanting to be sure, I went there—
       Though carefully; I crept so close I heard
       Them boast that birds would eat the Geatish bodies,
       And so I heard them speak of Sigelac,
       Of Modric, Byrhtwulf, and of many more
       Whom they had slaughtered with their Swedish swords.
       I dared not linger, listening to them laugh,

                For fear at morning light the foe would find me.
560   I tried to run, but I was tripped and torn
                By briars and branches till my hands were bleeding.
                At last I lay down, longing for the day.
                The night was full of noises; nameless forms
                Were gliding past, perhaps of ghost or ghouls
                Or shades of soldiers all too lately slain
                And haunting me or hunting for a home,
                A realm to rest in while their bodies rotted.
*   They had not heard of heaven's promised peace.
                I clutched my sword and kept it close at hand
570   And bent my back against the biggest tree
                But failed to free myself of horrid fears
                Of green-eyed wolves that gathered in the gloom
                And specters worse than that that set me shuddering.

             "When morning came, I meant to make my way
                Toward the south when sun's light showed me how,
                But clouds had covered it; I could not see
                And wandered woefully in trackless woods
                Until I heard, behind me, high above,
                The screams of eagles circling as they sought
580   For carrion corpses on the killing fields,
                And so I went away through wilderness
                Until I came to cliffs along the coast
                And followed them, although afraid of falling
                Where cracks and crevices lay covered up
                By tangled roots of trees; there was no trail.
                One day I did fall down and hurt myself;
                I stopped the bleeding; bound it with a bandage;

And so I limped the last few leagues to home."
His feeble voice then flamed up in his fury:
590 "But now we must assemble spears and shields
And all the other implements of war
And arm ourselves against the Scylfing scourge
And vow to gain revenge and victory."

But Wiglaf said, "I think that we should wait
And think before we start to threaten them;
So many wives are widows; warriors dead;
We all are in an agony of grief
And troubled by your tale. We need some time
To ponder and to plan. I would propose
600 We meet again tomorrow; meanwhile all
Must study what you said; shall we submit
At last to hostile Scylfing swords and spears
Or find a way to fight or shall we flee?"

When dawn came up next day, Wiglaf had drawn
A circle in the sand; he said to them,
"The lands are very large and we are little;
The Scylfings surely know our circumstance
And will be well aware that we are helpless
Before their fury. When their feasting ends
610 Their ships will sail and they will seek us out
And who will help us then? Where will we hide?
Our fighting men have fallen; we are few;
Our brothers, bold and fearless, have been beaten;
Their doom was death. Is that our destiny?"
But many of the men were murmuring

And Lofric said, "We cannot leave this land.
Our fathers were not frightened by their foes;
Our hearts and hearths and heritage are here,
So let us meet our doom and dare to die
620 As we defend our fields and families,
And win the warrior's wealth: a lasting fame."

Then champions cheered and chain mail hauberks rang,
But Herbrund said, "No fame can feed the famished
Nor does it make good milk in mothers' breasts
When babes are bawling and the cupboard bare.
If we cannot defend these fields, we ought to find
A place where we can pass our days in peace.
What glory do we gain by bearing grudges,
The ceaseless strife of Geatish folk with Swedes?
630 Why is it not as noble to ignore
The endless insults of an enemy
And follow peace to find a fuller life?
The dragon built its bed within the barrow
To rest on riches rusting in the ground;
As useless now as ever it has been.
What good is gold when we are in our graves?
I am a farmer first; my family
Is more to me than any mound of treasure.
When springtime comes and sunshine warms the soil
640 And soft rain washes winter snows away,
The sun unlocks the lakes, turns loose the streams
To flow down into rivers filled with fish,
And berries form on every bramble bush,
And children prate and play behind the plow,

I set out then to sow the bursting seed,
Inhale the odor earth is breathing out.
What more could any mortal man require?
Is that not all that anyone can ask?
But where the dead now dwell, they do not farm;
650 In hell they do not hold or hug their children,
Or swim in streams or stretch out in the sun.
If we are weak and cannot well stay here,
Then let us look for other lands to farm.
I love this land, but I will let it go
For peace and pay whatever price we must
To give that gift to those whose lives we guard."
Again some men were murmuring and many
Began to shout that they would smite the Scylfings
And find great fame and finally win glory.
660 Then gray-haired Aelric, gaunt and grizzled, spoke:
* "Where were these fighters, now so fond of fame,
When Beowulf was battling in the blaze
And suffering the swirling surge of fire;
He was our king, but comrades did not come
To stand beside him when the dragon struck
Or brave the battle, bolting to the woods
To save their lives. But now they strut their strength
And urge us all to emulate their conduct.
Such people earn our pity, not our praise.
670 I save my scorn for scoundrels such as these,
Who lack the loyalty they owe their leader,
Abandon him in battle. Beowulf
Would never need such noble earls as these.
But he is dead; indeed, he met his doom,

And now we need to find another leader.
The Swedes will soon be seeking for our blood
And Wiglaf is the one as we all know
Who long was loyal and who can lead us now."
But Wiglaf son of Weohstan, the warrior
680   While standing in the circle, said to them,
"I would not fight a war we cannot win;
I see that some of you still seek a feud,
But I would ask what course is best for all,
And I would rather rule our lives with reason.
I cannot be what Beowulf has been,
Who went to war as one against our foes
And often, even so, went out unarmed.
I cannot lead unless our lives are linked;
A hero has his strength, but I must hope
690   To fight with friends and find a way together.
I heard what Herbrund had to say
And feel as he does that these fields and farms
Are beautiful and hold the buried bones
Of forebears, fathers, friends whom we hold dear.
And yet, in years gone by, as you must know
Those forebears came from far to find this land
And when they came across the white-flecked whale-road
They found no fertile fields, but wilderness,
Deep forest filled with every form of life
700   But harsh and hostile to the human race.
Our toil has turned the sullen turf to bread
And made these frozen northern fields be fruitful.
We labored long to win this land, and yet
It was not always ours; it does not own us."

He moved to put some points well set apart
Within the circle, saying, "Swedes are here;
The Franks are here; and Frisians flourish there;
The dauntless Danes undoubtedly are here;
Our homes are here, but how much more there is!
710   Outside the circle I have drawn they say
Are islands and, it may be, other lands;
Some say the world is warmer in the west.
I hope to find such havens for my home
And call on you to come, and to discover
A place of peace and new prosperity."
Then Herbrund said, "I hope for happiness;
My family follows you to find this country
And look for life, not death, and lasting peace."
Then others echoed him and offered Wiglaf
720   Their loyalty, though some were sullen still.
Then Wiglaf warned that they should keep a watch
On Hronesness, on Götland's highest headland,
*   Upon the barrow built for Beowulf,
And set a soldier there to send them word,
If any evidence of enemies were seen,
A man to signal if the Swedish ships
Should come in sight along the curving coast,
An adverse omen. Then they all went home
To work with wives, to find out what they wanted
730   And gather all the gear to go with them:
The cups and crude spoons from their cottages,
And bowls and broaches, bits of jewelry,
Small heirlooms, all the family owned and valued,
And flax and cloth and flagons filled with mead

And shanks of bacon, salted beef, and bread
As food to feed them as they traveled far;
All these they brought down to the bay, where boats
Were safely sheltered on the rocky shore.
Then daylight dimmed, the disc of heaven faded,
740 And nighttime came to cast its heavy curtain,
As black as wings of ravens, baleful birds,
Upon the fertile fields and foaming shore.
The men then made their way into the mead-hall
While women called the children, kept them quiet
With tales of terrors in the tomblike night,
And sang the babies songs to help them sleep
Though they were threatened by the thought of change,
An unknown future and an alien soil.
The men had meanwhile gathered in the mead-hall
750 In hope of hearing what the future held,
What country could be found across the sea
And far away for weary wanderers,
Who hope for haven in a heartless world
And for a better future for themselves.
Then Wiglaf said, "The world is large, but we
Are not alone, our need unknown to friends.
The oldest of our soldiers often said
* That Hrothgar had pledged help to Beowulf
And said the realm he ruled and all its riches
760 Should all be shared across the seabirds' bath
Whenever needs were known to one another,
And ringed-prowed ships, across the surging seas,
Should bring our people presents, proofs of love.
He said they would stand firm toward foe and friend,

And always aid us in our hour of need.
The time has come for us to test the truth
Of all that Hrothgar said and seek for safety
Among our friends the Danes. I do not doubt
That many will remember still the monster
770   Called Grendel, gruesome fiend who grieved them all
Through twelve long winters, working woeful harm
And having his own way at Heorot
Until the son of Ecgtheow saved the Scyldings
And broke the bones of Grendel. Beowulf
Befriended them and fought that fearful monster,
Tore off his arm and nailed it up as proof.
So now, when Geats have need of help, I know
The world is large but we will find a welcome
Among the Danes." The doubters did not protest,
780   But many murmured still among themselves
And waited. Then came Yrfa, Wiglaf's wife,
Raised high her cup and hailed the heroes;
She went to Wiglaf, then to everyone,
And poured the amber ale for each to quaff.
Then gaiety began to grow and spread
Within the hall as heroes hailed each other
And men dispelled their doubts by drinking deeply.
A bard sang ballads of a bygone day
When Geats had gone to war and garnered glory
790   Against the Swedes with dagger, sword, and spear.
But soon he sang as well of storied journeys
To unknown, ancient lands beyond the ocean
Where dreadful sights are seen and dragons dwell;
He sang of sailors, those whose spirits soar

In pain and peril on the plunging waves,
When they can ride the swell of storms at sea
And dawn is darkened with the driving snow,
The frost and falling sleet and freezing rain,
Who love the loneliness and long salt-surge,
800 The storm-drenched eagle's scream and sea mews call,
That haunt the homebound sailor hopelessly;
He sang of wild and wailing winds and howling gales,
He sang of seas like mountains, surging tides,
And waves that washed a ship's whole crew away;
They struggled in the swirling sea and sank
To find the fish that feed on sailors' bones;
Their widows wailed and orphaned children wept.
At last he sang of loneliness and love,
The comfort of one's comrades and one's kin,
810 And friends in foreign lands, who never found
Their homelands anymore; their hearts were heavy.
He finished. Fighters slept upon the floor.
The sun was dim next day and clouds were dark.
The Geats were gathered on the shore in groups
Where Wiglaf went to them and warned them, saying,
"The hardest time is here; I had not told you
That we must set ablaze and burn our buildings,
The hearths and homes that we have held so dear,
Where babes were born and we have broken bread;
820 The houses we inherited, the hall
Where we have sung our joy and shared our sorrows.
We cannot leave the least of our belongings;
The Scylfings must not say that they destroyed it
Or be allowed to boast of beating us."

The fighters than pulled faggots from the fire
And turned to take the torches through the village
And there ignite each house's thick reed thatch.
The hungry flames spread fast and filled the air
With stinging smoke that drove the soldiers back.
830 The women meanwhile went about their work
Till ships were stocked and families safe on board,
The people in the boats. They pushed the prows
Away from shore where smoke and soot still rose
In grayish wisps against the gathering clouds
And left the land behind, not looking back.
The sea was quiet and the ships went smoothly
Across the water and the windswept waves.
Though lonely in the limitless expanse,
Unending aspect of the open sea,
840 They steered the ships toward the hidden sun,
A brightness breaking through the brooding clouds
And shining softly in the distant south.

The Scylfings saw the smoke while sailing south
And wondered what it was that would create
So dark a stain against the southern sky.
They brought their dragon boats into the bay
To find a fire-dark land. The flames had died
But smoldered still amid the smell of death
That rose around them from the ruined homes.
850 They stood and stared, amazed at what they saw;
The thought that came to all of them was this:
"The Franks or Frisians must have come here first
And gained a victory, so the Geats are gone."

They brushed aside the blackened thatch and beams
To look for any loot that might be left
But they found only ashes underneath;
No glory could be gained by gathering them.
Then some were saying they should seek their homes
Before the Franks or Frisians should go there
And make that unprotected place their prey.
The saddened Swedes returned then to their ships,
Their dreams of gold and battle-glory gone,
And, disappointed, put their oars in place,
And set their sails toward home–a sorry lot.

The Geats went on and soon began to glimpse
Through darkening clouds the distant Danish coast,
A low and purple line of solid land,
A welcome sight for wet and weary folk.
At last the ships came sliding to the shore
Where Beowulf had come to beach his boat
And help King Hrothgar who had long despaired
Of gaining peace. He stayed in Grendel's grip
So long as life stayed in that loathsome monster.

* The coast guard keeping watch upon a cliff
On horseback, hurried down to hail the Geats,
A mounted force of five, all fully armed,
Whose leader quickly called them to account:
"How dare you draw your prows to Danish soil?"
He asked; "I see that some of you are soldiers
And armed as I am, able to contend
With sentries such as we are, stationed here.
But I must tell you we have twenty times

As many men prepared to meet with you
Unless you leave our shore before much longer.
And yet I see that some of you are young
And you have women with you. If you want
To fight, I fear your families will suffer.
So now reply, and promptly, if you please,
Because you cannot otherwise come closer
890   Until you tell me what your titles are
And names and nation. I must know all this
For enemies are often on our shores
And we have suffered serious harm from some,
So we must warn our troops to treat you well
If you are friends, or fight if you are foes.
Who are you? I must have an answer now."
Then Wiglaf was the first to speak; "I will,"
He said, "Reply; our purpose here is peaceful.
You should be glad to greet us; we are Geats;
900   We boast that Beowulf has been our king.
Your realm was rescued from a reign of terror
When his strong hand defeated Grendel here;
The monster and his mother met their match,
Then Hrothgar gave our leader golden gifts
And promised peace between our peoples always
And aid if either one had any need;
But now our nation also stands in need.
My name is Wiglaf and I wish for words
With him who holds the throne of Hrothgar now
910   To ask whatever aid it may seem right
To give in gratitude for Grendel's death."
The coast guard said, "It is our king who can

Command concerning this; his throne is over there
Beyond those trees. I will send two to take you
Into the hall where Hrethor has his throne.
Choose ten to take with you and tell the rest
To stay here on the shore till we receive
Our orders. I must always stay on guard
And watch the water and the other ways
920 That lead toward our land. Now you must leave
Your sword and spear right here beside the ships.
Our king requires that we take utmost care."
Then Wiglaf chose some wives to go as well
And bring their babies so they'd seem to be
More like a family than a force to fear.
Two men in helm and hauberk hastened then
To go as guides for them to greet the king.

They followed these men from the floating ships,
Now reined by ropes and riding in the bay.
930 The stony street led straight up from the shore;
* They hoped to see the hall that Hrothgar built,
Its gables decked with gleaming gold, its glory
And splendor shone through sundry foreign lands,
But all they saw was empty space and ashes,
The blackened beams and empty, burned out shell
Of Heorot, King Hrothgar's feasting hall;
A sorry sight. They stood and stared in horror.
Around the hall's debris were humble homes,
A few of farmers and their families.
940 The sentry showed them somewhat further on
A larger house. "This is King Hrethor's hall,"

He said, and summoned others from inside;
A tall retainer came and talked with them.
He said, "I serve King Hrethor, and it seems
That you are exiles, asking for our aid,
With many mouths to feed. Why, may I ask,
Should Hrethor help you? He is often asked
By poor and piteous people, persecuted,
And driven here half-dead, in dreadful shape,
950 And we would willingly deal kindly with them
If we were safe ourselves. But you have seen
Our royal residence, destroyed, in ruins.
The Frisian forces came with flame and sword
To gain some glory; they did us no good.
They slaughtered some of our best soldiers
Whose constant courage we had counted on,
Destroyed and sacked our winter stores as well.
We drove them off, but damage had been done
That weakened us." But Wiglaf, tired of waiting,
960 Broke in to ask, "May I point out to you
That we are Geats, and Hrothgar gladly gave
Assurance of assistance and his succor,
Affirmed a friendship forged against all rivals
And loyalty lasting through the length of years.
We came to see your king in confidence
That Hrothgar's heart-oath would be held in honor."
Then Wittu answered them, a wary watchman,
A sentry certain to maintain in safety
His country's king, entrusted to his care:
970 "We often overlook the deeds of old
In troubled time like these, but I will tell

Our leader, Lord of Scyldings, you would like
To speak with him, and soon bring his response.
If you will wait, I will return at once."
He strode then swiftly to the seat of Hrethor,
A leader young in years and yet respected
By friend and foe alike, a forthright king.
Acquainted with the customs of the court,
He waited willingly; then Wittu said:

980 "Some comrades came today, a Geatish cohort,
Whose boats have borne them well above the brine;
Their leader, Wiglaf, wishes words with you
And brings to mind our bond with Beowulf.
It seems to me that you should meet this man
Although I think the stores we have are thin."
King Hrethor said, "I have most surely heard
Of Wiglaf, son of Weohstan, a Waegmunding,
And last of all that line, a likely heir
To Beowulf, most loyal and brave in battle.

990 His dagger gave the death stroke to the dragon
Whose rage and fury filled the Danes with fear.
I very much would like to meet this man,
This prince, now present here. So, please, go back
And urge him to come in and speak with us."
Then Wittu went to Wiglaf once again
And said that Hrethor had invited him
To draw near and address the Danish monarch.
He said to him, "You may present yourself;
So come; our king is curious to hear

1000 The story of your struggle and your sojourn.
His majesty remembers many tales

Of Beowulf and begs that you will bring
Some good news of the glory of the Geats,
A war-strong people whom he wishes well;
He gladly reaffirms our former friendship."
Then Wiglaf went with him; they walked together,
The steadfast soldiers in their shining armor,
And with them went their wives and children also,
Both tired and tearful from their traveling.

1010 The stalwart Danish sovereign, Hrethor said,
"I wish to welcome you most warmly here.
Our peoples promised one another peace
In former days; I would confirm that faith
And pray that both our peoples prosper always.
King Hrothgar held this throne by heaven's favor,
And made a mead hall, mightiest of all,
A splendid, stately building, standing here,
* But Grendel grieved him greatly with his raids,
A monster moved by hateful spite and malice

1020 Who ruled the royal mead hall ruthlessly
Until your uncle offered aid to us
And freed us from the fierce grip of that spirit.
But Hrothgar died and Hrothulf, Halga's son,
Usurped the throne and slew King Hrothgar's heir;
Then Heoreweard killed him and held the throne
Until his death. The Danes endured all this
But, weakened woefully, were warred against
By Frisians, then by Franks; the fierce Hetware;
And other enemies assaulted us;

1030 We fought the Franks but failed to drive them off
Till torch-fire turned the tragic hall to ashes,

A day of death and doom for all the Danes.
I saw the fire; the flames went flaring up;
They raced through rafters, roaring as they went,
Like winter wind, like storm-blown waves on rocks;
The light lit up all lands, but did not last;
And then the roof and rafters crashed in ruins
While men stood by amazed and women mourned.
When daylight broke, the blaze had burned it all;
1040 They searched the ashes seeking some remains,
A golden goblet or a bench still good
And in their hunt they found the horrid hand,
The grisly claw, of Grendel from the gable.
The hand had hung there at the highest point,
Unsoftened by the storms or summer sun
But forged to further hardness by the fire,
A weapon worse now than it was before;
The gold is gone but Grendel's claw remains.
It seems to be a symbol of our sorrows
1050 For fire and foe have left us few and weak,
But evil somehow seems the stronger for it."
King Hrethor halted, looking round the hall,
And said, "But now, my friend, I need to know
What sort of strength you bring to serve our cause.
Our forebears vowed a friendship for all time;
They pledged support; the need for it is plain.
You made your way here with your wives and young,
But Wittu says your ships brought soldiers too.
Your feud is with the Swedes; we fight the Franks;
1060 Alone it seems most likely we would lose,
And yet our youth and unity bring strength;

Let us makes vows of vengeance and win victory.
But Wiglaf said, "The women with me came
To seek your help, Lord Hrethor, in the hope
That ancient amity might open doors
For both our peoples, bound in brotherhood,
To look for and to learn new ways to live,
That all our families might be freed of fear.
Our stoutest men were slain by Swedish blades;
1070 We want no wars to weaken us yet more.
Our sovereign, Beowulf, was strong yet steadfast,
Not keen for combat if there could be peace.
The Scylfings saw no need to test his sword,
Contented to maintain a truce for years;
But when he died we dared adopt new ways
And Swedish blades drank up our bravest blood.
What good was that? What glory do we gain
By draining down our blood into the dust?
Do those in widow's weeds sing praise of war?
1080 I stabbed a dragon when it scorched my shield
But dozing dragons cannot damage us;
If Franks and Frisians are not fighting us,
Might we not let them live their lives in peace?
Come, Hrethor, help us now to heal these wounds.
We came here confident we could construct
A world where weak and strong might both live well
And people all might place their trust in peace."
Then Hrethor said, "I will not hide my heart
Which is most eager to distribute honor
1090 To gallant scions of the glorious Geats;
No doubt the Danes are very much indebted

To all who bear the blood of Beowulf
For daring deeds performed in other days,
But still we need to set a course ourselves
That looks at life now realistically;
So let us not conclude the case too quickly.
To those beside the ships food will be sent,
But I would ask that all now in our hall,
Strong warriors and worthy wives and children,
1100 Remain with us to make their evening meal.
Let bards retell the tales of former triumphs,
Of foes defeated and of friends sustained,
And I will call on careful counselors
To offer us advice." But Wiglaf answered,
"I'm sure, Lord Hrethor, that you seek to serve
Your people properly, improve their lives,
And not endanger any Danish dwelling.
You have a feud as well with foreign forces,
Marauding ranks who fell on you in wrath,
1110 Whose hate-fire has turned Heorot to ashes.
But I have other ultimate concerns:
A place of peace for people tired of war.
I think it best our band be at the boats
Prepared to push our prows away from shore,
Pursue our search with nations less concerned
With ancient injuries and harbored anger,
In lands and nations now unknown to us
Where feuds are few and folk are not oppressed
And righteousness bears rule throughout the realm."
1120 King Hrethor, listening, laughed a little, asking,
"Do any nations know another way?"

When darkness came, they did not join the Danes
To feast in fellowship or share their flagons
But stayed beside the ships and slept in tents.
When daylight drove the darkness from the heavens
The ravens roused them with their raucous cries
And Wiglaf sent the soldiers to the shore
To gather up the gear the Geats had brought
While women went to find the wandering children.

1130 Then Hrethor sent his soldiers, saying to them,
"We must not let our friends take leave so lightly;
Their arms would aid us greatly in the future."
But Wiglaf stood them off with spear and shield
Till they could drive their dragon boats from Denmark.
The sun in southern skies made bright the sea
As ring-prows, wind blown, made their westward way,
And followed swan-roads, skimming sea-gray waves;
The foam went flying as the sails unfurled;
The tall masts trembled and the timbers groaned

1140 As prows kept plunging through the piling waves.
All day they sailed with Denmark in the distance;
The sailors sometimes singing as they worked,
They hauled the high sails, heaved the steering oars,
As keels went cleanly through the ocean currents
And sea gulls soared above the shifting breeze;
But women worried for their children's welfare
And how soon they might have another home
Where brides might come and babies could be born
And table food be shared and tales be told

1150 And age be honored and the old might die
Amid the caring company of kin
And folk might find an end at last to fear.

               The third day they encountered thick white fog,
               No sun, no shore, no sign that they could see,
               A fog too thick to find a way to follow;
               And silent, as the fog absorbed all sound;
               A fog so thick it felt like winter fleece,
               The sails hung slack, nor could the helmsmen steer
               For lack of landmarks or a guiding light,
1160   And so they spent the night still lost at sea.
               When daylight dawned, the fog was driven off,
               The morning mist was melted by the sun,
               And then they saw a shore with sandy beaches
               And prows were pointed to approach the land;
               They wanted water and were tired of waves.
               The sailors ground their ships into the sand,
               But mounted men came riding up, demanding
               To know their nation and their names and purpose
               And waving weapons. Wiglaf answered them,
1170   "We have no nation nor are we renowned
               For wielding weapons or for skill in war.
               We put in here, a place, so it appeared
               Where we might find the water that we wanted."
               The riders raised their weapons to be ready;
               Their leader said, "Our lord has laid down rules
               And ordered us to ask all unknown people
               To leave at once, or wait beside the water
               As captives while we call for more to come.
               You must approach our prince as prisoners;
1180   No stranger coming straight into our streets
               Will have our help; these orders may seem harsh
               But safety is our chief and sole concern."

But Wiglaf said, "We will find water now;
So do withdraw your men and let us drink
And fill our empty water flagons first."
The spokesman, in response, drew back his spear
As if in anger, ominous to Wiglaf;
But Wiglaf drew his dagger, drove it deep
Into the horseman's side; he slowly slid
1190 From horse to ground; the gore came gushing out
And stained the soil; a dark pool on the sand.
The other riders rode off rapidly;
A horn was heard as if to call for help.
And Wiglaf said, "We will find water elsewhere."
They shoved the ships away from land and sailed
Along the coast, but kept a watch for coves
Where they might seek for shelter safe from foes.
They found, before the evening came, a fjord
Whose sides fell steeply to the salty waves.
1200 Tall pine trees stood, dark green against the ground,
And hemlock overhung the heaving waves
That rose against the rocks around the edge.
A hawk was hovering high above the water
And circling slowly in the silent air.
They came to level land, a little bay;
A brook came bubbling down the bank
And grass was growing where some deer had grazed;
A pleasant scene; they pushed the prows ashore
And, leaping out, they lashed the boats to land.
1210 The men then went to hunt, while women worked
To search for fuel and set up simple shelters
And children ran in rings around the clearing.

The valiant men provided venison
To add to evening meals as daylight ended,
And then they settled safely down to sleep.

They woke to hear a scream so shrill and sad
It cut the quiet air, made blood run cold,
And left them troubled, trembling in their tents.
The soldiers reached to find their swords and shields;
1220 Their eyes were open but the overcast
Had masked the moon above the mountain tops;
They stumbled, searching, but they could not see
What kind of creature caused their blood to curdle.
When light returned at last, they looked and found
A man was missing from among their number,
A soldier known as Selfric, sturdy, brave,
Who feared no fight and never fled from battle.
A trail of blood led back into the brush;
Some footprints led them further in the forest,
1230 But prints of such a size astounded them.
They knelt and noticed something none had known:
The footprints felt like frost, but air was warm;
They would not follow further in the forest
But went to Wiglaf, wanting his advice.
He told them they should try to track them later,
And meanwhile make their campsite more secure.
They spent the day still settling in that spot;
It seemed an ideal site from every aspect:
The fjord full of fish, the woods with game,
1240 The mountains making it remote from rivals
And sheltering the place from savage storms.

Some men began to mark and measure out
Locations they would covet for a cabin
And places they could put a garden plot.
While women did their washing, watching children,
Concerned about the midnight screams and Selfric.
That night they built a bonfire, set it burning,
And picked and posted proven warriors,
Selected leaders who would spread alarms
1250 If any sight or sound should startle them
Or any other outrage should occur
Or strangers should approach the sleeping Geats.
Then all went off in order to find rest.
They were not sleeping well when once again
Such screams were heard as shook their very souls,
A horrid sound that hurt and chilled the heart.
* The firelight gave a glimpse of ghastly beings,
As tall as trees and, terrible to see
Who grabbed the guards and ground them in their teeth.
1260 Their eyes were green, but all the rest like ice,
A greyish tone that glistened in the gloom,
Reflecting firelight from their frozen hearts.
The people standing paralyzed in place,
Were frozen fast themselves in fear and dread.
The trolls kept taking others in their talons
And munching them to make their hideous meal.
Then Aelric, oldest, wisest of them all,
Said, "Trolls, I'm told are terrified of fire."
So Wiglaf, went directly to the watch fire
1270 And seized a flaming faggot from the blaze
And, walking warily toward the trolls,

He flung it squarely in the first one's face.
It burst abruptly as a bubble does
And left behind a little pool of liquid
Reflecting faintly the surrounding flames.
Then others also brandished burning branches
Until the trolls in terror fled away.
Then Wiglaf would have gone deep in the woods
And taken torches to attack the trolls;
1280 He saw no reason to preserve the species.
But few would follow Wiglaf very far,
So most remained amid their families
While Wiglaf and two other warriors went
To find the frozen phantoms in their lair.
They tracked the trolls, pursuing with no trouble
The frozen footsteps in the forest earth,
And came to cliffs where there were ancient caves;
In far off times the trolls had taken them
From ogres who had always owned that land.
1290 Within the cold, dark caverns trolls could keep
Their species from dissolving in the sun,
And yet they had to hunt for human blood
Since none of them had any of their own.
The woeful creatures saw the comrades coming
And tore up forest trees to toss at them
But they could hide unhurt behind some boulders
And then move forward from the forest screen
Because the trolls had turned and taken refuge
Within the caverns, cowering in their caves.
1300 The soldiers, still pursuing them, came closer
And broke dead branches off the trees and set them burning

And dropped them down the caverns deep, black holes;
The howls they heard showed some had hit their mark.
They sent down more and seething steam came out,
An awful odor almost overwhelmed them.
They stayed there till the sounds of sizzling ceased
And then returned again to tell triumphantly
The saga of their sojourn, and the signs
That all their enemies were overcome
1310 And peace might prove now to be possible.
That night the families feasted by the fire
And hailed the heroes who had shown such valor;
They filled their flagons with the foaming ale
And joined in song and general jollity.
A bard sang sagas they had seldom heard
And let the lyre ring out its liquid music.
He told of how the trolls in ancient times,
When earth was cold and ice was everywhere,
Had crowned a king whose cavern deep in earth
1320 Was ringed with rocks that had a radiance,
A glowing light that let them build their lives
In safety from the shining of the sun.
The trolls were twice as tall as any man
And needed nothing for their nourishment
But ice, and oils that issued from the rock,
A timid, gentle tribe who never toiled
Or went to war; their wants were all supplied
Without an effort since their world's Creator
Had fully furnished all that folk would need.
1330 And so for centuries, they never ceased
To pass their time in peace and so to prosper;

They kept their caverns with the utmost care,
Embellished bountifully with brilliant jewels
Adorned and decorated with great dignity,
And finished in the very finest fashion.
But then a tempter talked to one young troll
About the beauties of the world above
Where there were fruits they had not found before
To touch and taste; the trolls knew only ice;
1340 One night this troll ignored his nation's laws
To find a way into the wider world
And come again with glowing sun-warmed gifts.
The trolls, entranced, returned and brought back more,
They lusted to enlarge their way of life
Though some assured them that the sun could kill.
Attracted by new treasures trolls rebelled
They set aside their ancient style of life
And risked the sun's bright rays to reap its fruits.
The peaceful kingdom came to grief in chaos
1350 As trolls attacked each other tooth and nail
And raided human regions for their riches;
They learned to like new liquids in their diet:
The heat of human blood to warm their hearts.
This feud the trolls inflamed by fierce attacks
Until the terror of their tribe was told
With horror everywhere in human homes.
The bard kept singing sad and haunting songs;
Till all the ale was gone and ashes glowed
And firelight dwindled and the dews came down.
1360 Next day they found some fragments in the forest,
The bits of human bone and body parts

Remaining from the meal the monsters made
And gathered them together in the glade
They brought great beams and branches from the woods
And piled the pieces in a funeral pyre
To honor all whose flesh the trolls had eaten.
The smoke rose up and sorrow smote them all.
Then some of them were saying to themselves
"We cannot build on land where bones are buried
1370 Or make a home where heroes have been slain."
Still other ached for unforgotten homes
And some were sure that Wiglaf had destroyed
Their lives and left them now with little hope
Of gold or glory—giving them no purpose.
They went to Wiglaf saying, "We must move
And search for some more suitable location,
The place of peace that you have promised us
Where families can flourish without fear
And all is guided by the gods for good.
1380 You killed some trolls and all is clear and quiet
But maybe there are many more beyond,
Who lie there lurking in some lonesome place.
Since some have fallen, all are filled with fear.
We only ask that we should now move on
To sandy shores or soaring peaks, but somewhere
Or anywhere at all that is not here."
But Wiglaf was not willing; he replied:
"I think that there is no place so unthreatening
It has no hardships we would have to face,
1390 No place on earth that does not pose some perils.
And would you want no work that tests your skills,

Or choose to raise our children with no challenge?
We may prefer to face a foreign foe,
But evil also lurks within ourselves;
I dread the danger lying deep within,
The foe we cannot often find or flee,
That swings no sword and throws no spear: the self.
So let us linger here a little longer
But send a single ship ahead to search
1400 For pleasant places where we might have peace."
Then they selected Laefstan as their leader
And formed a company of fifteen fighters
With skill as sailors, steadfast men of war,
And told them to return with truthful stories
About each area from every aspect:
The place, the people, and whatever prospect
They saw of settling there, constructing homes,
Of finding farmland, rivers full of fish,
Of raising children, rearing young folk rightly,
1410 Of the inhabitants, and who were hostile,
Indeed, of every danger to a dwelling
And every asset to an honest life.
So then they stocked a ship with spears and swords
In case they came upon a hostile country,
And various provisions for the voyage;
They started out to seek a place of safety
And sailed forth from the fjord they had found
And north through waters new, unknown, to them.
They sailed up fjords, found defenseless towns,
1420 And plundered people, pillaged as they went,
And gathered up the gold, neglecting nothing

That caught their fancy, making fearful figures;
The natives fled before them and their fury
While ravens, black-clad birds of battle fields,
Came flocking down to follow them and feast
On carrion corpses killed and left behind.
So when they sailed back south the ship was laden
With riches robbed from all throughout the region;
They sailed exulting in their great success
1430 And hoping they would have a hero's welcome.
Meanwhile their comrades, careful carpenters,
Had built with boards and heavy, oaken beams,
Some strong but simple shelters in the clearing
The soldiers had been sent to search for food
And brought deer back and several kinds of birds;
They smoked and salted some and ate the rest.
Each night they set a sentry for their safety,
Arranged a ring of fires around their camp,
But still they failed to find refreshing rest;
1440 The memory of missing men was strong,
And some of them woke screaming from their sleep;
The dread of death intruded on their dreams.
They watched as well to see the warriors
Returning from their travels; they would try
To see explorers sailing up the fjord.
The soldiers sent to scout the land ahead,
The comrades, came back down the Norway coast;
They found the fjord they had started from
And sailed the ship past cliffs of slanting rock
1450 To make their landing. Laefstan led his crew
To bring their boat into the stony beach

Where colleagues clustered round them, questioning:
"Where have you been? What booty have you brought?"
For some of them could see the treasure in the ships.
But Wiglaf asked: "What are you bringing us?
What land is lying out there which is like
The homes we had and which we hope to have?"
And Laefstan said, "The lands we learned about
Cannot oppose our prowess. We made peace
1460 With sword and spear and brought back their possessions
To deck our dwellings with this dazzling wealth.
We found no folk with strength to stand before us
Or keep us from acquiring all their country;
The gods enabled us to gain much glory."
Then Wiglaf asked, "And is this all you did?
You found some feeble people in the forest
And slaughtered them and stole from them their substance
And so you speak of peace. You silenced all
Your victims' voices with your violence
1470 And tell us tales of what you now call triumph.
But now the coasts of Norway, near and far,
Will be alert, on guard against the Geats;
Indeed, I dread the doom you bring on us
As others everywhere will seek us out
To wipe away the memory of your war.
And punish us, your people, for their pain."

Then Laefstan in his anger answered Wiglaf,
"But look what we have lost with you as leader:
Our hearths, our homes, and all our happiness.
1480 It's time we Geats should go to war again

And brighten rusted blades with steaming blood
Until the tribes around us learn to tremble
And we regain the glory that is gone."
But Wiglaf's words were warm with indignation:
"What good is gold and glory without peace?
What future can you fetch us with your fame?"
Then Laefstan called his comrades, bade them come
And stand with him and strive as soldiers should.
But Aelric asked him, "Is this how the Geats
1490 Have learned to act in loyalty to their leaders?
Would you win glory setting Geat on Geat?"
But Laefstan lunged at Aelric with his lance
And hit him in the heart with his full strength;
The thrust went through his body, thin and old,
And brought the blood out, spurting from his back;
He fell down on his face at Laefstan's feet.
Undaunted, Wiglaf drew his dagger out
And called on those with courage, bade them come
And face him fairly if they felt like Laefstan.
1500 But Laefstan stood alone. He looked for help
And found that there were few who were his friends;
For Aelric was an elder held in honor;
It grieved the Geats to see him in his gore.
Then someone threw a spear, assaulting Laefstan,
That landed just below his linden shield
And gashed his groin. Again a spear came flying
That hit below his helmet, he fell down
To earth and lost his life. So Laefstan died
As Wiglaf sought a way to stop the slaughter.
1510 He said, "This killing of ourselves must cease;

We are too few to fight." He faced them down,
And brought about an end before a battle,
A test between the two sides, could occur.
He ordered them to act in unity
And not to hurt their hope to find a haven
Where folk could flourish free at last of fear.
Again he gave command to go for wood
And build a pyre on which to burn the bodies.
Some murmured that they might have made two pyres
1520 A lesser one for Laefstan lest it seem
That he and Aelric earned an equal honor;
But Wiglaf wanted all to be as one
And not divide a victim and a victor
Since death, he said, was still the same for all.
Then folk went out to forage in the forest
And bring the branches back to build the pyre
They took the treasure and contributed
The helms and hauberks and the hilted swords
The golden goblets, wonderfully engraved,
1530 And other objects, torn from those who owned them,
And placed the costly pieces on the pyre,
A tribute to the two whose lives were taken.
Then Wiglaf spoke some words to them in wisdom:
"We honor all who died, but Aelric more,
Whose careful counsel we have counted on;
He went on board the boat with Beowulf
To meet the monster many years ago,
And heard King Hrothgar speak of heroes,
About the doom death brings to all who breathe.
*1540 'A short time,' said he, 'yes, and all too soon

Will sword and sickness come to sap your strength
Or fangs of fire or else the surging flood
Or sting of sword or else the spear in flight
Or agonies of age or else the eye,
Now dazzling, dims and darkens; all too soon
Will death, O warrior, work its will with you.'
So Hrothgar said, but is there something still
We need to know, or is there nothing more?
We piled our presents on the funeral pyre
1550 As evidence of honor they have earned,
But this is only fuel to feed the flames;
The gold we glean today is gone tomorrow,
And yet we yearn for something far beyond
These riches that will only rust and rot;
Our greed can never gain a lasting good
Nor fame, that also fails and fades with time,
For men are mortal, memories are short
And we forget the glory that was gained.
The deeds we do, however, will endure
1560 And form the future for our families;
Society is shaped by our decisions.
So Laefstan's lust becomes his legacy
While Aelric's wisdom is a gift to all
To guide the Geats wherever they may go."
He stopped, unsure his sermon had been heard;
"But now, he said, "the night is coming near
And we have work for all with willing hands,
So take your torches to the waiting pyre
And let us burn the bodies of the brave
1570 To honor all whose lives were joined with ours."

They fetched the fire and soon the flames leaped up,
A searing sister of the noonday sun,
That melted in its heat the men's remains;
They saw the bone-cage broken in the blaze.
The Geats stood gazing till the fire was gone
And ash alone was left of two men's lives,
Then made their evening meal with mournful hearts.

That night another troll came near their camp;
It seemed that they were sensitive to smells
1580 And came from far to find the human flesh
Whose burning smell was borne them on the breeze.
The troll had talons terrible to see
And eyes that glowed a ghastly greenish hue;
The troll attempted to attack the camp
But fearing fire it whimpered fretfully
And broke off branches blundering through the forest.
At last it came too close, and quickly burst,
Collapsing in a little pool of liquid
That sizzled slightly in a sudden wind.

1590 Next morning many women made their way
To Wiglaf wanting time for words with him,
The troll attack had terrified them all;
They could not feel secure in such a country.
The warriors thought that speaking was unworthy
And seemed to show too much uncertainty,
But they were thankful that the women's thoughts
Should be expressed. They were not bold to block them.
Then Wiglaf said he sympathized, but still,

"No place on earth is perfect; peace is rare;
1600   And if we found a land with fewer fears
          Where sleeping dragons did not seem to dwell
          And trolls had not been told of till this time,
          Where fields are fair and forest full of game,
          A place where people have not put their mark,
          With shattered shields and broken spears and lances,
          Yes, if there is an island without people,
          Whose shores are still unstained by human blood,
          It will not stay that way if we are there.
          We learned from Laefstan what our hearts are like
1610   And changing homes can hardly change the heart."
          But Yrfa, Wiglaf's wife, said, "We agree;
          Yet logic all alone is little use
          When hearts are hungry and the hearth is cold.
          We only know we ache for inner peace,
          To see our children safe beneath the sun;
          We have been hurt too much to call this home."

          Then Wiglaf sent for sages, senior men,
          Who by their careful counsel could assist
          In thinking through what things they ought to do
1620   And helping him decide how he should act.
          The first to speak was Fredgar, fond of fighting,
          And proud of his opinions and appearance;
          He said, "We should go home and do it soon;
          We do not need to dwell with danger here.
          This fjord feels to me like foreign soil;
          I am too old to understand new ways.
          In Geatland we were well established once,

With hearths and homes and good, familiar habits,
And even enemies we understood.
1630 It was not wise to leave our homes to wander;
It will be best if we go back, rebuild,
And let our children grow again as Geats."
Then Siric spoke, a seasoned warrior,
And one of two who tracked the trolls with Wiglaf.
"It seems to me," he said, "we should remain;
Why should we seek to face the Swedish swords
That killed so many of our closest comrades?
I fear not for myself, but some will fall,
And wives will wait to hear that they are widows.
1640 I am too old to look for enemies;
This is a peaceful, pleasant kind of place,
Well sheltered from the stress of violent storms;
The forests can be cleared for fertile fields,
A rich array of wild life roams the woods,
The fjord flowing by abounds in fish,
And if the trolls are troublesome at times,
A blazing branch will quickly beat them off.
So let us stay where we are settled now
And move no more until we truly must."

1650 The oldest of them all was Ethelbyrht,
A warrior well regarded for his wisdom;
He spoke more slowly, but with certainty:
"Not much remains of all that we remember;
The past is ashes, yes, and even if
We go to live in Geatland once again
And build anew what now lies burned and broken,

It will not work for us as once it did.
The circling sun cannot be sent back east;
No yearning yields our yesterdays again;
And we are not the same as once we were.
A life untroubled by the trolls is tame
And yet we should not simply seek excitement
Or linger long where trolls are known to lurk.
I am uneasy in this area;
I think we cannot quite be comfortable
Where deadly danger is a daily threat.
I am not fond of fleeing out of fear
But we are wives as well as warriors;
Our goal must be the good of all the Geats.
Yet if we are not able to remain,
I favor moving forward for our future,
To look for lands where we can live in peace
Until our tribe attains a larger size
And we can once again go out to war
And let the foreign people feel our fury
And garner glory for ourselves, the Geats."
The other soldiers shouted their assent;
They wanted war but saw the need to wait
Until the time when they could gain more treasure.
They had not heard of heavenly rewards
Nor did they rightly see how riches rot,
How little good is glory in the grave.

Then Wiglaf, son of Weohstan, chose words
And spoke with calm and quiet confidence;
Avoiding conflict, he unveiled his vision,

The hope he held to of a peaceful haven:
"The search that we are on is still the same:
Behind or yet ahead, we seek a home,
But words are weak; no one of us can say
1690 In measured words what means the most to us
Or paint the picture prized within our hearts.
It is what some have seen in battle-strife:
The courage then required amid the killing;
It is what some see staying safe inside:
The babies bawling while the kettle boils;
It is what some will see in country scenes:
The trees they treasure and the tors they know;
And some have seen it in the search itself,
Who hang their hopes upon a distant hill
1700 Yet relish more the route than the arrival.
But let us go together toward our goal
And step by step see what its shape may be.
Our children have their choice of challenges
But we must find our way, and go as one
To find the future of the Geats as friends.
So come, my comrades, act with courage now
And someday bards will sing about our sojourn."

Then Wiglaf said that soldiers should assemble
Their arms and armor, place them in the boats
1710 While other people should prepare supplies,
Should fill the flagons, and should gather food,
Should bake more loaves and bring them all on board;
And some should sew the sails that had been torn,
And paint the prows in colors proud and bright,

And make new masts if some could not be mended.
Still others, Wiglaf asked to make more oars
And see that they were smoothly shaped and sound.
Those skilled in hunting he sent out in haste
To find what fowl or other flesh they could
1720 And bring it back to be prepared to take.
A few brought fish and fruit that had been dried;
Some brought fresh roots and berries to the boats;
Still others cooked and cleaned and carried
Whenever others asked them to assist.
In two short days they did these various duties.
The final night they feasted by the fire
And told each other tales of weary travels,
The stories told by some and sung by others.
The bard embellished them as best he could
1730 And sang old songs long stored up in his mind
And made new words for many he remembered,
Entwining them so he could tell new tales.
He sang of princes placed in hateful peril
In other lands where ogres eat men whole
* And then he sang of Scyld, the son of Scef,
Who, though without a home, an orphan, outcast,
A foundling, taught his foes to fear his name
And grew to win great glory, glowing fame.
He sang of Scyld's son, Beow, brave in battle,
1740 And his son, Halfdane, high king after him.
Then Halfdane's son, called Hrothgar, held the throne
And he it was who built the hall called Heorot,
So fine a place its fame had spread afar,
Though only ashes of it now remain.

The fire was dying down, the song was done,
And Scylfings went to seek a place to sleep.

When morning came and men and women moved
Reluctantly to learn that it was light
The sun's rays sparkled on the shining water
And all things were as in creation's plan;
1750 Then some were gloomy, others glad to go.
The last of their belongings were collected
And carried, clothes and food and cooking pots,
To stow them safely on the waiting ships.
Then Wiglaf sent the soldiers out to search
Throughout the area for anything
Of value on their voyage or their venture.
They searched the ground and all the simple shelters
But they were empty, nothing anywhere.
So Wiglaf ordered ships to set their sails;
1760 They lifted leather sails along the masts,
All brightly painted, brilliant blue and red.
A fresh breeze through the fjord followed them
And set the ripples racing round the ships.
They gazed again at granite walls of rock
And falls of broken stones that faced the fjord
And watched the wind begin to whip up waves.
The current carried them along the coast
Then out at last into the open ocean;
The line of land grew lower as they watched;
1770 They left behind the hemlock covered hills
And headed toward the west as Wiglaf wanted.
The billow-rider bore them bravely on;

At last they were alone; no land in sight;
The women watched for serpents warily;
The men were more intent on seeing mermaids;
But all was calm; the sea was smooth and still
With just the faintest froth of lacy foam
And ships were sliding smoothly on the waves.
The sailors watched the sun and steered due west;
1780 At night they noticed skies with not a cloud
So they could set their steering by the stars,
And on they went, still working to the west.

The second day, a storm came from the south
At first they felt a freshening of the breeze
Then clouds were coming up to cloak the sky.
It was mid-day, but still the darkness deepened;
The wind began to grow with stronger gusts,
And then a clap of thunder threatened them.
The children cried and cowered under covers
1790 While sailors strove to strike the flapping sails
Before a blast would break the bending masts.
The rain came small and soft at first, in spurts,
But harder then, like hail, that hit with force,
Till rain was running down their clothes in rivers
And they were soaked and sodden with the spray.
Their clothes grew clammy with the cold and wet;
The salty sea-spray stung against their skin,
The wind was raging, rising to a roar,
Till they could hardly hear above the howling;
1800 It drove them on, half drowned and drenched;
They shook and shivered in the savage cold.

The rolling billows wrenched their narrow rafts
And boats were bending on the billows' crests,
The ring-prows rolling in the rising waves
And wind-blown water washing over them.
The sailors said they had not seen such waves
That heaved and hurtled down on them like hills.
The steering oars of some ships snapped in two;
To point the prows became impossible
1810 And surely, Wiglaf thought, some ships would sink
Unless some help should happen from on high.
That night and next day too they knew no change;
The swirling storm raged still in all its fury,
While sleepless sailors sought to stay afloat
And breaking seas still beat upon their bark.
They had no sun or stars by which to steer
Nor hope they might behold their homes again.
The next night came, the sea–surge seemed to slacken,
The storm-swell ceased to surge against the boats,
1820 The dreadful wind was dying down at last;
The fourth day dawned and finally the fleet
Could ride the rolling waves with restful ease;
The black and brooding clouds were breaking up,
And soon a warming sun was shining down.
The children crept out from their cloaks and coverings
And women went to work to look through baggage
To find some food to put in famished mouths.
So now they knew once more which way was north
They hauled up heavy sails and headed west
1830 Though all the boats were badly mauled and battered
With splintered masts and shattered steering oars.

They sought a place to put in for repairs,
A landing to relax and have some leisure,
For they were tired of tumult and of tossing,
More weary of the waves than words could tell.

As dusk came down, they saw a distant land
But Wiglaf wisely ordered them to wait
And sail in circles till the sun came up;
There could be danger driving on in darkness
1840 Of wrecking all their ships on rocks and reefs,
And if they sought to sleep on unknown shores,
Their foes might fall on them before they knew
What type of tactics would protect them best.
The moon had set; the sky was full of stars,
And Wiglaf, wakeful, wondered why it was
That stars in every land are still the same.

* When first the flush of dawn spread from the East
They slowly sailed the ships toward the land
As bright sails billowed in the early breeze.
1850 They watched for signs of life: a sentry stationed,
A farmer in a field, or fishermen,
Or smoke ascending from a single house.
They heard the curlews' cry and sea gulls' calling
But neither sight nor sound of human source.
The water went between low hills and widened
To bring them to a broad and spacious bay
Where many seals were sleeping on the shore,
A peaceful place where people might live well;
Yet still they saw no sign of human life

1860 Until they traveled to a certain point
Around a narrow neck of land, and knew
They were not first to find this far off place
Though still they saw no sentinel on guard
Or any evidence of other people
Except some boats abandoned on the beach
As if some fisher folk had fled away.
So Wiglaf let them land to look around
And search beyond the shore for something more.
Behind some hillocks, they discovered homes
1870 Where they were sheltered from the sea and storms.
The people there were poor and living peacefully
In shelters made of stone, with roofs of sod.
They welcomed Wiglaf's warriors as friends
And offered them some other, unused land
Where they could feel quite free to farm;
They had no taste for any type of trouble.
The Geats were glad to go ashore and rest
But wished to wait, conferring with each other,
Before deciding if the site was suitable.
1880 The natives noticed that their guests would need
To find some water and sufficient food.
They showed them near the ships a bubbling spring
And also showed them herbs that they could eat
And certain kinds of seaweed for a soup.
They said the land they lived on was not linked
To any other land; it was an island,
And occupied by peasants, poor as they,
With other islands all around their own,
And hamlets huddled here and there throughout,

1890 And farmers growing grain and raising goats;
But wealth and warfare were not known among them.

Then Wiglaf ordered off an expedition
To go and get some greater sense about
The island and its opportunities,
To try to find some unused fertile fields
And seek a sheltered place in which to settle
At least a little longer, days or weeks,
And so replenish food supplies and plan
A course of action all agreed upon.
1900 Then, meanwhile, most of those remaining,
Awaiting this report, would work with Wiglaf,
Rebuilding battered boats as best they could
And sorting out the stuff that had been spoiled
By waves and water washing over them.

The chosen warriors went away at once
And strode back into camp as sun was setting
Quite pleased and proud to come again with presents:
A goat which they had gotten as it grazed
Was slung beneath a spear two soldiers carried;
1910 While others brought two otters and some eels
Which they had speared while standing by a stream.
They also said that they had seen strange sights:
* A hill not made by any human hands,
A massive mound that had amazed them all,
And stones beyond the might of men to move
That stood on end and stretched toward the sky.
They thought it might be magic that had moved them

        But also wondered whether once there was
        A race of giants who could wrest such rocks,
1920   The standing stones that made them stop and stare.
        The mound they saw had made them all imagine
        A dragon's treasure trove with wealth untold
        Was stored up secretly and deep inside
        There must be golden goblets well engraved
        And sharp-edged swords wrought with the skill of elves
        And shining banners brilliantly embroidered
        And other articles once owned by men
        But buried by some bygone race of heroes
        And even now unknown and quite unnoticed.
1930   They said that they had searched for some way in
        But boulders far too big had blocked their way.
        Then Wiglaf asked, "What is it ails you all?
        Why must I now remind you of the meeting
        That brought a baleful death to Beowulf,
        The fatal fire that fell on many houses,
        Because a robber raised the dragon's wrath?
        You were not willing to reward him then,
        Allot your leader loyalty in his need,
        And stand beside him when the serpent struck.
1940   And would you risk arousing all the wrath
        That such a serpent might now spend on you?
        There is no time to waste on tales of treasure
        When we have work still waiting to be done."

        But day by day, when duties were assigned,
        The soldiers who were sent to scout out game
        To feed their families always found the time,

When they had speared some sleeping seals,
To dig and delve, work downward in the mound,
Until one tumbled through into a space,
An empty room lined all around with rock,
And nothing buried there but broken bones.
In anger then, they asked who else had come
In former times to take the dragon's treasure
And so they scratched their runes into the stone
And let the letters tell of those they loved
And anger at the absence of a hoard.
They made their marks for other men to see
And then they sealed the sepulcher with sod
And went away, but did not talk to Wiglaf
About the buried bones they had discovered.

But meanwhile other searching soldiers saw
Some hillocks here and there that had them puzzled.
Not far beneath the sod were slabs of stone
That seemed to cover caves or crevices.
The natives said they knew the grassy knolls
Or hollow hills were now the homes of draugrs,
The dwellings of the dead; they dreaded them.
Especially when the days were short, they shivered,
If hurrying home they had to pass such hills
For then the draugrs did such dreadful deeds
As filled the country folk with nameless fear.

For weeks the people passed the time in peace;
Assembling shelters from the stone and sod
And finding food, both fish and game, to eat.

        And yet they all seemed ill at ease and restive;
        The country made them quite uncomfortable
        In some uncertain way. They were not sure
        They really could arrange to put down roots
        And make their homes amid these hollow hills
        In dread of draugrs and in constant doubt;
1980   What hope could hold them in this haunted island?
        They went to Wiglaf to discuss these worries.
        "I have been hoping," Herbrund said, "to find
        A land to live in that is lacking nothing
        A farmer needs to shape a family's future.
        I think this country cannot quite provide
        The assets I would ask for in a home;
        I think the soil is thin, the clouds too thick,
        There are no trees to take for timber
        Or fell for fuel to build a fire for warmth;
1990   The brush and bracken that they burn
        Will hardly cook our food or heat our homes.
        I miss the sun-filled meadows and the mountains;
        I would prefer to find a fairer land
        And sometime soon, before the summer ends."
        And for the first time Fredgar felt the same:
        "There is no future for us in these islands;
        I see no glory to be gained or gold
        Among these peasants; people here are poor
        In war and wealth and knowledge of the world.
2000   There is no fame to find in fighting them;
        To kill or conquer them wins no acclaim.
        The warrior's way is not to watch the weather,

Appointing times to plow and plant and reap,
And using spears to set upon a seal;
I would not stay here eating eggs and oysters
If there is work for warriors in the world."
The warriors slammed their spears against their shields
Applauding Fredgar's words. They felt that fighting,
The clash of combat, comrades at one's side,
2010   The bucklers breaking as they bear the impact
Of swinging swords and lethal spears in flight,
The hammer blows on hardened, hand-linked rings,
And shimmer of the sun on shining armor;
Indeed, the death that is a warrior's doom,
Was better far at last than being buried
In such a placid, peaceful place as this.
Then others also spoke their minds; they uttered
Their varied viewpoints, vying to be heard.
Some seemed to think a southern route was safer;
2020 Some wanted to explore a westward way;
Some sought a better soil and others strife,
But most were of one mind, that they should move,
And looked to Wiglaf to select as leader
A future course on which they could concur.

Then Yrfa, wife of Wiglaf, spoke for women;
She said, "Our search has gone on for a season
But has not, here or elsewhere, found a home,
A place where we can plant our crops in peace;
This island also is not what we seek,
2030 But life's too short to spend it all on ships
So let us look for open, fertile land—

Not perfect, that's not possible, but proper—
We simply need enough for normal life,
The safe and simple things that satisfy,
And near enough that no more people die."
Then Wiglaf said, "I do not want to wander
Or travel all the time; we truly must
Stop roaming soon, arrive where we can rest.
But now we need to look a little longer
2040 Until the Sovereign shows us where to settle,
Almighty Maker of the Middle Earth,
The place appointed in his purposes
For us to occupy and end our journey."

Then Wiglaf ordered all to act at once
To bring their baggage to the boats again,
Sufficient food for every family,
Assemble all on board the ships to sail.
Then Wiglaf asked the islanders for insight
In looking for a land where they might live,
2050 A course they could pursue with confidence
To sites more suitable for settlement.
They said they knew of nothing to the north
Except some barren islands, bleak and bare
And washed by waves and constant, savage winds;
Still further north were islands all of ice
Where none would like to linger very long.
They thought the west led out to endless ocean
Where monsters, they imagined, made their home.
But there were certain sea-paths to the south,
2060 That offered other opportunities.

To those who dared, undaunted, all the dangers.
They said a larger land was lying there
With massive mountains that no man could climb,
Where snow was often seen and stinging cold.
They said the mountain folk were few but fierce;
They told of tribes so wild and turbulent
Their bitter feuds were famous far away;
A hateful, hostile, cruel, unconquered country
But one with running rivers rife with fish
2070 And crowded forests full of deer and pheasants.
They also told him travelers had returned
To say that they had seen a writhing serpent
That captured ships and crushed them in its coils
And snapped up sailors swallowing them whole.
This monster made its home among the mountains,
In glens where none dared go without a guide.
But further south, they said, were softer lands
With kinder climate and a gentle coast;
They had not seen this countryside themselves;
2080 The hazards they had heard of left no hope
Of reaching other regions at such risk.
But Wiglaf did not take the time to talk
With others, asking elders their opinions.
It seemed to him that sailing to the south
Was now the only option if they hoped
To find a final refuge fairly soon.
So Wiglaf mustered all the men, commanded
Equipment be secured and cargo stowed
And all the ships be set to sail at once.
2090 The breeze that backed them as they left the bay

Encouraged them and kept them on their course.
The standing stones were clearly to be seen,
A sight that overwhelmed them all with awe,
Amazed when they imagined giants moving
And shaping stones of such colossal size;
But they were thankful that they had not met
The makers of the massive monument
And had not stayed where some might set upon them.
Beyond the bay they entered open ocean;
2100 Waves crashed against the coastal cliffs behind
And rocked the ring-prowed ships with rolling billows.
The shifting clouds obscured the sun; the wind
Was whipping white waves up along the whale road
But still the sailors kept their course due south,
A heading that they hoped would have success
And lead them to the land for which each longed.
It seemed a short time passed until they saw
A line of land below a bank of clouds,
And then a high and harsh and rocky headland
2110 With rocks that ringed the base, and raging waves
That beat against the barrier; no boat
Could hope to find a harbor without harm
In such a surf. The sailors shifted course
And drifted down the coast throughout the day
But did not land for fear of finding foes.
As day was drawing to a close, they did
Observe a bay, a somewhat sheltered cove,
And steered their ships in through the pounding surf.
A river ran down falling over rocks
2120 And splashing softly in the sunless sea.

The shore was swampy and not suitable
To stay; too little of the land was level.
They bound the boats to stakes as best they could
And let some land but left the rest on board.
For several days they sailed still further south
While clinging closely to the rocky coast
And stopping sometimes to refresh themselves
And look for food and fill their flagons.
At times the sailors tried to terrify
2130 The children saying they had seen a serpent;
The boys were gleeful, but the girls began
To cry and cower while the sailors cackled.

One sunset, as they drew the ships to shore
And gathered goods together for a meal,
Attending to their tasks, they were attacked,
Quite suddenly assailed, by savages
Who had no armor, only bows and arrows,
But sent their shafts with horrifying skill;
Some fell before they fully realized
2140 That they were even threatened. Thick and fast
The arrows came at them, and quickly killed
Two warriors and one among the women.
The soldiers swiftly reached for spears and swords,
Their helmets and their hardened, hand-linked hauberks
To face the phantoms shooting from the forest,
The unseen enemy whose lethal arrows
Were raining down around them as they ran.
The battle-tempered soldiers bent their bows
To shoot but could not see the arrows' source,

2150　　Concealed and shrouded by the sheltering trees.
　　　　The shining armor-plate impeded progress,
　　　　Their chain-mail checked them as they tried to charge
　　　　Into the trees and tripped on tangled roots,
　　　　The brush and branches blocked their bold advance
　　　　And helped the hostile horde within the woods.
　　　　Then Wiglaf went himself into the woods
　　　　And with no bulky armor on was able,
　　　　Protected by the trees, to test his sword
　　　　Against the unseen, ghostly gladiators,
2160　　And swinging, stabbing, send them reeling back.
　　　　Then Waelric, one of Waelstan's stalwart sons,
　　　　The tallest of that tough and hardy tribe,
　　　　And one of those who went with Wiglaf
　　　　With burning branches to attack the trolls,
　　　　When he had seen the way that Wiglaf worked,
　　　　Took up his sword and set out in the same way
　　　　To find their foe and put them all to flight.
　　　　Attempting to protect himself with trees,
　　　　He forced his way still further in the forest
2170　　And battered bowmen with his blood-soaked sword,
　　　　Unable to take aim as he rushed on them;
　　　　He drove them down before they drew their bows
　　　　And left the landscape littered with their bodies.
　　　　The moon emerged from melancholy clouds
　　　　And shone down on a scene of pain and sorrow.
　　　　They brought thick branches from the woods to burn,
　　　　A funeral pyre prepared for those who perished;
　　　　The smoke ascended in the silent sky
　　　　While watchers wept and all bewailed their loss.

2180	The Geats kept guard that night against attack
	In fear the furtive bowmen who had fled
	Might come in quest of all their fallen comrades
	With further forces furious at their loss.
	When sunlight came the soldiers set about
	The task of taking food and tools and armor
	And bearing it on board the waiting boats.
	The comrades clearly could not linger there
	Or hope to make a home in hostile land.
	But Wiglaf told them, "We were amply warned
2190	That perils would appear along this path
	And dangers, as indeed they did last night,
	But we have set ourselves a certain purpose
	And have agreed to work to gain that goal
	And find what fate affords us, fair or foul.
	The world still turns, and testing times will come
	Along the road, till we arrive, and reach
	The promised place for those who persevere.
	The mist-filled mountains are diminishing,
	The high-born eagles' home and haunt of wolves;
2200	The land is lower now, and I believe
	The end of all our travels is approaching."
	Once more they slipped their moorings, raised their masts,
	And set their course toward the southern sun.

    The Geats, still gloomy, still engaged in mourning,
Were saddened by the sight of sullen clouds
That quickly cast a curtain on the sun
And hid the land ahead behind a veil.
The people never noticed now the sting of salt

Or how the wash of water wet their clothes.
2210 The mists that made them miserable before,
The constant cold, the crowding in the boat,
Were almost easy now to overlook;
The weary world they knew was always wet.
So on they went, and envied other people
Who stood on solid ground and saw their lives
As fixed, and felt no doubts about the future.

* At last they saw an island, lying low,
With cabins crudely crafted out of stone.
They found a shallow harbor on the sheltered side
2220 Protected well against the wind and waves
And brought their boats together in the bay.
On coming closer, they could clearly see—
Amazed—those moving on the isle were men;
There were no women, and they wondered why.
It seemed that some essential element
Was lacking in the lives these people lived.
They wondered, too, why not a one had weapons;
They had no arms; there was no armor on them.
They seemed to feel quite safe in their surroundings,
2230 As if they had no enemies at all.
These men came out to meet them as they moored
And answered easily the questions they were asked:
They claimed to come from countries to the west
And said their style of life was set by some
Who gave up everything they owned on earth
To find a treasure better far than fame,
A gift they said was greater yet than glory.

>   These people practiced poverty and prayer;
>   They had no wealth and waged no wars
> 2240   But tried to teach the children trusted to them
>   To write and read and mumble prayers by rote.
>   They looked for poor and isolated lands
>   To pass their time in peace apart from those
>   Whose lives were ruled by greed, whose goal was gain.
>   Then Wiglaf asked them other questions also
>   And stood there on the shore in conversation
>   While all about him people beached their boats
>   And waited, wondering what they were to do.
>   So Waelric spoke to Wiglaf sharply saying,
> 2250   "You cannot take the time now just to talk;
>   When folk are hungry, feeding them comes first,
>   And then comes time for those who wish to think."
>   "Why eat," said Wiglaf, "if you cannot ask?
>   To live is not worth much unless you learn;
>   The mind needs meat as much as does the mouth."
>   But then he laughed, and led them to unload
>   Sufficient for a few days on the island;
>   By now he knew that there was not enough
>   To hold them here where soldiers could not hunt
> 2260   Or farmers find a place to plow and plant.
>   The Geats could well have gone again next day
>   But Wiglaf hoped to have more time to hear
>   About the peaceful, brown-robed brotherhood
>   Who said they served a single, unseen God
>   And lived in loyalty to God alone.
>   They said their style of life was very simple;
>   They did not wish to waste time worrying

About the realm of things that rot and rust
But sought instead a country less uncertain,
2270 An everlasting life they longed for now.
To gain this wisdom, Wiglaf was prepared
To stay with them and seek to understand.
No tongue had told him of the true Creator,
The God who governs all things for our good;
He longed to linger on the island learning
The message that these men had made their own.
But Waelric warned him others would not wait,
That many of the men were murmuring
That even loyalty at last has limits.

2280 Then Wiglaf asked in anger whether any
Remembered how, not many months before,
The loyalty they owed their lord was lacking;
They did not crowd around our king in crisis;
The dragon's fire and fury set them fleeing
And some were sent to exile to their shame;
No happiness of home and hearth is theirs.
"Go tell those trouble-makers to be brave,
And sit in silence while I seek advice.
Our friends here travel frequently and far
2290 And know this coast and can provide good counsel.
They tell me if we travel two more days,
That we will come to cliffs along the coast
With headlands high above the heaving waves
And reach a river running to the sea
And forming there a harbor full of fish.
Above the sea the brotherhood has built

A place of prayer where they can live in peace;
And side by side there is a sisterhood
Where women also walk that way of life.

2300 They say that we would surely be received
And welcomed warmly as we go along our way.
And they have just suggested that we journey
Beyond that point till we approach a place
Where fields stretch flat as far as one can see.
They say that we could sail there in our ships
By keeping constantly upon our course
In six or seven days without a storm.
The place they picture seems to be appealing,
Because the fields are fertile and are full
Of streams that sailing ships could use with ease.
So we could make our home amid the marshes,
Well hidden from all harm and hostile folk,
And find the food we need by clearing farms,
But still could seek provisions on the sea.

Perhaps some clans now camping there will claim
The land is theirs and thrust at us and threaten,
And force our fighters to be firm with them,
And give them work to do to gain some glory.
And will our war-starved warriors be pleased
2320 To do their duty if that day should come?
But all this I have learned while seeming idle;
There is a time to talk, and pay attention
To men familiar with the many miles
Of landscape lying now along our way.

But now we know these things we need to move;
It seems to me that we should sail as soon
As your array of restless folk are ready."
So once again they gathered all the Geats
And told them that the time had come to travel,
2330 But now they knew the nature of the journey
And could be clear about the course ahead:
No doubt there would be danger every day
But at the end a home for all of them.

They packed the ring-necked prows with their supplies
And bade good-bye to all the brotherhood,
Who promised to support them with their prayers.
The sprays of water sparkled as they sped,
And hearts were high with thoughts of finding home.
A willing wind was with them all that day;
2340 The billow-rider, banners in the breeze,
Sped fast and fleet across the rolling foam.
That night they came upon a quiet cove
And sheltered there with sentries stationed round,
But none came near, annoying them that night.
The women dreamed of daily chores and duties
And sharing meals among familiar friends
In homes where hearths were hallowed by long use;
Young men envisioned valiant victories
As soldiers slew their foes in fierce assaults,
2350 But others' dreams were filled with fertile fields
And growing grain that gleams in summer sun.
They did not dream of distant, unknown shores,
But only of what they had always known:

Familiar things were what they missed the most
And hoped to have again to heal their hearts.
They woke to find a fog that filled the cove,
As thick as new-laid thatch; it held them there
A second day till they could see to sail.

The heaven-ruler, robed in clouds, arose
2360 And sent them scattered showers as they sailed,
But wet no longer worried weary travelers;
The dreamt-of destination drew them on
Across the constant cresting of the waves.
The puffs of wind propelled the painted sails.
Until they reached the region of the river
* And turning toward the tall cliffs flanking it
They saw some simple shelters on the ness
Along the river's southern side, and saw,
Above them on the bank, the brownish robes
2370 That marked the men whom they had met before;
But here there were some women wearing them
Because this colony included both;
The men and women met at certain moments,
Appearing at appointed times for prayer,
But staying otherwise in separate shelters.
The boats were brought upriver to a beach
And sentries set to guard the ships from harm;
Then Wiglaf went, and with him several others,
To climb the cliff and meet the comrades there.
2380 The Geats brought greetings from the northern group
And took some tokens to be recognized
And offered them as evidence of honor.

The members met them, made them very welcome,
Politely led the Geats to find their leader,
A well-known woman, honored for her wisdom,
Whose name was Hilda. Having traveled here
From Lindisfarne to found this fellowship,
She gathered in a growing group of folk
Who sought a stable center for their lives,
2390 A place of order in an unruled world.
She welcomed Wiglaf and his comrades warmly
And asked them each to tell her of their journey,
And so they told her stories of strange sights,
And tales of terror caused by hungry trolls,
And storms at sea, and struggles on the land
With arrows shot by unseen enemies.
They hoped that she might have the time to hear
Their bard sing ballads about Beowulf
If all their comrades could arrange to come,
2400 But Hilda said it seemed unsuitable
To bring so broad a group above the harbor;
She said they climbed that cliff to be secluded
And so the stairs they built would be too steep
And bothersome for any bearing burdens.
She said they would be glad to give the Geats
What help they could, and counsel on their course.
Yet, if they had an interest in such things,
She would be willing to provide them with
A bard whose ballads were most beautiful,
2410 A swineherd who had somehow learned to sing
When angels touched him, tuned his troubled voice,
Commanding him to make engaging music

To glorify the God who gave this gift.
Then Wiglaf would have been quite willing
Except that they were so consumed by travel
They needed now to rest and to renew
Their strength to sail and to pursue their quest.
Then Hilda had some counselors who were willing
To give the Geats advice on how to go.
2420 They said the sea was safer than the land
Because of kings engaged in deadly conflict
And so it seemed to them the Geats should sail,
Providing victuals for a lengthy voyage,
Expecting they would spend some time at sea
They told them to allow a longish time
To reach a place not plagued by war and peril.
They spoke of certain spots along the cost
Where they might hope for haven in a harbor,
And reefs and rocks that had caused many wrecks.
2430 The Geats were grateful for this useful guidance
And made their plans to move again next morning.

That night a gale began with gusts of wind
That tore the trees, and soon a tempest raged.
The Geats made simple shelters with the sails
But those who once were washed with ocean waves
Were made yet damper by the driving downpour
That seemed to soak them deeper than the skin.

Next day, the downpour did not cease
And two whole days the tempest still continued
2440 And then, too late to sail, the showers stopped

And Wiglaf sent some warriors to the woods
To forage in the forest for some food,
To get some game and give them all fresh meat.
They came back rather quickly, having caught
Two deer, a buck and doe, and dragging with them
A fellow they had found who tried to flee,
Which made them think he threatened them.
They captured him and kept him to be questioned.
But Wiglaf thought he was not worth the worry;
2450 He seemed to be a simple sort of man
Who had no weapons, was too weak to fight,
And held in both his hands a battered harp.

* With questioning, he said, "They call me Caedmon;
I have to herd the swine for Hilda's people.
But when they said that I must sing for strangers,
I feared, and so I fled into the forest."
"Are we so worrying to you?" Wiglaf asked.
"You came with clashing armor," Caedmon said,
"And warriors wielding spears and other weapons.
2460 My harp, against such force, would hardly help;
But I have been uneasy anyway
About appearing in a public place.
When, in the tavern, turns were being taken
And someone handed me the harp to hold
And lift my voice, I left and sat alone,
Afraid my friends would see me made a fool.
On one such winter night, I wept alone
To think I should be so ashamed to sing,
When, lo, an angel of the Lord came in

2470 And touched my tongue and told me I should sing.
The vision vowed my voice would now be strong,
And suddenly I sang a new and wondrous psalm.
In praise of God, the Giver of all good.
And yet, each time, the terror still returns
And strangers strike great fear within my soul
Until I take the harp and touch the strings
And God unlocks my lips, and I am lost
In praise of God whose power placed me here."
"I wonder," Wiglaf said, "if you are willing
2480 To sing your songs for some of us tonight.
Our hunters have brought home fresh game for us;
We can provide a visitor with venison."
"I cannot stay," said Caedmon; "they require
To have my presence up at Hilda's house.
A poor man herding pigs must know his place
And come when called, and so I cannot stay;
Nor could I dine on deer; we do not eat
The flesh of beasts; our food is always frugal;
We break our bread and drink our humble broth
2490 And call it quite enough. I cannot stay;
I thank you though for thinking of me thus;
Your clan is kind; and yet, I cannot stay."
"You cannot go," said Wiglaf; "captives can't
Just make their minds up that they wish to move.
I wish to warn you," Wiglaf said, "of this:
Our band of brothers brought you here to us,
And Hilda has already bade us hear you;
And so, at supper, we will hear you sing."

        That night they feasted on the fresh-killed food
2500   And beer the brothers brought to them from Hilda,
        And Wiglaf called to Caedmon, "Come and sing,
        Or else I too will touch your tongue."
        So Caedmon held his harp and hit the strings
        And sang the song the Sovereign Lord had given
        When first he found he need not fear to sing:

*   We give praise as we must * to the Master of heaven,
        The Creator's power * and purposes also,
        The Eternal One's work * and wonders as well,
        The Lord of Glory * beginner of all.
2510   First the Lord shaped * the shining sky-roof
        The Holy One made it * for human beings
        The bard then said, "I sing a song like that:
        It is a ballad Beowulf brought back
        From Hrothgar's hall when he had killed the monster.
        With that he seized his harp and struck the strings:

*   "I sing of human origins * in olden days
        When the All-Ruler * wrought the earth
        With glistening fields * girdled by water
        And set up in triumph * the sun and the moon
2520   As lights to illumine * the land and its dwellers
        And furnished all * the face of the earth
        With tree limbs and leaves. * The life was shaped
        Of every creature * that creeps and moves."

        "But can you sing us," Caedmon then inquired,
        "A song of sojourn and of travelers' searching?"
        "Of course I can," the bard responded quickly:

 *   "Weary and careworn * the wanderer travels,
Homeless and helpless * hiding from fate,
Grieving at daybreak * when dawn arises,
2530 Bringing the sunshine * and solace to others,
The death of his kin * and countless disasters.
Traveling the deep sea * swept by the breakers,
Feeling the blast * of bitter north winds.
Day after day * the dreams of the heart
Sends him on sea-streams * to shores far away,
Not knowing God's purpose * or plan for his fate.
All those know who bear it: * the bitter companionship,
Shoulder to shoulder, * sorrow provides
When friends forsake him * and his fortune is exile
2540 Without any gifts * of gold to reward him
And earth's beauty dead. * He dreams then of hall feasts,
The sharing of treasure * and triumph with friends
When his lord welcomed him * to wassail and joy;
Never again * will such gladness be his
Or the loving counsel * of his comrades and lord.

Here wealth is fleeting, * friends do not last,
Human life perishes, * passing soon away;
All of earth's fabric * fails at the end."
"Yes," Caedmon countered, "clearly you have known
2550 A sadness and a sorrow in your searching;
But have you heard, in everything that happened,
Of One who wills the good of wanderers
And guides them as they go toward their goal
Until the travelers find the end intended?

*   Let me sing of a wanderer * one who left everything
           A man called Abraham * an alien and stranger
           A herder of sheep * seeking a country
           Who crossed mighty deserts * doing God's will;
           Often he was hungry * homeless and weary
2560   But angels attended him * at his tent's entrance
           He took bread and baked it * broke it for the strangers
           He offered them curds * and a calf he prepared
           Then the Almighty * made him a promise
           You will have descendants * like the stars in number
           And in your offspring * earth-folk will be blessed.

           "Your harp-song helps me hold on to the hope
           That God may give us guidance," Wiglaf said,
           "The earth's wise Ruler always overcoming
           The foes we find and filling us with strength."

2570   "I promise I will pray that you may prosper,"
           Said Caedmon. "With your kind concurrence now
           —Delightful evening—I would like to leave
           And see that all my swine are in the sty.
           I trust that Hilda has not ceased to hope
           That she will see me safely back again."
           "Then go," said Wiglaf; "Give our grateful thanks
           To Hilda for your harp. You have been gracious;
           And may the One you worship walk with us,
           And guide the Geats, and govern us as well."

2580   Next day the dawn was dark, but no rain fell;
           The wind was with them as they went their way

And sailed a steady course toward the south.
For two whole days they did not dare to stop
For fear of fighting forces on the shore.
The counselors had cautioned them with care
To seek for hidden sites and make them safe.
So when they came to coves that were secluded
They ranged a ring of guards around their camp
Lest trolls or troops of archers should attack.
2590 And find the Geatish forces undefended.

They were not told that trolls would trouble them
But thought it best that burning brands be ready
Since no one knew what terrors stalked the night.
On certain days the morning sun would shine
And hearts were hopeful and the children happy,
But then a sudden shower would assail them
And drench their clothes and drive their spirits down.
A village on the shore was sometimes seen,
But Wiglaf was not willing to attack
2600 As some insisted they should seek to do
To take the unprotected treasure there.
But Wiglaf wanted them to think of Wolferth,
The sorrows he had suffered from the Swedes,
Who ambushed all his unsuspecting comrades
So almost none returned to tell the tale.
"We cannot count," he said, "from off the coast,
The warriors in the woods, or know what warning
Or message may have made its way to them.
We cannot be too careful, having come
2610 This far, to fail or be defeated now."

So they continued to take care until
* At last they saw such land as they had looked for
And brought their boats to land and breathed a prayer
That here at last might be their hoped for home.
The site they sought was not on open sea,
But flat and fertile land with open fields
And rivers running deep into the region;
A place where they could plow, and plant their crops,
And hope to build their homes, and reap a harvest,
2620 With access open to the ocean's waves
For easy travel to take part in trade
Which some would seek; while others sought a way
To raid the rival clans around them;
But Wiglaf would not let them go to war.
For some it seemed a strange and alien life;
They longed to sail their ships up foreign streams
And then to fall in fierce and sudden fury
On victims: vandalize a peaceful village,
Or wreak their havoc on a humble home;
2630 But, best of all, they thought, to battle bravely
With other men in armor like their own
And strike their spears against a linden shield
And hear the hammering of swords on helmets,
And deal the death-thrust in a fatal duel.
But Wiglaf would not let them go to war;
They questioned, carped, complained, and criticized
And yet, for many years, he would not yield.
The people prospered in a time of peace;
They worked to wall their homes with daub and wattle
2640 And then laid thatch in thick layers on the roofs.

They tilled the level soil and sowed their seed
And gathered in the golden harvest grain
Of wheat and oats and barley; others of them
Preferred to use their fields for flocks of sheep
And weave a warm, soft fabric with the wool.
As time went on a few men turned to trade
And sailed their ships in search of costly goods.
They took the finest fleeces they could find
And cloth the women wove from woolen yarn
2650 And carried cargo far across the sea
* To come back bearing bowls of bronze
And cloaks and silver cups and combs
And brooches, beads, and bottles made of glass,
And all the luxuries that ladies like.

The fields were fallow when they first arrived
But here and there they noticed humble huts
Of simple peasants scratching in the soil
And managing to make a meager living.
Some fled their fields in fear when ships arrived
2660 But others would not leave the land they loved
And swore sincerely they would serve the Geats
And owe them honor, aiding them in conflict.
In time, some smaller tribes came to them also
And so the Geats began to grow in numbers;
The realm they ruled became a wider region
And comrades called on Wiglaf to be king
And be for them what Beowulf had been,
But Wiglaf would not wear a royal crown;
He said they should find someone else for that,

2670 Until they told him all the tribe agreed;
Though people might oppose some policies,
They looked to him alone to be their leader.
Reluctantly, at last he let them do
As they required and crown him as their king.
He said he would defend them from their foes
But would not go to war for gold or glory
Since these were frail rewards and faded fast
When put in place upon the funeral pyre.

* Then Wiglaf warned them times would one day change
2680 And kings would come who only cared for war;
These kings would take their treasure up in taxes
And make them give their sons to gain more glory
And take their daughters to attend their wives.
But still they pressed him, so to please the people,
He let them call him king and make a crown
Though still he would not wear it willingly;
He seemed quite satisfied with simple things.

Then some of them began again to grumble;
They wished for one more warlike in his ways.
2690 And yet, with times of peace, the people prospered;
Their fields were flourishing, their flocks increased,
And bigger, better homes were being built.
It pleased the people that they could appear
To act like all the other tribes they knew
They built a handsome hall to hold their feasts
And celebrate their seasons of success,
A seemly hall where harp-songs would be heard

        And bards could sing the ballads that brought back
        The memory of many other moments,
2700   Of former days and all the friends and foes
        Who shaped the story that they so much loved.
        They gathered gladly to rejoice again
        And fill their flagons up with foaming ale.

        Then Yrfa, Wiglaf's wife, a gracious woman,
        A kind and courteous queen, beloved by all,
        And well attuned to tribal expectation,
        Brought bowls of beer and carried them about,
        To honor all who over many years,
        Surviving various trials while on their voyage,
2710   Had brought them here and helped create new homes;
        And first she went to Wiglaf with a bowl,
        In tribute to the leader of the tribe
        So he might drink a deep, thirst-quenching draft,
        And then she favored Waelric, faithful friend,
        And brought a bright and brimming cup of ale
        To him who steadfast stood beside his lord,
        And then to thanes who through their strength and wisdom
        Had given useful guidance to the Geats.
        The happy voices filled the hall; the harp
2720   Resounded, skillful bards sang ancient sagas
        And told new tales of how their tribe had traveled
        Surmounting many perils undismayed.
        They linked their lines as they had learned to do,
        Extolling with their wisely chosen words,
        The people who had proved their strength and prospered;
        And so they celebrated their success.

        They had not seen the hall that Hrothgar built
        Nor did they give the gables golden trim
        And yet they felt their feasting hall was finer
2730   Than any on the island where they lived.
        The fame of it spread far across the fens
*   Till Ranulf, ruler of the Saxon realm,
        Began to feel the Geats were gaining ground
        That should be under Saxon sovereignty.
        He called a counsel of his kingdom's leaders,
        Those skilled in giving sound advice, and said,
        "Another nation has annexed some land
        That we consider to be Saxon soil.
        We came here and we conquered British kings
2740   And made them all submit to our command,
        But now this foreign force is in our fields
        And growing great and gaining strength each day,
        And soon we Saxons will become their slaves
        Unless we can reclaim the land we conquered,
        And slaughter and destroy unwelcome settlers.
        Then his advisors vowed that these invaders
        Must all be overcome and driven out.
        So Ranulf rallied troops from all that region,
        Instructing them to come with shields and spears.
2750   To form a force of fearsome strength and size
        To go against the unsuspecting Geats.
        So, day by day, these troops were moving down
        Across the fens and coming ever closer.

        The land between the two opposing tribes
        Was flat and filled with slowly flowing streams

And so the Saxon forces moved by ship
Whenever rivers ran in their direction.
The marshes sometimes made such movement hard
And people had to pull their prows through swamp
2760 And operate with ramps and ropes and rollers
 To shift their ships to streams that served their purpose.
Yet, day by day, they kept on moving down
Across the fens and coming ever closer.

In Ranulf's plan, his power would appear
So suddenly the Saxons' first assault
Would wipe away the Geatish warriors
Who would expect assault to come by sea
But would not look alertly to the land
Or station sentinels around a side
2770 Where marshy places would impede the progress
Of troops intent on moving to attack.
 The Saxon strategy made false assumptions
Because the Geats encountered clans before
Who struck them suddenly from secret places,
The terrifying trolls and bowmen too,
And thus they always thought about such threats
And left some lookouts on the landward side
As well as sentinels to search the sea
For any evidence of enemies.

2780 These watchers at a distance were aware
Of smoke ascending to the clouded sky
As if from far-off fires across the fens
And noticed that each night the fires were nearer;

So then they went to Wiglaf with a warning
That troops of soldiers seemed to be assembling
And that the Geats should guard against attack.
Then Wiglaf made the men take certain measures:
To hone their swords and have their hauberks ready,
While Wiglaf, with some leading counselors worked
2790 To put in place a strong defensive plan
To stop the Saxons from destroying them.
Though now outnumbered, it was they who knew
The fields they farmed, the rivers where they fished,
The length and breadth and limits of their land,
And could control the time when they attacked
And pick a place that would impede the foe.

The Saxons, struggling in the swampy ground,
Were wet and weary well before they reached
Their goal, the solid ground where stood the Geats,
2800 But Saxon soldiers formed a seasoned army
Accustomed to the clash of arms in combat
And brutal battles with the British tribes.
The dread of them endured in distant places
Wherever some had seen their savagery
Or heard what havoc Saxon hosts had wrought,
Nor did they doubt that they could do the same
To grind the Geatish folk into the ground.
They saw themselves as sovereigns of the land
And would not willingly provide a welcome
2810 To strangers settling on the soil they claimed.
    For two whole days the Geatish troops had toiled
To ready gear which years of rest had rusted;

They sharpened spears and rubbed the grime from swords
Repaired their shields, replacing worn out parts,
The broken straps, and bosses that were bent,
And added other arrows to their quivers.
The two days full of tense activity
Had left them all on edge and out of sorts;
They often stopped and searched the sky for signals
2820 And waited warily to hear a sentry's warning,
But silence seemed to reign; the only sound,
The heavy hammering of human hearts;
But quiet often comes before a clash.

That evening, after all was set in order,
The Geats set guards in place and came together,
As Wiglaf wanted, when their work was done
To let the people all relax at last
With friends and foaming flagons, with no fear
Except the shadow of the strife to come.
2830 The bards sang ballads of the bravery
Of heroes who had once defeated hordes
And boldly beaten back the strongest foes
And crushed great kings and conquered provinces
And won renown, so now their names are known.
Then someone sang the saga of the journey
That brought them from afar to find this place.
He sang old songs long stored up in his mind
And made new words for many he remembered
Entwining them so he could tell new tales.
2840 He wove together certain well-known words
With newer names they had not known before,

With tales of trolls and terror they had caused,
And islanders who offered unused land,
And Hilda who had helped them on their way,
And those who died, who did not see their dream,
But who had fought to help them find these fields;
All these he sang in sweet and solemn tones
And let the last notes linger in the air.
The silence when he ceased his song was short;
2850 The cups went round; the clamor quickly rose
As men concealed their mood with merriment
And fled their fear with cups of foaming ale.
And somewhere near the Saxons also sang
And drank their draughts of ale to stifle dread
And brashly boasted of their bravery,
Until a time of quiet came for all
And sleep descended and a silence fell
Across the fens, and then a cold wind came
And families felt it far away, and feared.

2860 God's candle came up on a cloudless day
With sunlight shining on the sparkling grass.
* The Geatish warriors grabbed their battle gear
And soon assembled in a central place
And waited willingly for Wiglaf's coming.
A sentry stationed on a smallish hill,
Sharp-eyed could see the enemy with ease,
And how the Saxon ships were sailing nearer
Along the languid streams that led their way,
But though he thought the threat was imminent
2870 He took his time to tell them what he saw

Till he was certain they would soon succeed
In coming much too close to miss the quay
From which the Geatish ships had sailed the seas.
So then he waved a warning down to Wiglaf,
Who made his way amid the waiting men.
"We do not deal with dragons here," said Wiglaf,
"But men no mightier than ourselves though more;
Yet each of us is able to defeat
A single Saxon, and a second one,
2880 And then a third if that should be required.
When dauntless warriors do not fear to die,
They strike to save their homes, their sons and daughters,
And let them live forever in this land
That we have worked so long and hard to win.
Remember, dragons also die when doomed
By brave men willing to abate their breath.
So we will strike the Saxons such a blow
They'll rue the day they ran against our ranks
And Saxon blood will make the bards new ballads
2890 As Geats unite to gain again the glory
That once was ours, and will be when we win."
Then men began to shout and strike their shields
But Wiglaf called for quiet, cautioned them
That Saxons must not see them or suspect
That warriors were aware of them and ready
To strike as soon as they should step ashore.
Then Wiglaf ordered Wealric and his men
To hide themselves behind the little hill
That sloped down slowly to the marshy shore
2900 While he himself put all his armor on.

He laced the leather greaves around his legs
And hauled the hot and heavy chain mail on,
Its links forged long ago, a legacy
Of Eanmund, son and heir of Ohthere,
Whom Weohstan had slain in savage strife,
Unfortunate and friendless, far from home;
The helmet on his head was hardened iron
Embellished by a boar's head on the front;
He pushed his left hand through the leather loops
2910 Behind the shining circle of his shield
And grasped his ancient sword, an heirloom also,
And took his stand where he could see the shore,
Some halfway up the hill that hid his troops.
No sooner was he there than Saxon ships
Emerged, their masts above the marsh and reeds,
And soon their prows appeared, approaching shore.
Then Wiglaf slowly walked toward the ships
And said, "Be gone! This ground belongs to Geats;
We are a people proud to live in peace;
2920 Who would not willingly engage in war,
But neither will we simply step aside
To let our land be seized unlawfully."
Then Ranulf, riding in the lead, arose
And said, "We do not come here seeking something
That is not ours to hold by ancient right;
We are prepared for peace if unopposed
And only ask that you give us your arms,
Your swords and shields and spears and other weapons,
And yield a yearly weight of yellow gold
2930 Sufficient for the right to farm this land

As subjects should at all times to their sovereigns.
Bring arms and gold and we will gladly go."
Deriding Ranulf, Wiglaf raised his voice
And said, "It seems to me your ears are stopped;
You have not heard the half of what I said.
I tell you, none should ever talk of tribute
Except for masters and their sullen slaves;
But for a people fearless, strong, and free,
Your speech is surely unacceptable.
2940 So turn your ships and take your troops back home
Before they fall into the fens and drown,
For if they step ashore, you can be certain
That many mourners will lament your death
And Saxon widows will be wailing long
At hearing how their noble heroes fell.
So tell your folk the tribute you can take:
The tribute of swift spears and sharp-edged swords
And grim engagement with the guardians
Who love this land and call on you to leave."

2950 Replying, Ranulf pushed his prows until
They stuck in swampy water near the shore.
The warriors waded through the shallow water
And gathered on the drier ground to glare
At Wiglaf, watching them not far away
And taunting them to come and take their tribute:
"My bright sword's poisoned point will pay you well
And slake its thirst by sipping Saxon blood."
But Ranulf saw no need to haste or hurry;
He rearranged his ranks on rising ground

2960	And shaped his soldiers in a solid shield-wall
	Each fighter fitted out in heavy fur
	In keeping with the constant Saxon custom;
	Then, brandishing their burnished battle axes
	The Saxon shield-wall slowly moved up hill
	As big drums boomed their baleful cadences.
	Still Wiglaf walked ahead, but turned to wait
	At times and taunt the Saxon troops who trailed him
	And call their vaunted courage into question,
	Though they could hardly hear his hostile words
2970	Above the booming of the battle drums.
	As Wiglaf now approached the peak, he paused,
	And stretched the spear he carried toward the sky
	And waved it like a wand toward the Saxons
	To signal those concealed beyond the summit
	To fall upon the foe in all their fury.
	The hidden ranks now rushed down with a roar
	And smashed the shield-wall very near the center
	To break the battle line, unbraced, in two
	And send the remnant reeling in a rout,
2980	Retreating to the ships, a tattered army,
	Who found, aghast, a group of Geats behind them
	Whom Waelric had brought with him from the woods.
	He circled with a small group to the side
	In hope of hitting Ranulf from behind;
	But Ranulf rallied men around his banner
	And shaped their shields into a circle-wall
	To face their furious foe on every side.
	The Saxon slain lay scattered on the ground,
	A few had even fled the battle field

2990	But Ranulf was not ready yet to rest
	And Geats began to feel the greedy axes
	That swung above the linden shields and struck
	Through helm and hauberk, splitting hapless heads
	And sending sheets of blood down shields and swords;
	The grass was grisly with the steaming gore.
	The Saxons seemed secure within their circle;
	The war-storm raged around their narrowed ranks
	But now the Geats began to suffer grievously
	And tire of taking the attack against
3000	The fearful flailing of the fatal axes.
	The bowmen did their best to shoot above
	The Saxon shield wall with their stinging feathers
	And hit the gaps between the helm and hauberk
	But all too few the foes who fell before them.
	Then Wiglaf summoned to himself the strongest,
	The best and bravest of his battered troops
	And said, "The Saxon circle must be broken
	Or else the outcome of this day will be
	A Saxon victory, ourselves their slaves,
3010	And all the trials and troubles of our trip
	Be found a futile failure in the end.
	So, all too often, other nations lost
	The freedom they had fought for when they failed
	To stand with strength against usurping powers
	And loved their lives above their liberty.
	Let no one say we stepped back from the strife
	For fear of falling in the battle-fury.
	The goal of peace is more than gold or glory
	And we must win our way to that reward

3020 Through battle and, it may be, by our blood.
Let cowards quake, but let the brave men come!"

Then Wiglaf went again toward the wall
Of shields and threw his spear with all his strength
And rushed at Ranulf, ramming shield on shield,
And striking sword against the swinging axe.
The clash and clamor of their combat rose
While all around them other rows were raging.
The battle-rush was bitter; brave men fell
In either army, old and young alike,
3030 As soldiers strove to see who could be first
To deal out death to those whom fate had doomed,
For each side's aim was evil to the other.
A Saxon soldier thrust his sword at Waelric,
Who countered with a crushing, crippling blow
That hit his helmet on the top so hard
He dropped to earth and Waelric dealt the death stroke.
A second Saxon warrior struck down Herbrund
But Waelric went to him and with his spear
He pierced the hapless man upon its point;
3040 The spear went through his stomach, slaying him;
In clanging armor coat, he crashed to earth.
Then Waelric reached his hand to Herbrund, helping him
To find his feet and join again the fray;
He slashed a Saxon buckler, splintered it,
And broke the arm that bore the battered shield;
A second swing cut through his sword arm also;
The warrior could no longer wield his weapons
Or grasp his gilded sword now on the ground.

          A lethal stroke from Herbrund laid him low;
3050   He sank down slowly on the bloody sod.
          But meanwhile Wiglaf waged his war with Ranulf,
          A deadly duel which others watched with dread,
          As, circling, each one sought a chance to strike
          A fatal blow to finish off their feud.
          Then Wiglaf slipped, the soil was soft with blood,
          And Ranulf rushed in recklessly to kill;
          But Wiglaf, leaning to his left, eluded
          The eager axe and answered with a thrust,
          A stab, that bit the Saxon in the side
3060   And broke his charge and brought him briefly down.
          He rose at once and ran in rage at Wiglaf;
          His battle-blade came down with blinding speed
          And hit the helmet with such horrid force
          That Wiglaf fell face forward, floundering,
          And would have died, but Waelric went to him
          And stood above him struggling shield to shield
          With Ranulf, blocked his blade and beat him back
          Till Wiglaf once again regained his wits
          And standing, swaying, raised his shaking sword
3070   In time to take the Saxon's next attack;
          But Ranulf, wounded as he was and weary,
          Let slip his shield and Wiglaf's sword struck home.

          Then Ranulf fell, and all his fighters fled,
          The Saxon losers, lacking loyalty,
          Abandoned boats and fled the battlefield
          To leave their leader lying on the earth
          And flee on foot across the spreading fens,
          And so were swallowed by the swampy ground.

* But then they found that in the final fray
3080 An arrow aimed at someone else
Had missed its mark and somehow made its way
By chance to hit a chink in Wiglaf's chain mail
And hit him near the heart, a heinous blow
That doomed him, though he did not die until
He first had finished Ranulf's fighting days,
Then walked toward a wall where he could sit
And speak to those who stood around in sorrow
To see the lord who led them lying there,
The gallant Geatish leader on the ground.
3090 Then Waelric brought him water, wet his brow,
And held his head to help him as he spoke:
"We ventured on our voyage with a vision
And sought a place of peace where we might prosper;
The Saxons may not soon resume the struggle,
Returning once again to test our temper,
But rivalries will rise within our ranks
And some will seek to steal the wealth of others,
For now I know it is not in our nature
To help and heal and never turn to harm,
3100 For envy is our inner enemy
And greed for gain and glory guides too many.
I said I could not conquer all who came
Against the Geats and guard you by myself
Nor be for you what Beowulf had been,
Who slew the monsters by his single strength,
But that may be our benefit, not bane;
When work is shared, society is stronger;
Our world is weak when all depend on one;

                So seek for ways to share in leadership;
3110   And learn a larger loyalty that flows
                From each to all, from all to everyone;
                And dare a greater dream, still dim
                But not beyond the yearning of the years,
                That all of us who live here on this island
                May find a path to peace so all may prosper
                And flourish free of fears of worldly foes.
                I call to mind the country Caedmon sang,
                Where all our human hearts at last are healed
                And senseless striving is forever stilled.
3120   My journey is not over; I go on
                In hope to reach the Heaven-Ruler's realm.
                I want my body buried by my friends,
                Not placed upon a pyre like Beowulf's
                Nor sent off on the sea like that of Scyld,
                But dig my grave in ground that we have gained
                By valiant voyaging and victory,
                And make a mound there to remember me,
                And so that some will ask to hear the story,
                The ancient saga of our origins,
3130   And how we came in quest of quiet peace
                And slew the Saxon foe to save our freedom."

*   The grieving Geats began to carry out
                The wish expressed in Wiglaf's final words.
                They sought a ship that would be suitable
                And picked their proudest boat; its ring-necked prow
                Had brought them safely through the storm and stress
                Of ocean waves and weeks of wandering

And left them all at last in this good land.
So would the warrior and water-rider,
3140 Who crossed the seas and conquered ocean currents,
The wanderer who faced the world's strong waves,
Now sail again to seek a farther shore
Unwashed by waves, unwearied by earth's tumult.

They brought the boat about, bow end away,
Then, waiting till the tide had almost turned
To have the hull as high as possible,
They pulled the prow to place it in position
On rollers they arranged along the route
Between the tide and place they had determined
3150 To be the best to use for burial;
With ropes they rolled it up the river bank
To move along a fairly level lane,
Then up a steeper slope—the men now sweating—
To find the chosen pasture, flat and fair,
In which a crew had carved a cavity
With space enough to hold the splendid ship.
They rolled it up a ramp to reach this pit
And bring the boat above the burial place.
They weighted one end down and took away
3160 The rollers that were at the other end
So they could tilt the ship into the tomb;
Then mauls removed the rollers that remained
To let the ship subside into the space.
They braced the bottom then by bringing earth
And settling shovelfuls around the sides.
Inside the boat they built a sort of box

By putting planks in place and nailing them,
To make a room, a royal resting place.
Some sturdy pegs were set along one side
3170 To hold a cast iron cauldron and some cups;
A royal scepter, shield, and sharpened spears
Were wedged in place against the western wall.
Within the center of the space they set
The coffin, carried carefully the corpse
And lowered it with loyal and loving arms.
They fitted at his feet some folded cloth,
A hammer, drinking horn, and hanging bowls,
A pillow, gaming pieces, pair of shoes,
Some combs, a cap of fur, a coil of tape,
3180 Three burrwood bottles, buckles large and small,
A ladle, lances, and a leather bag;
They covered this collection with a cloak
Of woven wool that he had often worn.
They hammered home the top with heavy blows
Then laid a lyre upon the coffin lid
And cast another cloak across the coffin;
On that they set a shining silver dish
Embossed with beasts and bordered with a braid.
They offered all these objects to provide
3190 A truly worthy tribute to their leader,
The honor that was owed by all of them,
And also all that Wiglaf would be wanting
To fight and feast in unknown future years.
At last they placed a lamp and lighted it
And closed the cover of the room they crafted.

Then there was wailing of the women in their woe
Who feared that foes would fall upon them now
If Wiglaf was not with them as their leader,
While warriors stood about in solemn silence
3200 And watched the coffin, wondering how well
Another leader would allot their lives,
For Wiglaf always wanted one thing only:
A place where all could put down roots and prosper;
No trolls or troubles turned him from that goal;
He brought them through and beat their foes in battle,
But now they knew another leader must
Be chosen as their chief, to challenge them;
Would he seek wars to wage, would he be weak,
Would he make plans for peace so they might prosper?
3210 So much would be demanded of this man
Whom they would seek to serve with all their strength,
And so they faced the future, and they feared.

Then Waelric said, "I wish that Wiglaf would
Bequeath his questing courage to us all
But we must seek his spirit in ourselves
To face our people's future unafraid,
And hope that he who brought us safely here
Has left a legacy of loyalty
To give the Geats the gift of unity.
3220 We have no Beowulf to bear our burdens
So each of us must offer what we can;
So may we move ahead, and yet remember."

Then all the earth which had been taken out,
The sod and soil, was shoveled slowly in,
And other earth was added to the pile
To make the mound that Wiglaf had demanded,
A hillock high above the heaving sea,
That would be seen by sailors in their ships
Arriving with new riches on the river;
3230 The mast remained protruding from the mound
And held up high toward the heavens
A banner with a bear embroidered on it
Until with passing time the timber rotted,
Fell down, and disappeared, and memory dimmed,
And no one still remained who knew the name,
What body had been buried in the barrow,
Or how he died or deeds that he had done.

YRFA'S TALE

Attend! This time no smoke went twisting up,
No blazing fire consumed the bloody bodies;
Too often had we seen that sight. I spoke
Against the fire; I favored forms less harsh
And argued for the ancient way of earth. I said,
That burial was best since now our bones
Could rest in land that we would live in long.
I knew it was what Wiglaf wanted too
Since he had willed it with his dying words.
10   It seemed his strength came somehow from the soil;
His feelings first were always for this land
That he had sought for over swelling seas
And green things gave him gladness. It seemed good
That we should make a mound in memory
And let him sleep in land he so much loved
Yet sheltered in the ship that also shaped
His life. I like to think it serves to link
Our past and present with the promised peace
We yearn for far beyond our mortal years;
20   The mounds we make may bring to mind for others
In future years how futile fighting is
And I was glad his grave would still be green
So we might come and keep it carefully
And not forget the good times in our grief.
I had a husband who was brave and good
And lost his life because he lived for others.

So when the mound was made to mark the place
We wept a while and then we went away
Although I thought a part of me was there

30 　　　And would be always in that earthen mound
　　　　　And part of Wiglaf would be with me still;
　　　　　A body can be buried but it seems
　　　　　To me that there is more than earth that matters.

　　　　　That night my neighbors came; they knew, of course,
　　　　　I would be lonely. Lovingly they listened
　　　　　As I, still stunned, and overwhelmed by absence
　　　　　Both spoke and sobbed and sometimes simply sat
　　　　　Remembering how we met, the many times
　　　　　We faced our future unafraid although
40　　　　We sometimes could not see a safe way through
*　　　　The trolls and trackless seas and hostile tribes
　　　　　And perils that appeared along our path.
　　　　　My Wiglaf was not one to have his way
　　　　　By force of arms if any other means
　　　　　Would work as well. He sought to find a way
　　　　　Toward peace, as long as peace was possible,
　　　　　But combat came to him and he was killed
　　　　　And now I was alone.

　　　　　I never knew
　　　　　A house that held such happiness could then
50　　　　Be emptied out so soon; the echos ached
　　　　　And Wiglaf was in every one of them.
　　　　　Old crones and children came but could not fill
　　　　　The hollow house, nor could they heal my heart.

　　　　　A sound of singing came from somewhere near
　　　　　As warriors, Wiglaf's comrades, washed away

Their grief with foaming goblets and regaled
Each other as they tried to ease their hearts
By boasting of their bravery in battle
And sneering at the Saxon soldiery,
60 Revisiting our victory and vaunting
Their daring deeds that doomed the enemy.
But all that I could afterwards remember
About the battle and the burial
Was what I saw myself: a single man
Alone and leaning on his sword to let
The Saxons come. He stood there, and it seemed
To me that moment symbolized the man,
Who acted always from an inner strength
And never from a need to win a name
70 Or gain applause or praise by pleasing those
Who seldom sought for anything except
The gold that goes down with them to the grave
Or smiles that seldom last a summer's day.

I wondered then what Wiglaf would have thought
To see his comrades singing songs so soon
And with the mournful mounds reminding us
Of those dear friends who fell defending us
And who were heroes, yes, but husbands, sons,
And fathers first and our defenders second,
80 Who, having lost their lives for love of us
Are all forever absent from our world.
So how could hearts be healed so suddenly
That they could sing and sound high-spirited
In such a time of trouble and of trial?

But even widows would not weep all night
For all our many memories were mixed
And recollections led us on to laugh
Like grownup girls and giggle while we grieved.

All night we talked and told each other tales
90   Remembering so many moments past:
The land we left behind, and little things:
A toy or trinket with its tale to tell,
A simple chain a child had cherished once,
Still dear today although the child had died.

Each memory reminded us of more.
I told the tale of how I took some children,
My own and all the neighbor children also,
One summer day with sunshine smiling down,
To gather bramble berries in our buckets
100   And left them lying all alone at noon
Because we saw a stream and went to swim
And thought that later they would still be there.
We splashed awhile and sat there in the sun
At ease with all the world, and afterwards
Came back to find the buckets bottom up
And waiting with them, watching us, a bear.
We did not dare to drive the beast away
But went home from our failed trip fruitless
And brought the empty buckets back next day.

110   Then Gerda told of twisting twine one day
And weaving wool that we had newly spun

And leaving lots of it beside the loom
Because her daughter called to her to come
And fix some foolish thing that made her fret;
But while she was away and no one watching
A goat had gotten into Gerda's house
And eaten all the edges off her work.
She kicked the creature out, and sat and cried;
But later, looking back, she, too, could laugh.

120 We laughed until the tears came tumbling down;
So near to crying, could we call it grief?

We laughed because we could not cry all night
But we did grieve for all the good men gone
And spoke of some of whom the bards will sing
Whenever men are merry in the mead hall.
Some spoke of husbands who had held them close
And lost their lives in battles long ago
* And others spoke of Aelric, ancient warrior,
Whose one and eighty winters brought him wisdom
130 But more than any human mind could manage,
So in the end his thoughts were often addled
And no one knew what nonsense he might speak.
* We laughed, but he was loyal when Laefstan dared
To question Wiglaf's courage; he was killed,
But none who knew him would forget his name.

Such tales we told, and tried by weaving words
To hold each other up and help the hurting.
Then, one by one, the younger women went

            To chase their children down and do their chores
140   While still some women stayed who understood
            That what I needed now was not so much
            Their words or wisdom as their willingness
            To share my sorrow simply being there.
            For words are ways of being with a friend
            But we need more than words however wise
            And simply sitting silently is more
            Than any words that we could ever ask.

            They would not leave or let me be alone
            Until they had determined it was time
150   For them to cure my cares with quietness
            And slowly slip away and let me sleep.

            I woke, and wondered first where Wiglaf was;
            The deeds of yesterday seemed like a dream
            That soon would fade and free us as before
            To live our lives as we had liked to do.
            But Wiglaf was not there and would not be
            And I must learn to live my life alone,
            Though Karn and Weo would be with me still.
            A woman always will have work to do:
            To cook and clean and care for kith and kin
160   And somehow summon strength for them. And so
            I must begin again to gather up
            The shattered pieces and the severed strands
            Of life, and learn to look ahead once more
            And make a life with meaning for myself.

So dawn came up and all the duties of the day,
And then some came to me and called me "Queen,"
Which was my right when Wiglaf was the king
But somehow seemed to have another sound
When all the queen that I had ever been
170 Had come because of him. It now became
A title terrifying to my ears;
A queen as consort, yes; but unaccompanied?
I walked as queen with Wiglaf willingly
* Though he was hardly pleased to have the title
Of king and would not wear a crown; he warned
Of kings to come whose only care would be
The gold and glory to be gained in battle,
Whose will for war would weary them in time
And make them long for leaders less like kings.
180 He did not warn or see that Weo would
Become that king and gladly wear that crown.
They said, "Of course, we'll keep the cares away
From you; we would not worry you with wars
And strife and such-like serious challenges
To men who make their lives in Middle Earth;
You can be queen and have no cares at all."

I said, "You do not know me, not at all;
You cannot come and call me queen and then
Ignore me, make the name of no importance
190 And so, though silently, usurp the throne,
Pretend to give the title while the true
Authority is yours. I think the throne
Must represent a real and rightful power;

I could not claim to be a queen if some
Were acting otherwise than I would do."

And so we left the subject; I assumed
That one among the wiser warriors
Would call a council to select a king
And hoped to hear that he was such a one
As liked to lead by listening as well
And was inclined to turn away from war.
But time went by and no one took the title
Nor was a council called nor clamor made
To say that someone should be singled out
To be the one to bear that thankless burden.
It seems that sometimes when a strong oak falls
No other oak can fill the empty space.
But then a deadly dull routine of days
Went by: it seemed the sun no longer shone,
Each day became a dull and dreary round
Of morning, noon, and night with nothing new
(Or so it seemed to me), a senseless time
Of weariness that weighed me down. I wanted
To sleep all day; I seldom tried to speak
And I could barely go about my business.
Although I could not think, my thoughts would turn
To Wiglaf, wanting there to be a way
To turn the tide of time and live again
As fully as before our foes had come
And battle blasted all our better hopes.

The days went dully by; I do not know
How many more it was until one morning
A bard came by, a singer of our ballads,
A young man yet, for all his youthfulness,
The equal of his elders in devotion
And love for learning all the tribal lore,
The doom of dauntless heroes who had dared
Confront the phantoms of a former age
And battle brutal foes and fearful beasts,

230   The ghastly Grendel and his gruesome mother,
And terrifying trolls who tore their prey
With fangs so frightening all who saw them fled.
Such songs he sang while those who heard them shuddered
And drank more deeply from the foaming draught.

This man, so much admired for many skills,
Came quietly as I was cleaning clothes
And asked if I would ever have some time
When he might hear from me the history
Of Wiglaf's wars and many wanderings

240*   As only I of all the Wederas
Could tell the tale, the triumphs and defeats
But, more than that, my memories of the man
Whom only I had known through all his journey.

But I was angry then and answered him
Abruptly, "Bards have sung of Beowulf
And Wiglaf will be honored for his wars
So why should I do anything to add
Another ballad for the beer hall bards

                    Who glorify the fighting and the feuds
250   That bring us only blood and battle-deaths
                    And widows wailing for those wasted lives?
                    I think that there are better things to do
                    Than boast of bloodshed and of broken bodies.
                    Have you no songs to sing of sunshine days
                    With people all at peace and each employed
                    In farming with their families and friends
                    Or travelers who take their goods to trade
                    With foreign people, friends we do not fear,
                    But people who have pottery or pearls
260   Or amber or some ivory or bone
                    And carved work crafted carefully by elves
                    To offer in exchange for our best work.
                    Why must we magnify the men who fight
                    And not the women, wives who work at home?"

                    I may have made too much of this
                    And hit too hard, but I was hurting still.
                    The bard, astonished by my statement, stopped
*   And offered to return another time
                    But then he said that he could sing me something
270   More pleasing, possibly, if I were patient;
                    And he said, "Have you ever heard,
                    The epic I can sing of earth's creation?"
                    I knew it well; it's words were woven deep
                    In memory from many mead hall nights.
                    So I apologized and asked him if
                    He'd like to sing. I leaned my head to listen.
                    With sweet-voiced skill, he struck his harp and sang:

*   "In wisdom was the Maker's work begun,
         Almighty Maker of the Middle Earth,
280   Who sent the sun upon its ceaseless rounds
         And made the moon and all the myriad stars
         And set them in the sky to mark the seasons
         And made the Middle Earth and molded it
         With hills and hollows shaped by his own hand
         And set the surging sea within its bounds
         And garbs the garden earth with greenery
         When winter wanes and sunshine warms the earth
         And brought forth birds to fly above the earth
         And fish to fill the foaming seas below."

290   He sang as sweetly as the birds in spring
         But I could only think of other questions
         That tried and troubled me from time to time
         Whenever I had heard that ancient song:
         If all of it was good, why evil now?
         And why, when Hrothgar held his hall in peace
         With warriors making merry with their mead
         Did Grendel gorge himself in grim revenge?
         What fairness do you find in facts like these:
         That trolls should terrorize our tribe and take
300   Such men as Sigamund to make their meal
         And men as good as Wiglaf may be murdered
         And Aeschere and Aelric and the others
         Who lost their lives and left us all in grief.
         How can you call this kind of world the work
         Of a Creator aiming for our good?"
         I sat surprised to hear myself say this;

          I was not one to wonder; Wiglaf was;
          But as I said these words it somehow seemed
          That Wiglaf's words were welling up in me.

310   The singer stopped in some surprise and said,
          "You may be right, but music means enough;
          I will not worry much about the words
          And had not thought of things like that before;
*   My role is not to ponder right and wrong
          But simply sing the songs and tell the stories
          And leave the larger lessons for the hearers;
          Let others argue as to all of that,
          But still your story is a song that I
          Would love to learn, for I believe
320   The years go by too fast, and you are young
          No longer. You have lived an epic life,
          A tale that should be told while time remains
          And you remember moments and their meaning
          For us and all who will come after us.
          We need to know your story. No one else
          Has played your part, and that piece is important
          To help us hold the wholeness of our life."
          I said, "Indeed, I surely understand
          That you would like to listen and to learn
330   The history that has been often heard
          Of Wiglaf and his wanderings and wars,
          A tale our tribe must tell for evermore,
          But I have only ordinary things
          To say for I have never swung a sword
          That bites the bone and let the blood flow down,

Nor did I ever seek to duel with dragons.
My tale is Wiglaf's tale for we were one.
I did not stand beside him with a sword
But I was always in his heart and he
340 In mine, and though I was not there I think
I understood the utter agony
That conflict caused him with its need to kill.

"But I could also tell you other things
That I endured with all my daily duties;
Perhaps I have some tales you have not heard
Of chasing children and the household chores
And mending clothes and cooking constantly.
To love the little ones and help them learn
Requires commitment, constancy, and care.
350 Does this arouse heroic rhythms in your heart?
Yes, maybe I have memories in mind
That I might yield for you to take and use
To shape the sounds and make of them a song
That others everywhere might also learn.
My days were not all dull, for dangers came
And many moments filled with mortal fear
And terrors such as bards are sure to sing.

"I look around this land where we now live
So flat and full of endless fens and mists
360 Remembering the mountains and the moment
When deadly peril pressed upon our tribe
And trolls attacked us—you must know the tale—
And made their meal among our bravest men.

I think myself that it is safe to say
That Grendel too was of the tribe of trolls;
These fens at least are free of foes like that.

* "Oh, I remember: on that awful day
When Weo wandered off into the woods
While Selfric's screams still sounded in our ears
370 And no one knew what happened in the night
Except that Selfric, strongest of our men,
Had vanished, victim of some vile attack
By unknown adversaries in the woods,
That Wiglaf wanted one to go with him
So each might aid the other in distress.
'It is a fool,' he said, 'who feels no fear
And sets out seeking glory for himself
And blithely disregards the greater good
To find some fleeting bubble-dream of fame.'
380 So Wiglaf reasoned while I rushed around
In panic without any point or plan.
I did not seek for safety for myself
But only Weo's welfare, and I would
Have rushed off recklessly. I would have run
Unarmed and unprotected after him
Till Wiglaf warned me that I had no weapons
To deal with danger. I would meet my doom
And Weo would be worse off than before
If any monsters met me. I admitted
390 That he was right. It would be wrong to risk
My life that way and Weo's life as well.
I had dismissed the monsters from my mind
As anxious as I was at Weo's absence.

"So Wiglaf went to see where Weo was
And took the two who dared to seek the trail
Of frozen footprints on the forest floor—
So cold they were although the world was warm—
But failed to find the faintest evidence
That little Weo ever went that way.
400 When darkness deepened at the end of day
They came straight back but brought no boy with them
And felt that further searching would be futile.
I meanwhile had imagined many things
Since I could not go out in active search
And dull my dread by deeds however futile.
Nor could I cook or carry on my chores
While I imagined him a monster's meal.
He was so young and yet beyond his peers
In many ways; he was among the most
410 Aggressive with his friends, though good as gold
With us and other adults, always seeking
To please, win popularity and power.
Though only eight, his instinct always was
To lead, alert to every little trick
To find new friends and gain more followers
To go against another team in games
Or wage mock warfare with their wooden swords
Or search for sleeping dragons they could slay;
As fearless as his father, unafraid
420 Of man or monster in the Middle Earth;
A charming child and hard for us to chastise.
"The twilight came; no truant child returned;
The night grew darker; no one now could doubt

The terror-king had taken him. We told
Each other it was always possible
To hope that he was hidden somewhere near
And might still meet us when the morning came
Though inwardly we felt such faith was futile.

"But now my terrors took a far worse turn:
430   At midnight monsters came once more;
I heard the horrid screams, and huddled down
Within the simple shelter we set up
And waited, wondering if Wiglaf would
Return this time to tell me all was well
Or not come back, the bad news brought by others.
Karn somehow slept, untroubled by the screams.

"I later learned that Wiglaf led the way,
Attacked the trolls with torches till they fled
And found a few to follow after him
440   And kill the craven cowards in their cave
—a story you have surely sung before—
But meanwhile we found Weo near the woods,
Engaging in a game with girls and boys
As if no deadly doom endangered us.
I called to him to quit his game and come;
I asked him if he ever thought of others
Except to flatter friends and followers
And turn attention always to himself.
I raved and raged and ranted for a while
450   And screamed and scolded using scathing words
While Weo looked up lovingly and listened

Until the storm subsided into sobs
When I exhausted all my angry words.
Then Weo asked me if in any way
He could be helpful. How could I be hard
On him? It was his way; a winning way.
I made him stay with me all morning
And warned him Wiglaf would be angry and
When he came home, that he would hear from him.

460 "And angry Wiglaf was, and wondered where
And how he had been hidden from the trolls
And if he ever asked how others felt;
I seldom saw him speak so angrily
But Weo answered everything and asked
What he could do to make amends to mother,
And help, since he had caused such hurt;
His manner was, as always, meek and mild.
But Wiglaf's anger was not turned away;
He thrashed him thoroughly and added threats
470 To give him worse if he should go again
Without consent or any word to us."

"But what and where and why," the bard inquired
Of Weo: "was he in the woods all night
And did he dare approach the dreadful trolls,
Or did he hide, or hunt the hapless beasts?"

I smiled. "He said he slew the ones his size
And left the larger ones to deal with later,
Or let his friends and father fight them first,

              But honestly I am not sure. I asked
480   And he replied. I have no proof supporting
              My theory, but I think he followed them
              A little way into the woods and waited there;
              He meant it to remain a mystery—
              As Weo always was and would be still.
              In time to come, such tales were told of Weo
              That some would say he had a secret strength
              And could become invisible and call
              Upon impalpable, unearthly powers.
              We parents never know our children, nor
490   Did I know Karn, but Weo was the one
              Who sometimes seemed so far astray
              From us that I could only wonder how
              I might have mothered such a man as this
              —Though sometimes I could also see myself
              And Wiglaf in him well enough to worry.

              "But listen: this was long ago and I have learned
              A forest has no face, and so our fears
              Are magnified as we imagine monsters
              More terrible than trolls and twice as fierce
500   As Grendel, ghastlier and far more grim
              And dreadful than the dragon dealt with once
              By Beowulf and Wiglaf. War is worse
              Before we fight it than it is in fact.
              Our minds imagine more than we will meet;
              The phantoms that I fear the most are formless
              And hold their power in the human heart;
              It seems to me that shadows should not shake us,

> For evil is an aspect of our hearts
> That gains it grip because we give it room."

510 The bard sat still, astonished at my speech,
And I was also stunned at all I said.
That sort of somber thought is not my style;
My thoughts were wandering in Wiglaf's world,
Not mine; I had no mind to meditate
On why the grass is growing green,
From brown seed buried in the barren soil,
* Or why the same stars shine down from the sky
However many miles a man may go,
Or why a certain star is seen to move
520 While others always stay within their place.
It did not matter very much to me;
I had no burning need to know their nature
Or how to gain the guidance of the gods.
But it was always Wiglaf's way to wonder
And question constantly the course of things.

I learned at last to look at things that way
Myself: to see the strange surprise and splendor
In all the everyday and ordinary,
From time to time at least, as Gerda taught me
530 And others also, artisans who seek
To understand life's structures and to show
Relationships, the links that shape our lives:
How form and color can create new ways
To see and so enrich our settled ways.
So Gerda would explore the plants and pick

A fern or flower, from them making dyes
And weaving in her wool new worlds of color,
Like Wiglaf wondering and willing to upset
The habits handed down and now held dear,
540 The sane and settled way we live, and simpler
Because unquestioned, clear to all and settled.
So Sigelac assumed that swords and spears
Could answer any question. So, too, I
Assumed that women's ways were woven deep
In nature, known to all and never more
To change or to be challenged. Wiglaf chafed
At such and he, like Gerda, sometimes saw
New ways to work toward a better world.

My thoughts were far afield, but finally
550 Came back to where the bard sat by my door.
I meant to stop, but memories remained
So clear I could not keep them in. I said,
"I'll try to stick to facts: I see it still

* In dreams: the day when first the dragon came
And with it woe to all the Wederas.
The sun had set and shadows had grown dark
When first we felt a shaking in the floor
And then a roar and rumble came; we rushed
Outside and saw, high circling in the sky,
560 A shining, shimmering fire that shook the earth,
A fearful glory, glowing greenish-white.
I thought of Thor the Thunderer whose bolts
Light up the sullen sky when summer comes.
I stood and stared, astounded by the beauty

But felt no fear amid the falling fire.
I did not dread it as one might fear death;
I saw the savage splendor of its wings,
And I exulted in its awful beauty.

"It was the shine and shimmer I esteemed,
570   And if the evil had no beauty in it
And dragons did not also dazzle us,
Who would be won to follow evil ways?

"Then Karn, who crept outside, began to cry.
I scooped her up and smoothed her brow and smiled.
She whimpered while I whispered words of comfort
And sought to show her how the shining one
Was gleaming, glistening, oh so gloriously.

"When Wiglaf came he watched it warily;
I think he thought at once of how it threatened
580   An end of all our peace and unconcern.
And now I noticed, red against the night,
That fearsome fire was falling on our homes
And scorching them till suddenly it seemed
The blaze below was brighter than above.
The thunder stopped, but then a thousand fires
Sprang up wherever dragon-breath had issued
And flames were falling fiercely everywhere
As simple homes were seared and turned to smoke
And ashes, instantly and utterly
590   Consumed, a sad and sorry spectacle,
And we who stood and watched could find no words

For horror at the houses here and there
That burned and blazed beneath the dragon's breath.
I sometimes see those simple buildings still
And think of those who used to live in them:
And made their meals and laughed and mourned
And scolded children, scoured pots—now scattered,
No longer living in the land we loved
But, with the windblown ashes, wafted wide.
600 The dragon did his worst and came back down
And vanished from our view. A vapor rose
And smoke ascended from the cabins still.
We went with water and we worked to quell
The flares and flames the fire-worm left behind.
By now the dreadful night was nearly gone
And in the eastern sky that other fire,
God's candle, cast its light in cloudless skies.
The dawning day would doom our peaceful life."

The singer still sat silently, and I
610 Was listening too as tales came tumbling out
As if some other "I" were speaking now:
"First, Beowulf came bringing battle gear,
The ancient warrior willing once again
To act for us against our enemy,
The fiery flyer, fearful in his wrath;
He wanted Wiglaf and eleven with him,
So all went off to put their armor on.

"I went back then to wait with Karn and Weo
(I had assumed that they were sleeping still),

620 But Weo wasn't there; I wondered where
    He could have gone; when Karn had come to watch
    The shining serpent circling in the sky
    And we were unaware and did not notice,
    He must have managed then to make his way
    To some place more exciting to himself—
    Which worried me, for Weo was without
    A sense of fear and surely he would seek
    Whatever action he could find, and I
    Was helpless now, for how could I go hunt
630 For him and leave my little Karn alone?

    "Just then, a sudden sound of screaming came
    And hideous hissing, horrifying sounds,
    The roar and rattle of the dragon's rage.
    I went outside and saw the serpent soaring,
    His green scales glittering against the sun
    While I stood watching warily and wondered
    How far from us those dreadful flames would fall;
    He circled, then descended suddenly,
    Like doom and darkness, swiftly down he came
640 Where Beowulf stood bravely for the battle.
    I heard the horror of what happened next
    From others afterwards, though only Wiglaf
    Was near enough to know exactly how
    The dragon died and how his dagger struck
    The fatal blow that finished off the fire-lord.
    But all I wanted was to see if Weo
    Had dared to face the dragon and had died
    Before his father struck the final blow.

"I found the broken barrow; Beowulf
*650 Was sitting on a stone, as still and pale
As death, the life-blood draining slowly down,
His body blackened by the dragon's breath,
And Wiglaf was not with him as he sat
Surrounded by the wretched rogues who failed him.
But Weo was there with his wooden sword
Unscratched or stained with smoke that I could see.
At first I feared that Wiglaf in the fight
Had met his doom, a death-wound from the dragon,
And looked about the barrow for his body,
660 When out he came, and carried with him cups
And flagons, finely crafted, dishes filled
With jewels and rings, and wreaths, and helmets rimmed
With woven gold, all worked with skill, such wealth
As we had never seen; we stood and stared at it
But Wiglaf went to Beowulf, to wash
The king, beloved leader, last of Waemundings
While we who watched him stood aside and wept.

"We burned the body of King Beowulf
* And as the ashes cooled we asked ourselves
670 What fate would now befall us from our foes.
But all of that is known and nothing new
And long been listened to in many lands
So I can only add my own few words
Concerning what I saw. Yes, sometimes now
That dreadful day seems like a distant dream,
A vapor that will vanish from our view
When once again we waken to the world

Of daily life, so dreary without dragons.
But each of us," I said, "has other things
680 To do, and so we should, I think, now stop
Until we have more time. To tell my tale
We may need many quiet hours more."

"Quite right," the singer said; "so let us seek
Another time for you to tell your tale.
There is no need, you know, to go on now
About the bravery of Beowulf
Or of the day on which the dragon died;
You said yourself these songs are often sung,
But what we have not heard as yet is how
690 You came at first to call this country yours
As Wiglaf's wife, and so I think we want
To add all that, but at some other time."

So then we once more went our separate ways
And met again not many mornings afterward.
I took some time before I told my tale;
So much to tell, so many memories
From which to weave in words the world I knew,
So carefree as it seemed and quiet, calm,
Before the dragon came and darker days.

700 I said, "The story of my life must start
Before that day when first I found a spouse
It was not Wiglaf with whom life began
For me. Let me begin again and go
To early days and other lands when I

Was just a growing girl who had the gift
Of freedom to explore the fields and forests
While boys were being taught the battle skills,
The shield- and sword-play soldiers often need.
My playmate, Pira, went with me, exploring
710   And seeking water sprites and certain elves
Who could be captured on a quiet night,
When southern stars aligned, with silken thread
And so compelled to part with precious gifts,
Such gifts as golden rings that grant to those
Who wear them seven wishes wonderful
Beyond our years to understand or yearn for.

"One night when no one knew where we had gone
We found a fairy by a waterfall,
Encircled it with silken thread and said,
720   'Now give us golden rings and grant our wishes,'
But it had simply smiled and shook its head
And dashed our dreams—although we did not know
What hopes to hold or how to make the fairy
Provide our vision. We were very young;
We set our sights on things that seemed to us
Magnificent, things none of us had known
Like golden rings and gaudy jewels and gowns;
We pled for palaces and prancing steeds,
For kings to call us queens and give us crowns.
730   We did not know the grief that goes with glory.

"We kept the captured sprite and carried her
Back home and hid her under Pira's house;

We made a wooden box with woven wicker lid
Across the top to cover it and keep
Her safe from prying eyes and Pira's parents.
We asked her often if she would be kind
And give us golden rings and grant our wishes
But still she only smiled and shook her head;
We sometimes heard her humming happily
740 Though still she never sang or spoke to us.
But one day we had traveled far away,
Perhaps to hunt for other hapless sprites,
Or only to absent ourselves from any
Parental summons to assist in some dull chore,
And coming back we found the box was broken
And empty, all our eager hopes destroyed.
But Pira argued angrily that it
Was Bonric's blame, he must have broken it;
Her brother somehow saw us and assumed
750 That we were hiding heaps of gold from him.
We hid from him till he came home, and watched to see
If he'd go back to where the box had been.
He rode in, looked around, and went to rest,
But Pira placed herself in Bonric's path
And asked him if he knew of anything
About our box and who had broken it
And let our little water sprite get loose.
He stopped his horse and sneered at her and said,
'It's nothing but a butterfly, so battered
760 It failed to fly and fluttered to the ground.
I took it out and tossed it toward the forest
And when I looked again a little later

I failed to find it, so perhaps it flew
Or else an animal has eaten it,
But it was only something in your head;
Why so upset about a silly bug
That you imagined might be something more?'
And so his sister screamed at him and said,
'You hateful, horrid thing,' and hit at him,
770 But he just laughed and leaped aside and left.
We gathered up the bits of broken boards
And grieved for golden rings we would not get—
But later learned to look back and to laugh."

I stopped for breath and looked about; the bard
Was sitting with his eyes fast shut, asleep!
I walked away; I would not waken him.
I told myself I would not tell my tales
To singers such as that who could not see
How very vital such adventures are
780 To growing girls and boys, to give to them
A sense of self and strengthen them for life.
These moments mold us, make us what we are,
And bards should sing these battles boldly too.

The singer was ashamed when next I saw him
And begged me to let bygones be forgotten
And asked me if I would, some other time,
Resume my story—if he would not sleep!
I answered only I would do my best
To try to find a time when I could talk
790 But Karn was carrying a child and called

On me, her mother, more and more for help
Since she was often ill and I was needed
And did not like to leave my Karn alone.

And so for several weeks I did not see
The bard; I barely saw my bed or home
Because of caring for my ailing Karn;
Nor was I really ready—there's the rub—
To call to mind those conflict-crowded years
Or tell him without tears the tale I lived
With Wiglaf as a wandering wife and mother—
The tale of tumult, terror, tragedy—
Although I thought that I should tell these things
While I could see them still both sharp and clear,
Before they faded like the flowers on his mound.
Indeed I did, but sometimes also doubted
That lessons could be learned from lives like mine
Spent often only ministering to others.

So time passed by until Karn took a turn
Toward feeling better, briefly, and the bard
Returned. I took my tale up once again:
He heard me speak of happy times and hard
The mixed emotions and the memories
Of troubled times and terror, and of days
So peaceful that to ponder them is painful
—Somehow it's happy memories that hurt—
Recalling joys that cannot come again.
He had me talk some more to him of how
It was that I and Wiglaf came to wed;

And so I now explained to him the story
820 That even now and after all these years
Seems strange. I said that I was born a Swede
And therefore thought the Geats were threats to us
Because their coasts were close to ours
And they in large and little ways were like us,
And yet they dared to do things differently
And spoke the same words strangely, so we sneered,
But feared them, too, and fought ferociously
Until we tired of it and turned our thoughts to peace.

I said, "There truly were untroubled times
830 When Geats and Swedes were satisfied to sit
As friends at feasts and fight a common foe,
And so they sought to find a way to seal
Their friendship with a wedding. Then it was
That I was offered as a proper bride
*   For Wiglaf, son of Weohstan, a warrior.
I must assume," I said, "you know the saga
Of Beowulf and all his brutal battles;
His final strife was far ahead when first
We met and married. We imagined none
840 Of that. We looked for lives lived out in peace—
Or so I somehow thought, for I assumed,
Since we were one, that Wiglaf, too, would want
The same quite simple things that seemed to me
Important: peace and some small place to live
And form our own new family and flourish.

"But human lives are haunted by a history
Of deeds in days long gone and debts unpaid
That bind us all together, bone and blood,
And few can live in freedom from such fear.

*850 "The pact of peace expired because Othere,
The king, was killed. Onela coveted
The throne and therefore slew Othere,
His brother; ties of blood brought bloodshed.
His nephews fled Onela knowing he
Would kill them if he could, and so they came
To Geatland, once again begetting conflict
As Geats and Swedes resumed their sorry feud.
When Weohstan killed Eadgils Wiglaf knew
The Swedes would seek his life in satisfaction
860 And so he garnered glory with the Geats
And battled bravely there with Beowulf
And with his dagger dealt the dragon's death-wound
And finally put out the furious flames.
The dragon died, but we were doomed as well.

"I gave my troth and truly took the oath
To be with Wiglaf both in bed and board;
It was a magic moment, full of meaning,
And seemed to speak of peace for Swedes and Geats

"The feast that followed was a famous one;
870 They gave each other many golden gifts
And then a three-day feast that you might think
Would weld the warriors firmly into one.

The men drank many cups of mead
And bards sang ballads of the by-gone days
When some were slain by Swedish swords
And some had gone against the Geats and died;
They hailed the heroes who had won a name
By fighting furiously against their foes.
The bards sang ballads, too, of Beowulf
880 Who mauled the monsters that had menaced us
And set us free from fear of all our foes.
I came of course to know the Geatish king
Quite late in life when he was less than well,
And sometimes I could see his hands would shake
When he was drinking mead among his men,
And with the women I would wait on him
At banquets, bringing bowls of mead—
Those hands so huge they once had held the arm
Of Grendel, greatest of the foes of God,
890 And torn the tendons till the tyrant fled
And left his lifeblood leaking on the ground,
And dug his dagger deep into the dragon,
Its fiery breath grew fainter till it failed.
This massive man who sealed the monsters' fates
Now seemed a shadow of his former self.
I never knew this noble man when he
Was at his best, the ablest of them all,
But still so strong that none would strive with him,
And it was sad to see him so, and yet,
900 Though weakened by the weight of eighty winters,
He found a strength sufficient for the task:
To do one final, daring deed and die;
The sun has seldom shone on one so strong.

"But then the sun was shining in its strength
As we began a good new day together,
And Wiglaf was so wonderful to me,
So generous and gentle in our joy,
I had no hope of being happier;
Yet often in the morning I would wake
910 And find that he was up and far afield
And hunting hares and who knows what besides
And then returning to me with his trophies
And I would always offer him my praise
For conduct that I could not quite admire.
But I was very young as yet and yearned
To please my partner and to live in peace
And so would seldom fully speak my mind.
And now I wonder whether Wiglaf was
Commending me for manners he found strange
920 And that we lived our lives much less as one,
Less thoroughly united than we thought.

"I learned with time that men may look at life
In other ways than women. Wiglaf saw
His life as several intersecting circles:
He was a warrior, and a father, too,
And counselor to the king, occasionally
A sailor; sometimes all these circles met
And each one then enriched the others also,
But family, I felt, too often failed
930 To hold for him a status high enough
To satisfy my sense of what should be.
We argued often over all of this

But fortunately as friends, not foes, who know
What words will work to anger or to win.
It is amazing how a marriage makes
You change and grow in grief and joy together;
A man and woman merge in many ways
Yet still are quite distinct and separate.
"But I ignored, I never knew, the need
940 To talk together till we had attained
An understanding of the others goals
For we were young as yet, as you will see.
We thought that words like 'warrior' and 'wife'
Were all that any human being ought
To need to play one's own appointed part.
The warrior's work might take him far away
But he would have his wife to keep their home
And tend and till the fields till his return,
And then the wife would wash the warrior's wounds
950 And hope that he might help around the house
Till once again his work called him away.

"I would not ever want to be away
For long and leave the little ones alone
But Wiglaf often went his way to work for us
And fight in foreign fields against our foes.
For Wiglaf war was simply one more way
To serve his family, defend his friends,
* And do his duty, do what must be done,
Unwillingly if warfare was required.
960 Yes, men are made to play too many roles;
I cannot fault the fathers for these facts—"

But then I stopped and said, "I should not speak
As if expressing all my own ideas
For these are things that Wiglaf thought, and I,
So often have I heard these things from him,
Should speak for him, not say this for myself.
I'm wandering once more in worthless words,
But let me try to tell you of those times,
The wonder of the way we were made one
970   Creating out of our intense and true
Relationship of love another life.

"To be in love was both to lose my life
And still to gain and grow. I grieve today
For words that were not said along the way
And days that did not come because of death.
I often wish that we had found a way
To talk more truly and to tell each other
The feelings we had formed that found no words
And yet were true and stood the test of time,
980   To tell our dearest dreams and dreads as well.

"But I have always failed to understand
How he could bring to birth with me a baby
And then go off as if in other places
There might be more of meaning and of joy—
Yet always bringing back to me some baubles,
Some tiny trinkets that I treasure still,
As evidence that I was in his mind
And heart though he was far from home.

          He stayed away sometimes for several weeks
990   And then returned with many tales to tell
          Of strange and varied sights that he had seen,
          But now I noticed what I must have known before:
          What lonely lives our wives and mothers lead,
          How many wives and mothers make their way
          Through life alone with little help from husbands.
          A midwife's visit might provide advice
          But could not quite compare with husband's help
          When duties are divided day by day.
          My sisters sometimes spoke to me
1000   Of how their husbands hardly ever
          Took time to tell them of their frequent travels,
          Those wordless warriors whose weapons spoke for them.
          But Wiglaf wanted me to know his world
          As he knew mine and hurried home to share it.
          So often, in each other's arms at night,
          We lay in peace and let our thoughts go lightly
          About our busy lives, for both of us
          Were always eager to share the others cares.
          Our oneness went beyond the realm of words.

1010   One night I noticed something new as I
          Was holding him: my wandering hands discovered
          A scar that stretched across his shoulder blade.
          My fingers formed the questions for my tongue
          To speak but it was silent since my spouse
          Had felt my fingers asking for the words.
          I'm sure he sensed my fingers restless search
          For explanation and my need for answers.

         The words came one by one: "That wound," he said,
         "Was given weeks ago. I had forgotten.
1020   A warrior's welts come often unaware;
         The strife of battle somehow seems to make
         The senses dull, a dauntless man may die
         And not experience the piercing pain
         And aching agony but afterward
         We find the blood-soaked battlefield is filled
         With gallant warriors groaning in their gore.
         A Frisian found me from behind and struck
         And left me for a long while lying there
         In gore, as good as dead, or so he guessed,
1030   But soon my senses cleared and I could see
         To grasp my sword and get back up and give
         My careless Frisian foe a fatal thrust
         That sent him stumbling, silent, to the ground.
         For hours after that our armies clashed
         And many more good men on either side
         Fell down and died. I did my share of work
         And afterward we went and looked for weapons
         And gathered golden bracelets, gilded swords,
         And such like spoils that helped to soothe our pains.
1040   That scratch; it seemed so slight. I could not see
         The place to put a healing poultice on it
         And only after all the fighting ended
         Was I aware that I had unwashed wounds
         That ached when icy winds blew over us
         But softened soon enough when sun returned."

         There in each other's arms we lay as one
         And so expressed our love in simple ways
         And only afterward did I begin to see
         And feel the fury of the falling blade,
1050   The sudden thrust of sword and spurt of blood,
         And somehow felt assailed myself as if
         The furious Frisians also fell on me.

         I could not keep myself from crying out,
         And trembling, tears welled up, though Wiglaf tried
         To reassure me, speaking soothing words.
         I had not asked to hear just how it happened
         Or need to know the nature of the fight
         Or bring his battles into bed with us.
         At last we lay in peace and spoke our love
1060   Again and soon forgot the grief of battle.
         O Minstrel, Make these words of mine a song
         Of life and let your hearers learn there is
         A better thing to sing about than blood.

        "Should I recall the cruel tests that came
         Or should I sing for you a happy song
         Of marriage and its many joyous milestones,
         The cherished memory of cheerful children?
         This is, I think, a time to tell the truth:
         I do not yearn to see those youthful years
1070   Again or gaze on some forgotten, golden past.
         There is a certain sadness in my story;
         Indeed, I do not often live a day
         Unmarked by memories and 'might have been.'

"She was my wished—and waited—for first child,
As perfect as my plans and prayers had pictured.
Did Wiglaf want a boy? I did not ask!
I hoped for her and had my hopes fulfilled.
My life was centered now outside myself
And Wiglaf. We were one more deeply now
1080 Not simply in our slowly merging selves
But in this one who was all that we were—
One body in this baby, both of us
United now as we were not before.
We had the happiness you sometimes hear of
But seldom see beneath the noonday sun—
Until the second winter wore away
And snow grew scarce, but spring came late
To bring its gauze of palest green again
And sickness stalked our tribe and swept away
1090 So many, wives and warriors as well
As smallest babes, and she, my shining sun,
Was cruelly cast beneath its unseen cloud.

"Her face was flushed by fever's bitter fangs;
Her eyes were bright; her brow was burning hot;
She kept on crying, clinging to my arms,
And sobbing softly and incessantly.
The older women offered me some herbs,
Prepared a poultice, placed it on her chest
And soothed her somewhat with a scented oil.
1100 It hardly seemed to help; it hurt me most
That I could offer her so little aid.
I hate the helpless feeling that I have

With infants' illness; I as much as she
Was helpless; how can human beings fight
An unseen adversary? I as much as she
Lacked words or wit or wisdom to do more
Than cry—which could not cure or comfort her.
She cried; I could not help; I cuddled her;
I bathed her brow; I begged the gods to help
1110 And watched and waited, though I did not want
To see her gasp and struggle so to breath
More slowly and more slowly till she stopped
And suddenly grew cold; I cried out, called
Her name, but she could never answer now,
And then I cried, I cried and could not stop.
I so much wanted Wiglaf with me then
But he was hunting somewhere far from home;
My neighbor heard and knew that she was needed
And came and stayed and kept me company;
The older women came and others also
1120 And waited with me, wailing as they looked
At her, she looked so lovely lying there
And peaceful, too, no pain or peril now
Or other ills; I almost envied her,
To be at rest, beyond the rub and rush
And weariness of wending in this world
But I would ask the question none can answer:
Of all the evils in this life of ours,
The constant care and conflict crushing us,
Why has the Heaven Ruler high above
1130 Assigned the little ones to suffer so?

"And can you sing of sorrows such as that?"
I asked the singer; "Answer me, and I
Will tell you tales of other children taken
Although they battled bravely, but were beaten
While still so small, assailed and struck down too
By forces far beyond our feeble wit.
No soldier wages war without a weapon
Or seeks to slay an enemy unseen
But children, quite by chance it seems, are chosen
1140 To fight a foe they feel but cannot see
And so to suffer. Sing them, if you can;
Sing those who through no fault of theirs
Must suffer so."

                                  I stopped. We sat in silence.
The words had welled up from so deep a wound
It seemed as if another self had spoken
And formed my feelings into words—or fire.
The singer stood and slowly shook his head
And walked away. I sat there still and wept.

I found myself reflecting on the friends
1150 Who stood beside me as we said farewell
To her, and how it happened also that
It was just then that Weo in my womb
First moved. I made no mention of it then.
I knew, of course, that he would come, but could
Not deal with it that day when she had died.
As we began to leave the grave, again
He moved as if he meant to make it clear
That I should save a central space for him.

Just then I could not think of anything
1160 Except the greatness, grandeur, of my grief.
But Weo came, and Karn; I had to cope
With them and they left me no time to think
About my sadness, sorrow for myself,
And fear of further pain afflicting me.
There might have been as many as three more
But there was only awful agony,
Aborted births that left me bruised and beaten.
And so we formed a family of four
And learned to live our changing lives
1170 In peace; it was a pleasant, placid time,
Our tribe protected by the towering strength
Of Beowulf our buttress, bulwark, shield.

Next morning as I mended clothes my mind
Returned to that long past traumatic time
And found a feeling flooding in of peace
As if a hurt I held too long had healed.
I felt a freedom I'd not known before,
As if the singer somehow had absorbed
The sorrow that possessed me since that time
1180 And took it with him when he walked away.

I needed now no bard to help me name
My past and put it in its proper place;
And soon my mind went circling back; I saw
Once more so many moments in the past
* And thought of all those dark and dreary days
That wore away so slowly while we waited

           In hope and dread to hear what might have happened
           To Sigelac and those who sailed to strike
           Our foes before they came to fall on us.
1190   I spread the seed to satisfy the birds
           That clucked and cackled by the cabin door
           And made our meals and mended all our clothes
           And tried to turn my thoughts to daily tasks,
           But none of these were things that took much thought,
           And soon my mind was sailing with the ships
           And all the warriors who went away.

           One evening as I finished up my chores
           I saw the war birds circling in the sky,
           The carrion birds that come down on those killed
1200   And feast upon the flesh of fallen men.
           A dreadful fear came down on me that day.
           But meanwhile Wiglaf wandered woefully;
           He could not keep from caring for his kin
           However ill-advised their expedition.
           His mind was with them, many miles away.
           He hoped their heedless venture had not failed,
           But feared the fate to which their foolishness
           Exposed us, placing all of us in peril,
           Those waiting and those too who went to war,
1210   For Sigelac assumed we would be safe
           Until his troops returned again in triumph.
           He did not dream the danger we were in
           If other enemies came in his absence.
           But Wiglaf was most painfully aware
           Of how our homes were all at risk, and he

Saw clearly then the conflict that might come
When all our enemies, now unopposed,
Could fall on us with all their force and fury—
Such cruelty as we could not conceive
1220 For most of us could not remember more
Of combat, carnage, and the clash of arms
Than old men telling tales of triumphs past,
Of gold and glory they had somehow gained
By dealing death to men they did not know
With swords that bit the bone and steamed with blood
While friend and foe were falling on the field.
But all of this was unknown yet to us
And seemed like stories told to scare a child
For Beowulf had brought us blessed peace
1230 And none of us had known another way;
Through fifty winters we had not known war.
I think the thought that we were threatened then
Was hard to grasp and hold within our heads—
That unknown enemies might end our peace—
For who would harm us if we held no hate
Toward them or thought to threaten them at all?
We went our way as if the world were good
And peace could prosper with no care or plan.
Yet now so many of our men were missing
1240 And warfare-widows went about their tasks
With empty sightless eyes, or else with eyes
So focused on the fighting far away
They tripped on toys while doing daily tasks.

When darkness dropped its heavy curtain down
I sometimes spoke to Wiglaf of the search
For peace, a place where we might plant our crops
And grow, and he would grant my point, agreeing
That ceaseless death and slaughter made no sense.
But meanwhile we could only wait for word
1250 And try to be about our daily business.
I watched as Weo grew and went away
More frequently to find new kinds of friends,
And Aelric always took an interest
In Weo, working with him on his skills
In archery and other soldier's arts;
I wondered whether Wiglaf really wanted
His son so soon to study sword and spear
And all the other arts of war, but Aelric,
The oldest and the wisest of us all,
1260 Was taking time as well to teach him first
The basic law of loyalty to leaders.
And yet I wondered whether Weo was
Repeating and applying poetry,
Interpreting the teaching to himself,
In other ways than Aelric understood.
I listened one day to some lines he learned:

*
        The leader does well * to be wise in this world;
        He must always be patient * impulsive never,
        Not wasting his words * nor weak as a warrior,
1270   Not reckless in battle * nor riddled with fears,
        Never begrudging * glory to others.

"Dear Weo, you are yet a youth," I said;
"These goals are good for those who are full grown
And chosen for maturity by champions;
I wish you would be readier to wait.
Did Aelric also teach you other lines,
Some words of warning I remember well.
When I had grown enough to go and give
The cups of mead that make the warrior merry,
1280 The bard would sing this song, both sad and wise;
I heard it then and held it in my heart,
And now you need to know its wisdom too:

*
    Trouble is constant * in kingdoms of this world,
    All of this middle-earth, * more every day,
    Weakens and falters * failings increase;
    No one of conscience * calls himself wise
    Until he has lingered * long in this life.
    Money is fleeting, * friendship is fleeting,
    Kinsmen are fleeting, * mankind is fleeting,
1290   All the world's wisdom * comes soon to waste!"

Politely Weo listened, looked at me, and asked
How soon he should begin to study all
The arts that only come with years and age
And could they come to him more quickly if
He started studying while still so young?

Instead of answering I asked him if
The words of Wiglaf were not wise as well:
"A soldier seeks in every way to serve
And loyalty to his lord controls his life?"

1300 He looked surprised and laughed, "But I'm the leader."

Sometimes our children take us totally
Off guard—again and yet again. I gaped
And was not quick to counter, but I questioned:
And is it Aelric's teaching I now hear
That eight-year-olds are asked to serve as earls?
He laughed again and paused, then, looking down,
In just that way that Weo often would
He smiled and shrugged but never said a word.

But I had friends who felt quite fervently
1310 That it was good to give their sons to go
And smash with swords and spears
Till blood would run in rivers steaming red
And widows wailing would replace our songs
But Wiglaf led reluctantly, for lack
Of any other man to act as leader.
Our Weo did not wait, he was the one
The others always followed; it was I
Who tried and failed to turn him somehow to
A peaceful path and more constructive purpose;
1320 But Karn would follow me; she'd find a flower
And pick it to present to me as "pretty"—
A word she learned and liked to use a lot.
It seemed to sum up something of herself:
She somehow saw what Weo did not see,
The beauty in a bit of braided ribbon
Or peaceful patterns in a passing cloud.
I loved them both, but learned when they were little

>   We cannot chain our children to our choices
>   For each child is an individual
> 1330 And will be who they will. Though we may try
>   To force them to conform and forfeit freedom,
>   I know it will not work; I wanted Weo
>   To be like Wiglaf, but he would not bend;
>   He loved to lead, and from the first believed,
>   As if an instinct shaped his inner self,
>   That followers had flaws that he could find
>   And twist and turn to his intended end.
>   He was so young in years and yet so wise.
>   His goals were good at first, but gradually
> 1340 He seemed to shift and to concern himself
>   That first and foremost all should follow him.
>
>   I asked Karn on a later morning if
>   She thought of those who never threatened us
>   But sheltered us and shared their food and showed us
>   A way of life, of liberty, unlike
>   Our custom-crowded lives so filled with cares
>   And daily duties draining out our souls
>   And always more demands that we must meet—
> *   Of Hilda, how she helped us in our need
> 1350 And put us on our path so peacefully.
>   But, no, she knew the name and nothing more.
>   But questions came to Karn as we were chatting:
>   "My memories," she said, "are mostly moments
>   So silly it's surprising that they still
>   Come back when bards ask you about those days:
>   A special soup you made when I was sick

Or how I hated Weo when he hit me
(He wore that wooden sword and hit me with it);
The fear I had when you and Father fought
1360   About some minor thing, it seemed to me—
But you were angry, yes, and yelled at him
And then he walked away and would not speak;
I dreaded days like that and deep inside
Are scars I somehow sense may shape me still.
But I remember many brighter moments:
A bracelet Father brought me, bright and shining:
I loved it dearly but I lost it later
So Father fashioned one of yellow fibers
And gave me that because the gold was gone—
1370   I learned my lesson even if too late;
It meant so much to me since Father made it;
Such simple stories, still I think of them.
But, Mother, why did monsters make us move
And did we dwell in Denmark? Other children
Have told me tales, but is it really true?"

I smiled that stories such as that were told;
"We were not Danes," I said, "who dwell in Denmark
Where mothers sang their sad and woeful stories
Of monsters in the mists on distant moors,
1380   Marauders in their rage who ravaged them,
Whose hateful deeds brought havoc to their homes
*   As wives put on their widow's weeds and wept
For valiant husbands who had won their hearts
And left them chained to children and their chores.
We never knew the fear and gnawing dread

That paralyzed those people with despair
For many years while monsters made them cringe."

I told her of the time when trolls attacked
When she was small and screams disturbed our sleep:
1390 "We trembled terrified within our tents
And shudder still to see them in our dreams.
But many anxious moments now amuse us:
You fell into the fjord with the fish—
I saw you splashing but I could not swim
And called for help to come, and quickly too.
They drew you out half drowned and dried you off."
She smiled at that and seemed more satisfied;
And so I quieted her cares but kept my own
Concealed inside where they were seldom seen;
1400 So it had always been.

                                        What else could I
Or others do when somewhere soldiers struggled
And we could only wait and wonder how
Our future would be formed on fields so far
From all our homes, our hopes in hazard there
With every slash of sword and thrust of spear?

* At last the lone survivor limped back home
And told us tales of terror, how the Swedes
Had ambushed all our host of armored men
And struck them down in such a savage slaughter
1410 That all their red blood ran in steaming rivers
So deep he did not dare to try to cross.
He fled in fear and finally found his way

To us, a shattered shadow of himself.
Then Wiglaf was the one they turned to; he
Had seen how Sigelac had led astray
The warriors who wanted one thing only:
To battle bravely till their breath was gone
And know their names would now be sung by bards;
Their lives were lost in loyalty to their lords
1420 But few remained now to defend their families.
Then Herbrund spoke for some who sought for peace
And hoped to find a haven to build homes
In peace where they might prosper unopposed.

*   I dream still of that dreadful day we left
Our homes—our hearts—behind, and I
Remember well the mad and mournful scene
As soldiers spread the flames and smoke went up.
I could have cried to see the cabins burning
But could not take the time just then
1430 While boats were being readied to embark.
I could not cry because such chaos reigned
And Wiglaf wanted me to work with him

To calm the crowd and clear away the last
Pathetic piles of things that they had left
And get the baggage all aboard the boats;
Just then I wanted Wiglaf with me most
To grieve together as the gray smoke rose
And mourn the many memories remaining,
But each of us was fully occupied
1440 Until our tasks were done.

                                              I took my place
            And suddenly the sea was on all sides.
            I looked down as we left the land and saw
            The boat, it seemed, rise up above the bottom
            And even further up; it felt like flying,
            As if a broad-winged bird had borne us up.
            We seemed to soar above the sinking earth
            And foam was flying past like flecks of cloud.
            The crew, accustomed to the curling waves
            Saw nothing new at all to make them notice;
1450   They saw the surface only as they skimmed the waves.
            For others of us everything was new
            Since waves had never formed a woman's world,
            The white-capped whale road which the warriors knew
            Belonged to men; our land had narrow limits
            And so we saw this surging world, the sea,
            In constant motion, marveling the most
            At how this soft and unresisting stuff
            Was hard enough to hold our hollow boats
            With all that weight of wives and warriors.
1460   We felt like foreigners, like fish on land,
            Like bears who borrow wings to fly like birds,
            But filled as well with fear to find ourselves
            Held up by water in which anyone
            Who cannot swim will sink—except when they
            Are bourne aloft by fragile, bended boards.

            I noticed Weo with his watchful eyes,
            Attentive to the sailors' varied tasks
            But studying as student, not as stranger,

                The work that one day would be his as well,
1470   Alert to learn a little more each day.
                He sat where he could see the sailors work
                And how they heaved the sail and hauled the oars.
                But Karn just crept into my lap and cried
                As if she somehow sensed she would not see
                Again the hills, the high hills, of our home.
                We both looked back and could not see the burning
                But saw the smoke ascending up to heaven,
                A growing smudge of gray against the blue,
                And knew that none of us could now go back
1480   And live again the life we once had loved.

                The children were enchanted by the churning
                Of waves and widening wake we left behind;
                They viewed the voyage as a great adventure
                And would have run and raced around the boats
                Except that some of us made sure they sat
                By bringing all our bluntest words to bear
                And laying down the law for little ones
                To make quite clear what conduct we required.

                And so we sailed on smoothly for awhile,
1490   The chastened children champing at the bit
                And sometimes needing still to be restrained
                Until they tired of teasing one another
                And settled down to sit in sullen silence
                And finally to fade and fall asleep.

And so began the story of our search
For haven in a harsh world, haunted always
By formless fears of unknown foes beyond
Our narrow land whose names we'd always known.
We crossed wide seas and came to other countries,
1500   To places where the people were prepared
To treat us as a target to attack.
Why are the multitudes of men so made
That they assume a stranger seeks their blood?
So often on our journey others sought
To strike us first and seek our purpose second.
In warfare no one wins except the worst.
*   And oh, the trolls, the tales I often tell
Of green-eyed ghosts appearing in the gloom
And seizing soldiers, swallowing them down;
1510   Of seas that rose and surged and swamped
And broke our fragile boats, our billow-riders;
So many tales told time and time again.

God's candle cast its radiant light across
The mist-soaked meadows when the morning came,
And Weo, now a warrior, walked with me
As I set out to offer aid to Karn.
I told him he should try to trace his thoughts
And see what stories he might still recall
About those distant days and dragon-danger.
1520   He stopped and stared at me as if to say
That few things could be further from his thoughts,
But smiled and shrugged his shoulders and replied
His memories were mostly of the moments

When he and Karn had quarreled and had come
To me to mediate and make it right
And Karn would cry and I would cuddle her
And he would storm off by himself and sulk.
He laughed a little, lowering his head,
In just that way that only Weo would,
1530 And then said he would think of other things
And tell them to me at some other time.
But we had reached Karn's door and Weo went
About his business, briefly greeting Karn.

I found that Karn was crying, having cramps,
But it was early in her pregnancy
And so I sat and soothed her, showed her ways
To let herself relax. I lingered there
All day; I swept and dusted, washed some dishes,
And sent her spouse to find some meat for stew
1540 (I wanted all his worrying away
From Karn; I could not keep her calm if he
Was in a frenzy, fussing frantically
And causing chaos in his care for Karn.)

So while I worked, I talked, as women will,
I chattered on to cheer her and to chase
Away my futile fears and free my mind
Of dread so I could do my daily chores.
I also tried, since I was telling tales
And searching back for stories for the singer,
1550 To question Karn on what she could recall
Of growing up in Geatland, or of going

In search of peace and so of settling here,
Of moments that I might not now remember
That brought her joy, or just more generally
That seemed significant in some small way
Or large. She laughed at that and then a light
Came in her eyes in place of all the tears;
She said, "Oh, I could tell you tales to turn
You gray, but not by going back to Geatland.
1560 We left that land when I was little
And all that I remember of it is
The stories bards would sometimes sing for us
And tales they told of ancient times and lands,
Of Swedes and Geats who swung heroic swords
And broke their blades on helmets, shields, and bones.
It seemed to me almost a magic land
Where kings and queens wore crowns of gold
And monsters roamed the misty, gloomy moors
And dragons dwelt in dens on piles of jewels,
1570 And I would gladly go back there again
If only it were so—but I have doubts
That Geatland grass is greener than our own
Or kings and queens more courteous than here.
I had not seen such heroism here
As bards still sing, or battle bravery,
Until the time that father faced the tribe
Of Saxons by himself and saved our homes.
And I have doubt that dragons do exist
Since I have never seen a serpent fly;
1580 I know that sometimes northern skies at night
Will flare with flashing light that falls like fire

And think that some might see a serpent there,
But dragons, do they fly except in dreams?
These fens seem free of phantoms, fierce or tame
And is it likely we have less than lands
So far away that we are free to fill them
With monsters we imagine in our minds?"

I almost intervened to say that I
Had seen the serpent for myself; that I
1590 Had seen the fiery flames that fell and I
Had seen its broken body by the barrow.
But Karn had stopped quite suddenly to say,
"Perhaps I have a tale that you should hear:
They said that there were serpents in the swamp—
At least we little ones believed there were
And sometimes scared ourselves by seeking them.
One morning, as I did my daily duties
And went for water so that I could wash
The floor and flush away the filth, I found
1600 A boat that seemed abandoned on the beach
And went and found a friend to follow me.
We found a pole and pushed the prow away
From shore and suddenly were swallowed up
In reeds that rose around us on all sides.
I called it 'boat' but coracle is closer,
A small and simple thing of skin and frame,
So light that, like a leaf, the littlest breeze
Would send it skittering across the surface;
To stand and pole soon proved impossible,
1610 It tipped and tilted till we nearly fell

And feared to find ourselves among the fish.
We sat and reached for reeds within our range
And pulled on them to push our prow along
And work our way toward water with less weeds,
But soon were lost; the reeds all looked alike
And every opening only led to more;
Our flimsy floater moved across the fens,
A widening world of water and of reeds.
Then, suddenly, our ship rose up and stopped
1620 As if some animal were underneath
Determined it would tip and tilt us out.
It banged against the bottom of the boat
And sent cold shivers running down our spines;
A little less relaxed than we had been.
I grabbed the pole and plunged it in and pushed
With all my strength, but still we seemed held fast,
Our little, leaf-like coracle like lead;
But as I pushed the pole, the prow came up
And something struck against our underside.
1630 My friend, afraid of monsters, screamed in fright
And terror. I let go my grip again
Upon the pole and put it by my side
And tried to look below our little boat
To see what sort of serpent had attacked.
A bard had sung about how Beowulf
Had met a monster that had mauled his ship
And swallowed several soldiers easily.
We thought of this and so imagined that
A serpent seven times a warrior's size
1640 Could just as quickly crush our coracle

As I could sweep a spider from its strings.
But what I saw was something else instead:
Attached and trailing from our tiny boat
I saw a rope now wrapped around some roots
Entangling them and tied now to our boat
In such a way that we were weighted down
And could not move. The more I made the effort
And pushed my pole to pry our boat away
The more the roots and log arose and rapped
1650 And banged against our bottom boards
And pushed them up as if some ancient beast
Were rising under us. But it was us
And we had scared ourselves, expecting what
Our minds imagined more than what was real.
So then we laughed, a little nervously,
For now another fear emerged: unknown
To friends or family we were here, stuck fast
With not a knife, with nothing sharp at all
With which to cut the cord that kept us there,
1660 The rope that ran into a ring and knot
All covered with a crusted coat of pitch.
Once more, with all my might, I tried to move
The prow by pushing harder with the pole
But still I simply raised the sunken log
Which ground against us in a ghastly way.
And made me fearful that the fragile fabric
That kept us cradled in our coracle
Might split in two and spill us out to swim.
I could have cried—and did—but kept my head
1670 Enough to know we needed new ideas.

My friend had sat in silence; now she said,
'If we should work the boat the other way,
The rope now wrapped around the roots and log
Might just slide off as easily as on.'
It did. I don't know why I didn't think
It would be possible to push the pole
As easily in one way as the other.
We hauled the hawser up to have a look
And found a light-weight anchor at the end
Designed to snare and snag and so to hold
The coracle against a common current.
We brought it up on board our boat and wondered
That we had fared so far before it caught.
We sat there silent in the mid-day sun,
The ranks of reeds around us ramrod straight,
Unbent by any breeze or breath of wind,
So still it seemed to me that time had stopped
Until I felt a tear come trickling down
My face and fall at last toward my feet.
My friend said, 'Stop; the fens are full enough
Without you adding any more.' Just then
A sudden sound of splashing startled us
And ripples ran toward us through the reeds.
Too scared to scream, we held our breath and saw
A water rat that worked its way toward us
And came as if inclined to climb on board.
I disapproved, and punched it with my pole
Until it turned and took itself away
Which left us more alone and at a loss
And fearful of the phantoms that might find us,

Imaginary monsters making meals of us,
Our problem not the peril we supposed
But wraiths arising from our restless minds.

"What mattered more than mythic beasts was this:
That no one knew we were not now at home,
And we had no awareness of the way;
The reeds in silent ranks around our boat
All looked alike—and we were truly lost.

"'My friend—' I stopped her short and said, 'My friend?'
Why is there not a name to know her by?"
"There is," said Karn, "but I have kept it close
For should you know, I think she'd be ashamed.
But I will always think I owe her much;
When I was filled with fear and frantic,
She told me, 'Karn, be calm; we cannot find
Our way if we don't think and use our wits.

"'I now remember, Mother went with me
Some weeks ago to gather green, fresh herbs.
We wandered widely through the woods and fields
And foraged ever further from our home.
At last we looked and saw that we were lost,
The woods around us roadless as these reeds:
A terrifying, trackless territory.
We heard a horrid creature somewhere howl
And shuddered; I was sure some savage beast,
Another forager, had found some food
And we were earmarked as its evening meal.

But Mother merely motioned me to come
And follow her. We found a forest glade
1730 Where we could see the slowly darkening sky
And there, against the gloom, a smudge of gray,
The smoke that signaled supper time at home
As families fueled their fires for evening meals;
So we knew then the way we had to walk
And soon were safely back. It seems to me
It is as easy here: that you and I
Can wait and watch until the wood-turned-smoke
Unfurls a flag that we will see and follow.
So there's no rush; let's rest and try some riddles
1740 To take up time until we see some smoke.
I'll start; let's see how much you understand:

*
  I swallow the wind * from a warrior's lungs;
  Sometimes I call * with my clarion voice,
  Soldiers to the wine-hall * warriors to the battle,
  Sometimes to rescue * ranks of the hard-pressed
  And put foes to flight. * Find out who I am.'

"I answered, 'That one's easy; it's a horn.
My father tried to tease us with such tests
And I can ask you others just like it.
1750 So here's one not as hard while we are here:

  I live at the seaside * sand all around;
  Heels in the sand * head in the heights
  Lonely is my house * humans come rarely;
  No one had told me * the time would come

>   I should speak at the mead bench * mouthless as I am
>   For the point of a knife * and a powerful hand
>   Carefully made me give * a message to one
>   That two might not hear * and tell it to others.'

"'That's easy also,' said my friend, 'it is a reed.
My mother used to make so many things
By weaving reeds and we would work with her
Arranging reeds and rushes for her use.
But here's another one that's new to me;
I learned it from a family friend last week:

>   I saw a creature * in a cabin of humans
>   With many teeth * all turned downward
>   Daily it goes * out to the garden
>   Never impatient * it picks its way
>   Finds the infirm * lets the fair ones stand.'

"I thought and then I said, 'I think I know.
I guess a garden rake.' She said, 'That's good;
But would you think that weeds are really weak?
They seem to shove the better plants aside
And eat them up unless we interfere
And rip their roots out with our hungry rakes.'
"But 'hungry' made us both remember meals
And wonder whether we would see a way
Before too long to find our families.
The sun was lower now and soon would set;
The dangers of the dark filled us with dread.
Who knew what monsters—real ones—might emerge

In grim and ghastly shapes to gulp us down
Or drag us to their dwellings in the depths?
My friend and I so feared the fall of night
We could not keep our fading courage up
For long unless we found some sign of land.
We searched the sky for smoke, a signal fire,
Or other evidence but best of all
A swirl of smoke against the evening sky
1790   To give us guidance to our homes again.
"My friend and I were sitting face to face
Since each of us was sitting at one end
And so my friend who faced the sun was first
To see against the sun the sight we waited for:
A thin and trembling thread of smoke and then,
As mothers made the fire for evening meals,
Another and another till we knew
Which way it was that we would need to go.
I took the pole and pushed the prow that way.
1800   "So we returned in time, but told no tales
Of serpents in the swamp we might have seen.
I did not dare to speak of things like dragons
Or ogres or of other apparitions
Which some would speak of superstitiously
And green-aged girls might give some credence to.
I do not doubt that others do believe;
I simply say they are not seen today."

She smiled at me and sat back satisfied
For Karn and I had often argued thus.
1810   She could not credit creatures such as Grendel

      Which she herself had never seen or heard;
      She thought that I was old and out-of-date.
      It seemed a poor time to dispute the point
      And so I simply smiled and said, "And yet,
      You must remember, I've seen more than you
      And dragons do exist, though you may doubt.
      I think your fears were fully justified.
      This world is odd; there's evil always lurking
      And suddenly it strikes and sorrow follows."
1820 But I had no desire to argue it
      And wondered if she might remember more
      Of various events: our voyage here,
      The ship, the storm, the saga of the trolls?
      She answered there were only episodes
      That could be conjured up occasionally:
      "I most remember how the great sails moved;
      We little ones were lying with the legs
      Of sailors, sitting with their linden shields
      Above us in the bottom of the boat
1830 Where we could notice nothing more than knees
      And sometimes sails that soared against the sky
      Like clouds held captive by some clever trick.

      "I often ask myself what else took place;
      The bards still sing the battle Beowulf
      Once fought with foes so powerful and fierce
      Their wrath and rage meant ruin for us all,
      But where were we? What happened next? And why
      Did we come here and have to build new homes
      On soil the Saxons seem to feel is theirs?"

1840 I answered I was sure that she had often
      Heard singers who recite the story told
      Whenever any bard is asked to sing
      Of how your father dealt the dragon's death-wound
      And how our king was killed. "You question where
      Were we? You were asleep, but Weo went
      To see, and so I sheltered you at home."

      But Karn reminded me of moments when
      I, too, I told her, was in trouble when,
      "A few of my close friends, young Freya, Hilg,
1850 And I went wandering in the woods, where we
      Discovered cold, dark caves and crept inside
      And deeper down into the darkness there,
      And Freya wondered whether wolves might well
      Be living there. We laughed, but listened, too,
      And gave a call; an echo answered us
      And then a rumbling roar that shook the rocks
      And sent cold shivers down our spines; we screamed
      And fled, so frightened we were falling down
      Until young Hilg said, "Trolls!", and terror took us.
1860 We fairly flew, our feet not touching ground
      Until we came into a quiet clearing
      And there collapsed full length in helpless laughter,
      And gasped and giggled on the stoney ground.
      We lay there listening and alert to hear
      The fall of footsteps following behind;
      A squirrel stirred a leaf and Freya screamed;
      We laughed, a little nervously. The light
      Was fading fast and we were far from home

And were not eager for a watch-night in the woods
1870 Where trolls might truly come and taste our blood
And now we knew we did not know
Our way for we were well and truly lost.

"But in that moment came to mind remarks,
A saying somehow held inside my head,
That Father always emphasized: if ever
We lost our way to look for streams to lead us.
We found a flow of water, followed it, and found
Quite soon a stranger who could show our way.
Like you, we saw the curl of smoke ascending
1880 As mothers made their family's evening meal
And no one knew that we had not been home
All day and doing all our daily chores."
I stopped and smiled. I said I sometimes knew,
As mothers may, much more that might be said;
It isn't always wise to ask about
The various adventures out of view
And lasting lessons that we learn alone.
"A troll or two," I said, "can teach you well
Beyond what you can learn in years from parents
1890 And be remembered more than mother's warnings.
So you without consent went seeking serpents
And no one knew, or noticed you were gone."
I said, " I'm sorry it's too late to send
You off to bed without your evening meal,
But I will ask you only to remember this
When someday soon you have a child yourself
And cannot keep it close within your care
Amid the daily dangers we endure."

　　　　　　　Karn wondered if I knew where Weo went.
1900　　　　I said he slipped away quite suddenly
　　　　　　　As if some urgent business of his own
　　　　　　　Required his coming. Weo, unlike Karn,
　　　　　　　Had never liked to live a simple life.
　　　　　　　But Karn was quite content; no questions came
　　　　　　　To trouble her or turn her from her tasks.
　　　　　　　It seemed to her a simple thing to see
　　　　　　　That woman's work was just to be a wife
　　　　　　　And make her husband's mead and mend his clothes;
　　　　　　　She loved the little things of life, the joy
1910　　　　Of children, peaceful chores, the changelessness
　　　　　　　Within which everything is always new.
　　　　　　　But Weo looked for ways to shape the world;
　　　　　　　He dared to hold a different kind of dream
　　　　　　　And sometimes saw himself in battle garb.
　　　　　　　Undaunted, he would dare to battle dragons
　　　　　　　And shake his shield at them and shout defiance
　　　　　　　And face the searing flames and find a way
　　　　　　　To overcome the evils of the world
　　　　　　　And dominate its dangers: monsters, dragons,
1920　　　　The scenes he saw seemed safe enough to him
　　　　　　　And monsters melted in his childhood mind
　　　　　　　Before his smoking sword and seething spear.
　　　　　　　But other evils were not in his ken
　　　　　　　Because he had not known the human heart.

　　　　　　　My words with Karn had kept me still recalling
　　　　　　　How we, the Geats, in wind-blown water-riders
*　　　　　　Had hoped to visit Hrothgar's famous hall

Where Beowulf had been engaged in battle
Against both Grendel and his gruesome mother
1930 But saw instead the cinders of the place,
The ruined remnants, and a king whose reign
Had brought his people pain instead of peace.
This king of ashes called on us to come
And help him fight the foes who fell on him
But Hrethel's goal was simply getting gold
And conquering and killing as required
So Wiglaf led us back to board our boats
And look for lands where peace was likelier.

It seemed so strange to stand there at the side
1940 Of warriors as they waged a war of words
And struggled to assert themselves. I watched
As women seldom do when warriors meet.
I looked and listened as our leaders talked
And was not sure if Wiglaf wanted peace
Or simply to preserve our tattered tribe,
But hearing Hrethel helped me understand
That there are some whose center is the self,
Whose goal is gain or glory for themselves.
I well recall how Wiglaf told me once
*1950 That Herbrund, hearing soldiers howl for war
Opposed them, pleading that they plan for peace
And weigh the wisdom of a way of life
That brings no benefit; it baffled him
That some would seek for conflict and for strife
When peace was possible.

                                                    But it appeared
            That Hrethel had no hope of anything
            Except new onslaughts of his enemies.
            We were not willing to take up his wars
            And so we sailed to seek a place to settle
1960   Untroubled by contending, hostile tribes,
            And found ourselves assailed instead by trolls.
            We fought them off with fire and fled the fjord,
*   But nature next annoyed us with a tempest
            That drove us on through dreary days and nights.
            Through seas that rose and surged and nearly swamped
            And broke our fragile boats, our billow-riders,
            A swirling storm that nearly sank
            Our boats, that beat upon us, breaking masts
            And spars and shredding sails and dampening spirits.

1970   Sometimes it seemed as if the sailors had
            Forgotten us; beams groaned and water gurgled
            And sloshed around our ankles, splashed and swirled
            And flew against our faces and our feet;
            Whole rivers ran about and raged at us
            And sometimes mountain seas came streaming down
            And heaved the helpless children here and there;
            They could no longer cling to us or cry
            Or moan amid the maelstrom; underneath
            The canvass covers we were constantly
1980   Assailed from every side but could not see
            Or hear or use our hands to help the children
            Or ourselves or others any way at all.
            All sense of day and darkness disappeared

Since noon was now as dark as any night.
We could not think within the thud and thunder
As walls of water beat against the wood
And bent our boats and bruised our beaten bodies
We could not doubt our doom was to be drowned.
My chief concern: my own most cherished child,
1990 My Karn was carried off; I could not see
Her hand to hold it, hear her cry. It seemed
That she was gone, I grasped my neighbor's girl
And hoped that someone held and helped my own.
Young Weo did not hide from wind and wave
But struggled to assist the sailors' work
And play a part—or so it was reported—
In all their anguished efforts to repel
The billows and to bring us back to land.

And still the ships were sliding up and down
2000 The monstrous mountains that were mauling us,
That roared and raged against the ring-prows sides
And rocked them side to side and stem to stern
We held on helplessly while heaving seas
Still surged and tossed and swirled the ships around;
But huddled, helpless, in the heaving storm
We women, with a oneness most men lack,
Were linked at least by flesh with loving arms
And hands to hold us, hopeless though we were,
But sailors all are forced to face their fears
2010 Alone and lacking that sustaining love
That keeps our courage up. The crew had each
His task to toil at tirelessly, alone,

And each man acting in his own position
In silence, seldom speaking out except
In trouble to entreat a comrade's aid
And seek assistance in some special need.
One strained and struggled with the steering oar,
Another wrestled with the writhing ropes,
One bent down with a bucket, bailing out
The seas that swept and swirled incessantly,
Intent on tasks that left no time for terror
And freed them from the fear that filled our hearts.
All night the tempest tossed us to and fro
Nor did the dawn dispel the dreadful storm
Until we lost all sense and track of time
And did not know how many days we drifted,
And then at last the light returned; we looked
For children and a shore where ships could stop
And mend the sails and make new masts
And let the land allow us to relax
As all were sick of struggling with the sea.

As best they could they kept us on our course
Which now we knew. I never will forget
How all our ears still echoed with the roar
Of wind and waves; the calm and stillness were
As strange to us as strife and storm had been.
We had become accustomed to the clash
And brutal battle with the breaking waves
But now we looked for land, and life again
Seemed possible. We pointed battered prows
Toward the west and watched for evidence

Of any shore that might seem safe for landing.
A dreary dawn it was, but distantly
A greyish line of level land appeared.
We found a bay where boats would be secure,
A wild and wind-swept place it seemed, but we
Could bring our boats in safety to the beach
And set a guard against unwelcome guests.
We gladly got our feet on solid ground
2050 And searched for food to feed the famished mouths.

The men had gathered gear together in the sun
And most were mending shattered masts and spars
Then Weo came and with a winning smile
Told how he helped to haul the sails and pull
The ropes to bring the boats up on the beach;
What filled my heart with fear was fun for him.

The men, so mindless of the things that matter
Went happily to hunt, as if that helped
When after all that endless agony
2060 It would have helped us more to hold and hug
And find ourselves as family first of all.
But men have minds for many other things;
They brought the boats to land and then abandoned us.
I went to Wiglaf to complain and so
He stopped and helped me set a shelter up
But then went back to work on broken boats.
I would have liked to leave all that for later
And simply see him now the storm had passed
And take the time to talk of trivial things,

2070	Be glad to be together once again.
	We live with men but still have lots to learn;
	They keep so quiet when they come inside,
	So seldom share their thoughts or speak their minds
	While I am always reaching out in words
	With never time enough to try to tell
	Some other all that I have thought about,
	The myriad things my mind is musing on:
	Of how the breakfast bacon almost burned,
	And how I cannot cope with Karn's complaints,
2080	And why my neighbors make such noise at night,
	And if I ought to ask them why they do,
	And why this stew seems not as savory
	As others I have often more enjoyed,
	And whether colic can be cured with herbs.
	Such thoughts as these must thicken into words,
	Take form, be shared, and so shape human lives.
	This is a word-made world we wander in
	Where lives are linked and lived by language shared.
	My sisters share their lives in all they say
2090	And make community among us as we talk;
	The chirp and chatter men look down on changes
	Our selves, reshapes our souls, assimilating
	The little things of life that are so quickly lost,
	And much we would have missed immersed in self.
	Men live such lonely lives, yet like it so:
	The wordless wandering in the woods for game,
	The patient pacing as they plow their fields,
	And then the smashing of their shields and swords

When war replaces words. But would you think
2100 That breaking walls down builds a better life?

For warriors, words are weapons to be used
To fight or forage, often leading far
From lives that lean on theirs, relationships
That fail or flourish as we feed or starve
And nourish them or not with what they need
To grow together well: the glue of words.
But Wiglaf would object that words lose weight
Unless sustained and strengthened with the space
We need to muse and meditate the meaning
2110 Of actions and events before we utter words
For words are only worth the work we do
In thinking through our notions thoroughly;
But so much careful thought conceals our selves;
Men hide behind their silence; who can tell
Their goals? What good is that? We need the guidance
That comes to us from constant conversation,
Unplanned, impulsive words, not well prepared,
That tell the deepest truth with untamed tongues
And open each of us to everyone.

2120 I thought these things but there was seldom time
To wonder much as Wiglaf did in silence.

The island we arrived at known as Orkney,
A strange, mysterious, and haunted strand
Where ancient stones were standing in a circle,
Enabled us to rest from all the anguish

And strain and struggle that the storm had caused
And many might have wished to sail no more.
The natives had made known their willingness
To see some strangers settle in their midst
2130 But others argued that we ought to go
And look for land more like the land we left.
The weather was the worst part of the place;
The shifting fog would settle on our shelters,
Then, briefly, bursts of sun would burn away
The clouds that came in clusters from the west
But rare the day that was not rife with rain.
And so we sailed again and traveled south,
Still hopeful of a haven for our hearths,
Along a coast forbidding, barren, bare
2140 Where we were set on suddenly by some
Who feared our feeble force and left us fewer
In number. Not much further on another
And warmer welcome waited us; we found
An island all of men who offered peace;
No warriors, they warmly welcomed us
And gave us guidance we were grateful for;
They said that we would shortly see a harbor,
A river running in and, rising up
Above it, buildings on a barren headland
2150 That overlooks the sea. They said to seek
A holy woman, Hilda, who had made
Herself the center of the settlement
Where men and women worked in many ways
As one, the men not waging constant war,
Foregoing greed for gold and selfish gain,

         The women, freed from futile fashion's bonds
         And all the chains of childbirth, household chores,
         And daily duties that can dull the mind,
         United now in service to the needs
2160   Of others. Often have I ached with longing
         To go again and gain a deeper knowledge
         Of that community and those who thrive in it
         By seeking not themselves and selfish goals
         Nor waging war, but wisely seeking peace,
         And making their community a model
         For men and women weary of the wars.

         I would have gladly gone to gain some knowledge
         Of all their ways; but Wiglaf went with just
         A few to hear what Hilda had to say
2170   To us, and I was always occupied
         With chores and children—as I chose to be.
         So Wigaf was the one who told me of
         Their ways and left me longing for a life
         So free of fear.

                                    At last we found our way
         Along the coast to land where we could live;
         It was a place where we were free of war
         And deeds that make dramatic memories
         But families found their hopes and dreams fulfilled.
         There were no wolves to worry us; the flocks
2180   Could graze in peace upon the growing grass
         And sheep were sheared and all received a share
         And women carded wool and wove the cloth

And farmers plowed deep furrows in their fields
And children chased the chickens from their nests
And gathered eggs and scattered grain and grew
Like sprouts that shoot up in the springtime sun.

Why do we sing of sadness, grief, and sorrow,
Of woeful times and wasted lives and war?
Is there no praise for periods of peace?

2190 When Weo was fifteen, we wanted him
To learn of other lands and how folk lived
And be aware of other worlds and ways.
Our keels went constantly across the sea
And so we sent him on a trading ship
About to sail abroad to buy and barter
Along the edges of the eastern sea.
They went in peace, pursuing profit only,
And Wiglaf warned them to beware of those
Who might have minds set more on robbery,
2200 Enticing them to trade but then attempting
To hold them hostage, far from home and help.

They brought back amber beads so beautiful
And carved so cunningly that Karn and I
Were awestruck when he offered them to us
Along with golden goblets glittering,
A horde beyond what Hrothgar might have had,
"Because," he said, "I could not come away
Without some evidence for us of all
The strange and splendid sights that I had seen."

2210   I took him off and said, "Now tell the truth.
        I will not wear some other woman's wealth
        If it was seized by stealth or in a struggle.
        You went to trade, but did not take such treasure
        As would have won for you such wealth as this."
        But Weo seemed surprised at what I said;
        He told me they had tried to trade their goods
        But suddenly were set upon by soldiers
        And fought back only to defend the fleet.
        Then, later, when they looked, they found no life,
2220   The foe all fled or fallen, no one left,
        And so decided they should try to save
        Some few things for their families and friends.

        We thought he would come bravely back and boast
        As usual with young men who have yet
        To see themselves as others do and so
        Who feel they are the first to find a way
        To build a bridge across a certain brook
        Or scale a hill and see the other side,
        Though older eyes have often seen the place.

2230   But Weo was not ever one to boast;
        He came back quietly and kept his counsel;
        He understood that everyone would ask
        About his battle skills and bravery
        But even if they asked, he answered briefly.
        And so the story came at last from some
        Who went with them and were their witnesses
        And told a tale so strange it must be true:

"We set out sailing toward the rising sun
With sailors so familiar with the sea
2240 They ruled the rolling waves and raging sea
As easily as if the ocean waves
Were simply drifts of melting, spring-time snow
That prows could pierce and push aside with ease.
At last we neared a land where monsters live,
So frightening and fierce that few have dared
Approach that place and put their lives at risk.
But tales were told as well of treasure there,
Of gold that could be gathered from the ground
And priceless pearls to pick up on the shore
2250 Like polished stones that tumble in the surf,
And agates, emeralds, and other gems.

But wild or not, it was what Weo wanted
And so we set our sails toward that shore
And anchored off the coast, an arrow's flight
Away and waited there. We were not sure
What type of terror might patrol that place.
From dusk to dawn we did not see a light
Nor did we see from dawn to dusk a sign
Or any evidence of other creatures,
2260 No birds above the trees nor nests on branches
Nor smoke to show us someone might be there:
A dreadful silence as of death and doom,
A seething sense of something evil there
That lurked malignantly below our view.

"That night a sickening tremor struck the ship
And made us all imagine that some monster
Had struck the ship to send us to our doom.
We heard a hollow echo as it hit
And then the ship rolled sideways suddenly
2270 As if a hidden hand had hurled us toward the shore.
We slept no more till morning's beams emerged
And with their warming glow awakened us
To gaze again at billows gliding past
And search the shore for any sign of life.
The dawn revealed no damage had been done;
The ship was still as strong as it had been.
With morning light we marveled all the more
At how the silence seemed to sing of danger.
Some said they heard a sound so deep and strong
2280 It was as if the earth had open wounds
That gave its grief a voice and groaned aloud,
A sound so strange it seemed like silence,
An awful emptiness that hurt our ears.
But if there was no life, just emptiness,
Why should we fear to step out on that shore?
Young Weo, never one to waver, urged that we
Should land and look around without delay
And told us tales of treasure to be found.
We pulled the boat in bravely to the beach
2290 And disembarked in dread, but dared to follow
As Weo walked ahead and we fell back;
He had no fear of finding unknown foes.
The silence still increased in strength, and we
Could feel the force of it beneath our feet

As if the ground were groaning out its grief;
The air grew thick; we thought it was as though
A doom of darkness had come down mid-day.
Then suddenly the silence shrieked at us,
Its power pierced our ears and penetrated
2300 So deeply death itself could do no more
To horrify the ones it comes to hunt
When life's brief loan of years is done at last.
Then terror took control; we ran until
We saw our ships again upon the shore
And clambered breathless back on board, away
From such a shore and something still unseen;
As on the day the dragon came, a dozen
Brave soldiers set themselves to seek for safety
And not to face some fearful foreign power.
2310 But Weo was not with us; he went on
And disappeared in darkness, scorning danger,
The youngest of us all in years, and yet
Most careless of the cost or consequences.
Through all that day we did not dare to hope
That Weo would survive to come away.
We all acknowledged no one near or far
Could fight against a force we could not feel
Or strike at something that we could not see.
But Weo did, before the day was done,
2320 Return; we saw him standing on the shore
And calling us to come and help him carry
A dragon's hoard that he had hauled away.
We pulled the anchor up and sailed back in
To shore, and suddenly the silence ceased,

        The birds were back above the trees
        And squirrels scampered in the shrubbery.

        "It seemed a spell had somehow been dissolved
        And we were bold enough to bring our boat
        A second time to shore to see ourselves
2330   The treasure trove and hear as well the tale
        That Weo told; and we, who wanted most
        To hear what happened there, and how he came
        Again with gold and other splendid gifts
        Are waiting still, for Weo would not tell us.
        'You stayed behind,' he said, 'and so you did not see
        My deadly dueling with the ancient dragon
        Or face the fury of the fire-worm's breath
        Or climb the cliff to reach the cavern's mouth,
        Its entrance sealed by elvish spells for ages,
2340   Or take up torches to fend off the trolls
        Who fear no foe except those armed with fire
        Or joust with giants who oppose your journey
        And tear up towering trees to toss at you
        Or swing your sword against assembled ranks
        Of heroes in their helmets and their hauberks,
        Each larger than the last, and you alone—'
        He stopped and stood in silence. Then he smiled
        And asked if any of us had some food
        For he had missed his morning meal and now
2350   The sun was rising high and he was hungry.
        We went on board the boat and brought him bread
        And mead. We well remember how the men
        Stood hoping still to hear exactly how

Our Weo won himself such weight of wealth.
He said no more; we could not make him murmur
Another word. We have no knowledge now
Beyond what you have heard from us, and yet
We wonder whether Weo could have found
The famous dragon hoard his father found?
2360 We did not go to Geatland; memories grim
Had kept us from that country. Could it be
That somehow in that silence we were swept
Back to another time or traveled there?
We felt the ship move sideways, so we thought,
But did we move much more than we imagined?
Or did the dragon's dwelling come to Weo?
And each of us has sometimes thought of other
And stranger ways to shape the story but
The facts are far beyond all finding out."

2370 When Weo came home Wiglaf was away;
Our men were making many journeys then
And Wiglaf often went away with others
To trade and treat with many other tribes
And keep our coasts at peace and clear of foes
And barter goods we made and bring us back
Whatever others offered that we liked.
But trade attracted more attention too,
And other nations often envied us
Our peaceful, prosperous appearances
2380 And wondered whether we used weapons well
Or trusted in our treaties to be safe—
A risk that Wiglaf always was aware of.

But he soon heard from me what happened, though
It was the wife of one of those who went
Who told the tale to me as it was told
To her, not by her husband—he refused—
But by his brother, one who loves to brag
About adventures very few have viewed
Or can believe. I couldn't quite accept it,
2390 And so I said to Wiglaf, "Some say this
And others offer stories all at odds
With it, but here I have these beads which he
Brought me, and more. Do you remember
*   The golden hoard you gathered once in Geatland
And brought to Beowulf, the burnished gold
And other objects from the ancient treasure?
These look so like those others I'm alarmed."

So Wiglaf went to see what Weo brought
For all the others of his company
2400 And saw gold cups all curiously carved
And braided bracelets burnished once again
And came back soon to say that he was certain;
"For you have asked of years ago, and yet
Such scenes are seared and sharp within my mind.

*   How well I remember * many years later
The fire-breathing dragon * dead at the seaside
And Beowulf sitting there * breathing his last
I remember how he called me * craving to see the dragon hoard
And sent me into the barrow * to bring out the treasure.
2410 There beneath the cold stones * I stared at red gold,

> Glittering treasure * I gazed at on the ground
> Much of it rusted * ruined by time
> Golden beakers * their garnets broken off
> War-worthy helmets * heaped up in piles
> Golden cups and dishes * dust-covered, unpolished
> All this I brought forth * as Beowulf had asked

It seems as if it is the very same;
No other objects I have ever seen
Display such skill—the elvish art that shaped
2420 These pieces perished in a puff of time
And no one now has kept that ancient knowledge.
But what dark magic moved that monstrous pile,
The robber's refuse I condemned to rust,
And let it lure all those who lust for gold
And still corrupt the sorry, wretched race
Of those who think to threaten our long peace
And make that useless mass of moldy metal
A honey pot enticing human hearts,
A dazzling dream that draws men to their doom."

2430 "Is Weo one?" I asked. But Wiglaf turned
His back and beat his fists against a board.
"My son," he said, "My son; so strong and skilled,
Such native charm; and now—I do not know."
He stood in silence for a space, then said,
"It may be that we make too much of it,
Assume the worst of Weo without cause.
The time will come when we can test the truth
But now, though who can know, I see no need."

　　　　　　He halted with his head between his hands
2440　　　And speaking very slowly finally said,
　　　　　　"I cannot weigh my words when we're alone;
　　　　　　I can't be careful when I care so much
　　　　　　Or take the time to temper what I say;
　　　　　　I cannot weigh the words that somehow wound
　　　　　　And leave a lasting scar where only love
　　　　　　Was meant. We men were never meant for words."

　　　　　　For three more years we thought that there was value
　　　　　　In sometimes sending Weo out on ships
　　　　　　To see the world, that wide and woeful place,
2450　　　And find a way to face our foes and yet
　　　　　　To build a better life than warriors boast
　　　　　　Who glory in their gashes and their gold.
　　　　　　The windblown water-riders carried Weo
　　　　　　To lands along the coast and later on
　　　　　　Again to unknown eastern areas
　　　　　　In search of something new, not seen before:
　　　　　　Two-headed horses, humans with three legs,
　　　　　　A boiling sea, a beast with bones of gold.
　　　　　　All these the sailors said could still be seen,
2460　　　"And fortune frowns," they said, "on fearful folk
　　　　　　Who sit at home and never see such sights."
　　　　　　Our Weo felt no fear, but found no other world
　　　　　　Or sights so strange they might not all be seen
　　　　　　In any land.

　　　　　　　　　　　　　　　　　　　　But he did learn to lead
　　　　　　And bent his bow in battle more than once.

Our scouts had learned to look before they landed
For sometimes arrows flew from folk who feared
All strangers, shooting first, and only secondly,
When killing stopped, inquiring why we came.
2470 But Weo was an expert with the bow,
His arrows, bright-beaked birds that sought for blood
And sang a song of death that some would hear
But once before they fell to feed the ravens.
He throve on that and thanked us that we gave
Him so much chance to learn. I said I still
Was worried that he would know only war
And nothing of the normal life we'd known
Since coming to this coast at such great cost,
But he replied that peace was to prepare
2480 For battles that were bound to be our lot:
"It's vain just to survive; we must prevail."

I turned away. My time was taken up
With Karn, who now was old enough to know
Some men and make us think about a marriage.
I called her once to come and help me clean
And as we worked, I idly asked if she
Had someone she considered very special.

Young men, she said, were mostly on her mind
When girl friends gathered and began to talk
2490 About the boys they knew who bored them most.
"We laugh a lot about a boy who has no beard
And one who walks in such a funny way
Or stutters when he speaks or sneezes often;

But marriage is another matter, Mother,
Requiring careful thought. If I could choose—"

She stopped and stared at me as if she saw
Me for the first time and, surprised, she found
That we could truly talk. "It's true," I said,
"That there are many men who make you think
2500 It would be wiser surely not to wed.
But is there someone special you have seen
Whom you could care for, courteous and kind,
A man who makes you smile, who moves with grace,
Who fears no foe yet never needs to fight?"
And so she spoke of several young men
She sometimes watched. She wondered if they would
Be kind and comforting, or only care
For self; she asked if I knew any of them.
"O Karn," I said, "I cannot counsel you
2510 But we do wish you well and will arrange
A match you with a man to make you happy
—As far as foresight can effect these things."

I spoke with Wiglaf; we then went to meet
With Herbrund, since he had a handsome son
Of Weo's age. We wondered: would there be
An interest in an understanding reached
By mutual consent to make a marriage?

He said it seemed to him quite suitable
And asked if he could offer us some land
2520 And sheep and several goats and suchlike things

As dowry? Did we deem our Karn would gladly
Accept his son as suitable for her?
He knew his son had noticed Karn one night
And mentioned more than once her merry smile.
Our families were friends. He felt that we
Might well approach the pair for their approval.

And so, to simplify, we celebrated
A five-day festival, two families
United now in one new family.
2530 We gave each other splendid golden gifts
That would not change or wear away with time
But last, as love should last, through lengthening years,
Enduring, all our days, till death shall come,
In spite of sorrow, sickness, scarcity,
And all the other ills that flesh is heir to.
The songs of bards resounded as they struck
Their harps and hailed the couple's happiness,
The two united now in new-found joy.

What happened next is known to all by now:
2540 The Saxons sent us messengers who said,
"The land you live on all belongs to us,
So give us gold or we will gather it
And let our battle axes bite your bones."
We told them to refrain from vain attempts
To force us from our land and fertile fields.

And so the strife we sought to flee resumed
And we were once again, against our will,

Involved in violence. In vain, it seemed
Were all our efforts to find peace on earth.

2550 But Wiglaf wanted Weo far away
Lest evil arrows find their opportunity.
He thought that Weo was too young for war
But could not keep him from the clash of arms
Except by sending him away on some
New mission making more of him as leader
And offering also opportunity to fight—
Though Wiglaf hoped it would not work that way
But might remove his son from most or all
The brunt of battle. But he made his plan
2560 And told him he should take a troop of men
And find a place not far off in the fens
Where they could hide behind some reeds and hillocks
And be prepared to pounce upon the foe
When Wiglaf with his men had worsted them,
Said, "Stay there till the Saxon soldiers come
In flight, then fall on them with all your force
And see that no survivors sail away
Who might remember us and make another raid."
But Wiglaf hoped the plan that he had hatched
2570 Would save his son from any central role
And fighting would be finished well before
He saw the Saxon soldiers flee the field.

It did not work that way, for Wiglaf died
And so the Saxon soldiers who survived
Were able to escape quite unopposed.

Some fled into the fens and fell and drowned
But others, in their ships, made off in safety.
I was bewailing Wiglaf at the time
And so I had not heard of what had happened
2580 Until this tale was later told to us
By Burgred, one of those who went with Weo.

"The Saxons setting out to flee in ships
Were unaware of Weo's waiting force
And so they stumbled straightway into ambush.
The eager arrows ate their leader first;
The bolts that bit him came with blinding speed
And others also, eager for the blood
Of fleeing Saxon soldiers, struck them suddenly;
They fell before the horn-tipped feathered war-shaft.
2590 One boat then turned about and bore away
But one turned straight to land to seek the source
Of all those deadly arrows of attack
And landing, came to look for us who lurked
In readiness behind the ranks of reeds.
The Saxons swung their axes, seeking us,
And came too close to counter with our bows.
When Weo bent his bow he battled best,
And yet for years he had been using swords
Of wood and with them Weo and his friends
2600 And playmates often practiced thrust and parry,
So now the needed skills were not unknown.
When Weo swung his sword a Saxon fell
And then another, and a third, thrust through;
Still Weo's sword, unsatisfied, sought more.

We beat them back toward the marshy beach
And sent them staggering into the sea;
Their armor dragged them down, and so they drowned;
The sea and sand scrubbed off the stains of blood.
"A second ship meanwhile had sought to flee
2610 And was quite far away when we were done
With those who set themselves against our swords,
But Weo thought that they remained a threat
And ordered all his men to board the other,
The now abandoned boat that brought our foes,
And follow, find, and finish that boat too.
By nightfall we had not come near enough
For us to reach them with our eager arrows,
And when God's candle came across the fens
Next morning, the remaining mast was gone.
2620 We tried to track them down for two whole days
And sometimes thought we saw some sign that they
Had passed that way and pulled their serpent prow
Through mud and mire and marsh and made a way
Where surely even serpents could not slide,
But we were weary of the constant wet
And still we gained no sight or sound of them
And finally felt the fens would finish us
If we held on to such a hopeless hunt.

Yet Weo would not waver in his quest
2630 To kill or capture the remaining crew
And drove us daily on till nearly dead
Ourselves. Then suddenly we saw the Saxons,
A frightened crew of five who sought to flee

But could not budge their boat, embedded now
Immovably in muck where it remained
Till we caught up. We called on them to come
And said our swords were still unsatisfied
And needed now another taste of blood.
They had no stomach now for strife, but still
2640 Fought back as best they could and beat down some
Of us but Weo worked his way past sword and spear
To sink his sword in Saxon flesh until
Nobody breathed who bore a Saxon name.

"We turned our prow toward home and pushed and pulled
Our way through weeds and marshy growth, the water,
It seemed to us, was sometimes just as solid
As land, but less reliable; what looked
Like earth the most was almost always false
And sent us sprawling, sinking in the mud.
2650 And yet our borrowed boat did bring us back;
A week at least it was that we were gone.
When we returned, clothes torn and bodies tired,
We hoped to find that we were hailed as heroes
But found instead that few had felt our absence
Or still remembered there were missing men
For Wiglaf's death had dimmed your days so much
It left you little time to seek the lost."

"Oh, yes," I said, "and yet we did miss you,"
For I had known, and others also, surely,
2660 That Weo's troop of ten had not returned
And well we knew that Weo was not one

> To hide behind the house when danger called
> Or lag behind or look for other leaders."

And now, in need of leadership, we noticed
That, young or not, he yet was used to leading.
We missed him as we made the mound and mourned
For Wiglaf, and we wondered where he was;
But in our agony we did not ask.
Perhaps we had remembered how he once
Had wandered in the woods but was not lost
When trolls were taking grown men in their teeth.
So we assumed that we would see him soon.
And so we did, the missing men among us
Soon told their tale of battle and of triumph
And learned about our loss, our leader dead.
They went to Wiglaf's grave, and warriors wept
For he had been their bulwark, brave and sure,
And none till now knew how they needed him.

The months went by but memories in my mind
Are wound together; woe and weal are all
Connected now forever, each so near
I cannot quite believe they came to me
As separate segments in the stream of life.
The days went by, and both the bard and I
Spent many moments in remembering
And telling tales of other times and places,
But conscious, too, of Karn, the child to come,
And looking forward to a future filled
With hope. The Heaven Ruler helps us still

2690 To dream when death has darkened life. We wept,
But learned to laugh again and look ahead.

They woke me well past midnight with the word
That Karn was dead; the infant too; they did
Whatever any of them knew to do
But it was not enough; and now they came
To me to let me mourn and, once again, to make
A plan to do what must be done when death
Reminds us middle earth remains
A land where life is loaned a little while
2700 And must be given back again to God:
The Heaven Ruler has his hidden ways
And sorrow, oh so sudden, sharp, severe,
And cruel can come at any time. Oh, Karn!
I found my hope and happiness in her.
I wept and wailed for Wiglaf and for Karn,
My life, my love, my little one, all lost.
And so we needed now another mound,
But this one small, no ship in which to sleep,
No treasure to be taken to another world,
2710 A simple mound just made for them, the mother
And baby, birth and death here brought together,
As if a birth were but a better death;
But death in springtime seemed so strange a thing,
As if the winter ice still owned the earth
And ground the green things down that sought to grow.
Reluctant still to leave them there alone,
We wailed and wept and stood and kept our watch
Until at last we left them lying there
To sleep, and wait some second spring of life.

2720	Then Weo came with comforting and kind
	Assurances of sympathy and strength:
	Whatever I should need, if I would ask.
	But now I did not know my need myself;
	I needed one whose wisdom went beyond
	The common kindnesses and courtesies
	So easily released, that do not last.
	The women came and kept me company
	And mourned with me and made me laugh
	But others came and called on me as "queen"—
2730	They called me "queen" but did not come to me;
	They went instead to Weo, he who was
	The heir, and eager to take on the task
	Of leadership alone, and license, too,
	To turn our tribe from peace and take us down
	Another road, but not one we had known.

	They called a council and the warriors came
	To look for leadership. They listened while
	The wisest warriors, worn with many winters,
	Expressed opinions: what appeared to them
2740	To hold most hope for future happiness.

	Then some were saying, "Strike the Saxons now,"
	While others wanted us to watch and wait.
	I thought of Herbrund, how he helped us choose
	The path of peace that brought us to this place,
	But Herbrund had no heart to plead again
	The way that we had taken once before,
	And women were not welcome with the warriors

So no one said, "It sometimes seems to me
That we might well live better without war;
2750 We beat the Saxons back, so let them be
Or let us try to trade with them until
We wean them from their warlike way of life."
In vain I hoped that vision would be voiced
But it remained ignored, unnamed, unknown
And Weo was the one at last who spoke
—At least he was not ever loathe to lead—
And summed up simply all their sentiments.

"Who longs for peace," he said, "will pay a price
By being weak and weaponless when war
2760 Comes on us fiercely, as it always will.
We cannot trust for truth in other tribes;
A serpent's safer than a Saxon soldier.
My father fought our foes when forced to do so
But still they wait and scheme to strike us down
So now we need to let the Saxons know
That we are here and will not go away.
Our safety stands in striking Saxons down;
Our peace depends on planning now for war.
When springtime comes we will assemble such
2770 A force that we will fill their hearts with fear
And bring back booty from our beaten foes."
The warriors struck their shields; they wanted Weo.
But having won their hearts, he hesitated;
Professing fear of failing in so great a task
He told the warriors he must take some time
To think the challenge through more thoroughly;

He wondered, was he worthy of their trust.
It seemed a strange and sudden shift to make
For he had hidden his humility
2780 So well till then that none had noticed it.

That night my lamp burned low; I sat alone
When Weo came, for "counsel" as he called it,
And pressed me for approval and support
But also asked that I should be his guide
Remaining both his mother and his mentor.
He said that I was honored so by all
That I should keep my court as tribal queen
And he would help me, hunting down our foes.

I answered I was unaware of foes
2790 Annoying us and needing new concern.
I said, "You sent the Saxons swimming home
And filled the fens with all their floating bodies,
So those who limped back home have learned a lesson
And are so weak they will not worry us.
Our enemies will hear of how much harm
The Saxons suffered and will surely fear
To take up arms and test our tribe again.
What foe so frightens you that you are fearful?
You seem to seek for Saxons everywhere.
2800 Oh Weo, O my son," I said, "my son;
I cannot wear the crown and be the queen
If you insist on seeing Saxons everywhere.
The sword has swallowed some of our best men
Why must we make still more go after them?

What is it in you that is uncontent
With peace, a time to plow and plant; what good
Can come from constant conflict? Can we reap
The fallen bodies that would fill our fields
And turn their bones to bread to feed our babies?
2810 What evil is there in an enemy
So deep we do not dare to live in peace?"
"Your words are wonderful," said Weo;
"I long to live in such a lovely world
Where peace would be a part that all could play:
No tears or terror, love and truth for all.
Yes, Mother dear, indeed you must not doubt
But hold these hopes and help us seek them also.
My purpose, too, is peace, but in the past,"
Said Weo, "We have waited for our foes
2820 To come; so let us learn from history
And now resolve that we will seek our safety
And peace by power and prepare ourselves
To threaten them before they think of us.
I often ask myself if it was wise
To wait as Wiglaf did for wars to come.
I long for peace, but let us look with care
At others, always asking, 'Have they earned
Our trust?' And meanwhile, Mother, we must make
Our way within a world that works by force.
2830 The paths that lead to peace are paved with swords;
With strength to conquer comes tranquility."
And still he spoke persuasively of how
He longed for peace and looked for ways to live
In friendship with our foes—by force of arms.

He made his argument: that men will fight,
That simple safety for ourselves suggests
We keep control by killing while we can;
That power assures the safety of the strong.

I sat and listened sadly as he spoke;
2840 Had no one told him tales about the time
When Sigelac assailed the Swedes and how
He lost his life and we then lost our land?
I felt he feared the future we had fought for
And saw his safety only in the sword.
At last he left me, lingering to say
He needed me, for no one else he knew
Had such respect and so could reassure
Those lacking loyalty to him as leader.

I could not sleep that night; I sought for some
2850 Way forward from that futile conversation.
They called me Queen but did not come to me;
They turned to Weo, one who longed for war
And asked me only to endorse his acts.
I could not be that kind of queen, because
I knew that it would make demands on me
In conflict with my conscience; it was clear
I could not satisfy my son and be myself.
How could I be the queen, I thought, and counter
My son, resist his leadership and seek
2860 To move the minds of men and make them peaceful?
But then I thought, how can we live and thrive
With views and voices so at odds, divided?

And suddenly I saw I could not stay;
My presence would appear to give approval
To Weo's actions, wise or otherwise.
And I must leave the land I loved,
That Wiglaf worked for with his final breath.
I thought of this for several days and then
I sent a word to Herbrund, seeking some
2870 Advice; I hoped for Herbrund's help to find
A path to follow for my future life,
To get away from Weo and his wars.
But Herbrund urged that I should think no ill
Of him if he should hinder me, for "Who,"
He asked, "will plead for peace without your presence?
Who else is able to go in to Weo
And quietly request that he take care
To think of those whose happiness is threatened
When husbands don't come home and children's hearts
2880 Are broken by the news of battle-death?"
I ached with all my heart to answer him
With words that would be welcome to his ears;
My sorrow was, it seemed not so to me.
I tried to tell him when we talked one day
How many times a mother's mind reviews
Her children's choices, how she hopes to change
Their ways, but often sees herself in them
And knows that nothing nature plants is swiftly altered.
So Weo was the child I bore and weaned—
2890 I said I sometimes wondered how I suckled someone
My son and weaned a warrior, one in love
With death; why had he not inherited my hopes?

                I wanted him to work as Wiglaf did
                For peaceful possibilities, not power
                That cannot come except by cruelty.
                "But still he struggles to assert himself,"
                I said, "If I remain, so much the more
                He will oppose me and, to prove his point,
                Make peace the victim and my vision vain.
2900   But in my absence all will rest on him
                And then I hope that he might hear at last
                Advice from those whose valor vindicates
                Their words in praising love of peaceful paths.
                Yes, Weo needs to grow; my going gives
                My son the space he needs, and who can see
                The future he will find if, finally,
                He learns at last true leadership includes
                The weak as well as those who go to war?
                A wife might widen Weo's vision, too,
2910   Far more than any nagging mother might.

                I wove my words and Herbrund listened well
                And offered at the end to give me aid,
                Not gladly, grudgingly, but giving way
                Before the flowing flood of words that I
                Released. He would allow me now to leave
                But asked what hope of haven did I have,
                A single woman in a world so wicked?
                And how abandon burial places both
                Of Karn and Wiglaf? Could I care for them?
2920   He asked, and I could give no easy answers.
                I said, "The graves in Geatland, too, are green

As Wiglaf's and I wail for them as well,
But Wiglaf saw the same stars shining down,
As near us now as in our native land.
Perhaps the Heaven Ruler holds us all
Within her arms wherever we may go."

"And yet," said Herbrund, "you must yield me this:
The world is wide and hostile to the one
Who goes without a goal; that way lies grief;
2930 To seek a haven in a heartless world
Requires great care and could be all in vain."

I knew that he was right, but now was not
The time to answer everything. For I
Was wearied with our words, and wanted time
To answer him for, in all honesty,
I had no plan prepared, no place in mind.
I could not wander off into the wilds
Nor find a home with Saxons or with Swedes;
I simply knew I could not safely stay
2940 For Weo's sake and for my own as well.

I think some three days passed and then I woke
One morning and remembered from the mist
Of dreams that dimmed when daylight came
* That Abbess Hilda had appeared; my heart
Stood still, and then she seemed to signal me
To come and claim the comfort that I sought.
I woke and wondered: was the vision true?

　　　　　I had not heard of Hilda since we left
　　　　　The bay at Whitby where we stayed when we
2950　　　Were fleeing Sweden. Suddenly I saw
　　　　　The possibility of peace; the path
　　　　　Was long and hard but led to hope at last.

　　　　　I sent for Herbrund, for it seemed I should
　　　　　Make plans and pass on what I now proposed
　　　　　To someone I could trust. I told him
　　　　　I hoped to find a home at last with Hilda
　　　　　And sought a ship to take me somewhere near
　　　　　The place. I said that I would pay my passage
　　　　　If he could help me. Unhappy though he was
2960　　　He went away, returning with the news
　　　　　That certain seamen he had spoken to
　　　　　Turned down his gold; they darkly spoke of danger
　　　　　And warnings Weo gave that made them wary.
　　　　　So he would hold me here against my will?
　　　　　I sent another friend to speak to seamen
　　　　　Who found a ship that soon was sailing north
　　　　　And was not worried by what Weo threatened
　　　　　Since they had no intention to return.
　　　　　They asked that I be ready after dark
2970　　　When they would come as quickly as they could
　　　　　And take me to the harbor for the trip.
　　　　　My friend assured me that the ship was safe
　　　　　And trusted them to take me to my harbor.

　　　　　They came so carefully and quietly
　　　　　By stealth that suddenly I sensed

That they were there but then I knew no more
Until I woke and wondered where I was.
I felt the floor beneath me rise and fall;
Some kind of cloth, it seemed, had covered me
2980 But slipped sufficiently that I could see
A dim light as if day would soon be dawning.
And knew my nameless captors now must be
Transporting me to some place as they planned.
Then voices vehement and very angry rose
In accents I was unfamiliar with
And sounds of fighting, furious and fierce,
Continued for some time. I tried to see
But strands of strong, thick rope restrained me.
Then quiet came. The cloth that covered me
2990 Was shoved aside and I was made to stand.
Then one man spoke, a strange and foreign sound,
A language new to me, unknown, mere noise,
But stern and savage sounding, so I smiled
In hope that he would not be hostile to me
But saw no softening nor any sign
Of friendliness, a fierce and angry face.
He signaled me to sit and stay, and turned
Away and went about his work. The crew
Ignored me then and through the day. Unthreatened,
3000 I sat considering these strange events
And pondering what plans these people had
For me and what the meaning might have been
Of all the angry sounds that I had heard.

The southern sun and western coast were showing
A northern course, I knew, though no one spoke,
And gave me hope of reaching Hilda's home.
And so we sailed on slowly to the North;
At first they tied me tightly and took turns
In guarding me but gradually they grew
3010 More careless since a captive cannot well
Abandon ship and swim to shore while tied.
At night we slept ashore beneath the stars;
They let me wander in the woods at will
Quite confident I could not scale the cliffs
Or find my way through trackless forests
Beyond the beach, and yet I yearned to find
Some safety from these strange and silent men.

One night a lookout saw us land and raised alarms;
The seamen, suddenly surrounded by
3020 A larger troop, made no attempt to test
The warriors' will or skillfulness with weapons
But offered everything if only
They might not lose their lives or liberty.
So they abandoned me, unbeached their boat,
And left me not alone in this strange land
For now a new and unknown force had come.
They seemed to understand my speech and I
Could glean their meaning though I missed as much.
They told me they would take me to a place
3030 Where I could ask for aid and find a welcome.
I followed them through fields until we found
Some humble homes and then a higher hall,

*   One carved of stone, a stately, stunning mansion
           Unlike the wooden hall that Hrothgar had
           Or anything that I had ever seen;
           This house or hall was made of hewn stone carved
           In frozen forms of birds and flowers and trees.
           The soldiers let me step inside; I stood
           In awe unable to take in such beauty;
*3040   The windows in the walls were wonderful,
           Containing glass stained green and red and gold;
           I stood and stared, struck speechless by the sight.
           Such glory did their glowing give the space
           That even heaven could hardly hold more beauty:
           Like frozen flame, like flares of dragon fire,
           A rainbow radiance, gold, and red, and blue,
           Held eyes entranced while awestruck tongues were tied.
           Who knew the sun itself could shine so splendidly?

*   A Brother Benedict came out to bid
3050   Me welcome and to wonder who I was
           And how I came; he said the king was careful
           To guard his shores as I had surely seen
           But here they had no enemies; they hailed
           A peaceful king whose throne and power depended
           On love alone. He asked if I would like
           To stay awhile and tell them whence and where
           My journey was. I would not willingly
           Refuse such friendship. For some days and weeks
           I lingered in their midst and met there men
3060   And women with a wealth of wisdom that
           Went far beyond my family and friends

Or any others I had ever known.
And yet they yearned to hear unusual accounts;
Indeed, the dragon's death and Grendel's doom
Delighted them; they loved to listen often
Till Benedict forbade such bloody stories;
Perhaps it held them from their holy work.
But Benedict, I learned, had been abroad
And traveled to the east and had his tales
3070 Of popes and places where the pilgrims go
But did not see a dragon dead or living;
He closely questioned me about the claws
And fangs and fiery breath and how it flew;
He seemed to doubt but did not dare to say so.

In every audience, with ears attentive,
* There was a boy named Bede, a child so bright
He sometimes seemed more seventy than seven,
So young and yet much wiser than his years
And always eager to inquire of others
3080 And know whatever news was notable
Of kings and queens and countless other matters.
I had to tell him tales of Hrothgar's hall
And all about the battles Beowulf
Had fought. I finally sent him forth to play,
But how he loved to listen and to learn!

* At night the brothers sang their service strangely,
Not like the bardic beauty but with chanting
That seemed to rise and sink; the brothers said
That Benedict had brought it back from Rome.

3090	It seemed ill suited to my Swedish ears.
*	The walls had painted pictures of some people
	Who lived quite long ago in distant lands
	And had gold haloes fastened to their heads.
	Among the men one woman they called Mary
	Seemed honored over all the others there
	And called the queen; there was no king except
	The Heaven Ruler whom they placed on high
	But thought would come in clouds to claim his kingdom.
	Their treasures were what travelers might tell of
3100	Who spend their time in seeking splendid things:
	Some silken cloaks and clasps and cups and crosses,
	A dragon hoard they had of holy objects,
	But Benedict was born of royal blood,
	Accustomed to the court and costly things,
*	And honored both by Oswy and by Ecgfrith
	Who gladly gave him gifts of land and wealth.
	One day the soldiers sent us word to say
	A ship had just been steered in to the shore,
	And strangers came inquiring for a captive
3110	Whom one called Weo wanted brought to him.
	The soldiers said it seemed so strange a matter
	And somehow threatening that they thought it best
	To tell the truth but not the total story.
	They said the ship they sought had sailed on north
	A full six days before, but failed to say
	That Yrfa was not on it at the time.
	I brought my fears to Benedict about
	The way that Weo was pursuing me
	And he sent messengers in haste to Hilda

3120	Who said the strangers also searched at Whitby
	For me and left at last with great reluctance
	But well aware I was not in that place.
	It seemed to her I surely would be safe
	With her; she would be happy to be helpful.
	She sent two sisters back who could assist me
	And Benedict found brothers, men of brawn,
	Who carried cudgels with them cut from oak
	And strode beside us silently but watchful
	To keep us company in case of danger.
3130	He said it seemed much safer that we go
	By land and be alert for lurking spies
	Or ships just off the shore, but try to stay
	In forests far from firths or open fields.
	We left at dawn next day in damp and wet
	And moved through marshy ground all morning
	But early in the afternoon we found ourselves
*	At Wearmouth Abby; we were welcomed there
	And I was asked that night to entertain
	The monks with tales of monsters I had met.
3140	I told them how the trolls had terrified
	Our clan but, wet and weary as we were
	From travel, left some tales untold that night.
	The ship that Weo sent had stopped here, too,
	But they, although so near the coast, knew nothing
	And sent them on to seek us somewhere else.

From Wearmouth we went westward for awhile
And followed paths that forded frequent streams;
God's candle cast its beams through cloudless skies.

We came occasionally to caves, and I
3150 Remembered all to easily the awe
With which I saw the dragon stride the sky
And how I had to wait at home when Wiglaf
Had taken men to track the dreadful trolls.
These caves were quieter; I did not care;
I had no need for new adventures now.

We came to Whitby where the white waves break
Along the coast and climbed the sturdy cliff
As we had done once in the distant days
When we were seeking safety from the Swedes.
3160 They welcomed us and gave us every honor,
But Hilda whom we chiefly hoped to see
* Had died that day, such was the doleful news.
My hopes were centered so on seeing her
That now I could not keep from crying.
They said that sickness had assaulted her
For many years and yet she never yielded
To her infirmities but, full of faith,
Continued still to teach and train all those
Who came from far and wide. Her wisdom was
3170 Sought out by abbots, bishops, even kings.
As death approached, she prophesied of peace
And said that on this island all shall live
In peace, but few will farm, and foreigners
Will come to live among us; kings and queens
Will work for peace and peasants will have power
To shape their lives in liberty at last
And women will have power in that world.

Such fantasies had filled her friends with doubts,
Amazed at all her mind's imaginings;
3180 Perhaps, they thought, she'd had a glimpse of heaven;
But meanwhile men and women must go on
With life and leave such tales for leisure times
When chores are done and children can be charmed
With dreams of other, strange, and distant days.

And I was also left to wonder if
My voyage, vast seas crossed, had been in vain,
* But one called Aelfflaed kindly questioned me
And listened well and learned my fears at length;
She was a woman welcoming and wise,
3190 And who would follow Hilda as the head.
She said there was no safer place to stay
In all these islands; Ecgfrith was the king,
Her brother also, brave in battle, loyal
To her and Hilda's whole community
Had forces to defend them from their foes.
She told me also of the unknown men
Who carried me as captive to the coast
Of Wearmouth. Weo's warriors, in pursuit,
Had come to Whitby, closely questioned them,
3200 And told the story; so they understood
Just how it was that Herbrund had arranged
For certain men to steal me to their ship
So Weo would not think I willed to leave,
But then the captors quarreled; it occurred
To some that Weo would reward them well
To bring me back and so the two groups battled

And Herbrund's hired assistants had been beaten.
My captors then sent threats to Weo, thinking
That he would give them gold to get me back,
3210 But Weo sent his warriors in their wake
And she supposed they still were sailing north.
"Let men do what they must," she said to me;
"Our purpose here is peace and we are pleased
To welcome all who wish to work with us
And hold the hope that Hilda kept before us.
We look for life beyond the limitations
Of feeble flesh and human foolishness
And meanwhile as we offer up our praise
To God who gives us life and all our goods
3220 We seek to serve the simple folk around
And we would welcome you to work with us."

And so I settled here, a stranger still
As I have always been in Middle Earth
Amid a people pledged to seek for peace.
Their faith, it seems to me is for the few
But if my efforts aid them, I will stay.

They say of some who never seek to share
Or work for others' welfare in the world
"Nobody is the better for their birth.
3230 Is Weo one of those? I will not judge
But grieve for him, and more for her who had
So little life, whose loaned time was so brief
Yet held for ever in my aching heart.
The bards may sing of blood and buried gold

>   But I would only ask to see my own
>   Alive again and laughing with her love.
>   The singers like to say that life is loaned,
>   It isn't ours to ask about or question.
>   I do not know; I would not dare to dream,
> 3240   For who can guess what God intends to give?
>   I have no answers; I have only lived
>   Somehow, the Heaven Ruler helping me,
>   And done each day what needed to be done
> 3244   And taken time to tell you now my tale.

END NOTES FOR *BEOWULF*

1 – Beowulf begins with the word "Hwaet" which is related to the modern "What" but in Anglo-Saxon English was a word calling for attention and might be translated "Listen" or "Attend." The same word begins *Beyond Beowulf* and *Yrfa's Tale*.

5 – The Beowulf poet is, unfortunately, more interested in genealogies than most modern readers who would like to get on with the story. He can also assume a knowledge of names and events that can leave the modern reader bewildered. Briefly, the Danish royal line begins with Scyld Shefing. A legend told of how he was found as a baby in a ship sent out by unknown hands. His son was Beow who was the father of Healfdene. Healfdene had four children: Heorogar, Hrothgar, Halga, and Yrs, a daughter, who married Onela in the Swedish royal line. Hrothgar was the great king who instigated Grendel's raids and Beowulf's heroic response by building the great hall, Heorot.

43 – see above

58 – Scyldings are descendants of Scyld and therefore Danes in general.

83 – "Blazes yet to come:" this reference foreshadows the destruction of Heorot after the end of Beowulf but before the story in *Beyond Beowulf*.

93 – One of the questions debated by scholars is the extent of Christian influence on the Beowulf poet. Obviously the story of Creation in the Book of Genesis lies behind these lines.

107 – The reference to Cain is, of course, Biblical (cf. Genesis 4) but the notion of monsters descended from Cain is not Biblical.

175ff. – The transition from pagan to Christian times is reflected in the temptation to return to pagan ways in the face of Grendel's rage, but the poet thinks of pagan gods in terms of Satan, "the Slayer of souls."

194 – The Geats: Beowulf's people, a tribe living in southern Sweden.

261 – Hygelac: the Geatish king, is one of three sons of Hrethel. A daughter married Ecgtheow (Edgetheow) and was the mother of Beowulf.

299 – Wederas: another name for the Geats, who are also called the Weder-Geats.

348 – Wendels (Vandals): a Danish tribe.

454 – Weland: also known as Wayland, the blacksmith of the gods.

460 – Heatholaf: a Wulfing warrior killed by Ecgtheow (Edgetheow)

461 – Wulfing: a Germanic tribe

Weather-Geats: another name for the Geats meaning Storm-Geats.

471 – Wylfings: another Germanic tribe

499 – Unferth: a member of Hrothgar's court. The name is sometimes taken to mean "Un-peace," and Unferth is then seen as a symbolic figure created as a challenger of Beowulf's credentials.

506 – Brecca: chief of a tribe known as the Brondings, a young contemporary of Beowulf.

521 – Brondings: possibly a Scandinavian tribe but nothing is known of them.

601 – Spear-Danes: the Danes with an honorific addition.

612 – Wealhtheow: Hrothgar's wife.

875 – Sigemund: in Beowulf, Sigemund is called the slayer of a dragon, but in other Norse narratives it is Sigemund's son who killed the dragon.

1019 – The hint here at future treachery is a complicated subject and scholars hold different views as to exactly what is being suggested. There is some discussion of the subsequent course of Danish events in *Beyond Beowulf* lines 930ff.

1068 – Howell Chickering calls the Finnsburg Episode (1068–1159) "notorious for its obscurity" and "a permanent field day for quandary lovers." (Chickering, pp. 332–331) There is a fragment of another poem (The Finsburg Fragment) by another author that does throw some light on the subject. Perhaps it is sufficient here to say that a group of Danish warriors and a group of Frisian warriors become involved in a fight for possession of a banquet hall. When neither side can gain the upper hand, a truce is offered and accepted. The episode is set in contrast with past and future events in the Danish court. As usual, Chickering is an excellent resource for further study.

1931ff. – The story of Modthryth raises a number of problems for specialists. "Thryth" means anger or arrogance and Mod-thryth could simply be an adjective meaning "arrogant in manner" and not a name at all. The two Offas known in history are a fourth century king of Angles in northern Europe whose wife had no such reputation as "Modthryth" and an eighth century king in England whose wife seems to have had a bad reputation, but the eighth century is too late for Hygylac to be telling a tale about her. Suffice it to say, Hygd's character is shown in contrast to that of a less attractive woman.

2204 – Scylfings: the Swedish royal family and therefore all Swedes. The Scylfings occupied territory north of the Geats in present day Sweden.

2247ff. – "The Lay of the Last Survivor" repeats a frequent emphasis in Beowulf on the futility of human striving to possess. Hrothgar had spoken of it to Beowulf (1757–68), and the same note is struck at the end when Beowulf's survivors bury the hoard again, "as useless to men as it was before." (3167–8)

2602 – Wiglaf appears here for the first time and it is noted that he is a Scylfing, or Swede. His father apparently sought refuge among the Geats because of an earlier feud within the Scylfing tribe.

3075 – The Old English speaks literally of the "owner's legacy" but leaves it unclear whether the "owner" is God or the dragon. Some of the experts read it one way and some the other.

END NOTES FOR *BEYOND BEOWULF*

1 – "Hwaet!" The first word of Beowulf is variously translated "What!," "Lo!," "Indeed," "Attend." Although it is the ancestor of the English word "what," its purpose here in a formulaic opening is to call for attention and we have therefore begun the sequel also with that word.

1–19 – The final passage of Beowulf describes the funeral pyre on which he was cremated amid expressions of fear for the future.

20–32 – Beowulf had met his death in combat with a dragon which had been ravaging the countryside in vengeance for the theft of a cup from his treasure trove.

33–41 – *Beowulf* begins with the tale of how King Hrothgar built a great mead-hall named Heorot to celebrate his victories.

48–53 – Wiglaf had come to the aid of Beowulf in his final combat with the dragon. He is described as the "son of Weohstan" and Beowulf speaks of him as the "last man of our tribe, the race of Waegmundings." He is, then, the logical successor to Beowulf. He and Beowulf are the only named characters from *Beowulf* who appear in *Beyond Beowulf*.

65 – Grendel is the name of the monster slain by Beowulf early in his career.

80–84 – These fears and forebodings are discussed at the end of *Beowulf*.

197–212 – The reference here is to a speech in lines 2900–3028 of *Beowulf* and, specifically, lines 2922 and 3001 that speak of a threat from the Swedes. The Geats, the tribe of Beowulf and Wiglaf, lived in Sweden, perhaps in the area now known as Götland, and south of the area inhabited then by the Swedes.

233 – Hygelac (also given as Higlac and Higelac in translations) was king of the Geats at the outset of Beowulf and is Beowulf's uncle. He is the one character in Beowulf whose existence is confirmed by other sources. He was killed during a raid on the Franks about the year 521 a.d. This would place Beowulf's death toward the end of that century and somewhat early for the events described in *Beyond Beowulf*. Beowulf reported back to Hygelac after his victory over Grendel and Grendel's mother.

234ff. – Hygelac's death, in the battle at Ravenswood (Hrefnes-holt), is described by the Messenger in lines 2419–2496.

242ff. – This tale of Beowulf is not to be found in the original and seems to draw on later tales of Eric the Red and Leif Erikson—but perhaps they were moved to sail west by tales of Beowulf's voyage.

361 – A bard sings of the creation of the earth in Beowulf, lines 91–99.

405ff. – The fight mentioned here is described in more detail in *Beowulf*, lines 2354ff. and lines 2500ff. Beowulf is said to have swum back to Sweden from Frisia carrying the armor of thirty warriors in his arms.

459ff. – see lines 2920ff. of *Beowulf*

471 – The Scylfings are Swedes; not to be confused with the Scyldings (see line 763 below), who are Danes.

497ff. – The descriptions of this battle and other later battles draws on the Old English poem The Battle of Malden as well as battles scenes in Beowulf.

519 – "He had no breath to boast of battle-deeds." A common device in the Old English poetic style, a feature of Beowulf in particular, is *litotes*, a deliberately strong understatement, often negative in form.

568 – A subject much discussed by Beowulf scholars is the significance of the references to the Bible in *Beowulf*. While the Beowulf poet probably inhabited a Christian world himself, he seems careful not to imply a similar level of knowledge for those of whom he writes—but he does make reference from time to time to the limits of their knowledge.

661ff. – This incident is referred to first in lines 2596–2599 of *Beowulf* and again in lines 2864–2891. It is one of many places in which the importance of loyalty is emphasized.

723ff. – The building of Beowulf's barrow is recorded in lines 3156–3159 of *Beowulf*.

758ff. – Hrothgar's pledge is reported in lines 1854–1865 of *Beowulf*.

773 – The Scyldings, descendants of Scyld (also spelled Scild in some translations), are the Danes. Hrothgar is Scyld's great-grandson.

791–812 – Here I have tried to reflect the language of two Old English poems known as "The Wanderer" and "The Seafarer."

874ff. – This episode is modeled on the story of Beowulf's arrival in Denmark (*Beowulf*, lines 229ff): he was greeted by a wary coastguard, sent up to Hrothgar's hall, greeted again by a guard, and finally admitted to the king's presence.

931ff. – The burning of Heorot is foreshadowed in lines 82–85 of *Beowulf*, immediately after the report of its building.

1018–1022 – In Beowulf, lines 815–824, we hear how Beowulf tore off Grendel's arm and in lines 834–836 how he nailed it to the gable of Heorot.

1257ff. – There are various traditions concerning trolls. Some say that they turn to stone if exposed to sunlight; others that they melt when exposed to fire. I have followed the latter tradition.

1540–1546 – This is my translation of Hrothgar's speech in lines 1763–1768 of *Beowulf*.

1735-1742 – This history is given in the opening lines of *Beowulf*, lines 4–79.

1847ff. – The following episode is set in the Orkney Islands, north of the Scottish mainland.

1913ff. – The reference here is to the Stones of Stenness and Maes Howe.

1949 – The guide books say that Vikings broke into Maes Howe about the year 1153 c.e. and scrawled runes on the walls in frustration when they failed to find treasure—but perhaps the Geats had broken into it earlier and reacted in the same way.

1960 – The "hollow hills" of the draugrs are a part of Orkney folklore.

2217ff. – The community at Lindisfarne was founded by St. Aidan, who arrived from Iona in 635 a.d.

2366ff. – The Abbess Hilda founded the community at Whitby in 657 a.d. It included both men and women under her rule.

2453ff. – Caedmon was a member of Hilda's community. The story he tells here of how he became a poet is all that is known of him.

2507ff. – This is my translation of Caedmon's hymn to the Creator, the earliest English poem. Here, as with the subsequent bardic songs, I have conformed much more closely to the pattern of Old English poetry. Each line has four stresses and there is a caesura between the two half lines. The first stressed syllable of the second half line provides the alliterated letter which is then matched by one or two of the stressed syllables in the first half line.

2516ff. – This is my translation of a passage in *Beowulf* (lines 91–98). The similarity between this passage and Caedmon's hymn is striking.

2527ff. – This poem is my composition but based on an Early English poem called "The Wanderer."

2555ff. – This poem also is my composition but has parallels with Old English poems based on the Bible.

2612ff. – Sutton Hoo is an historic site in East Anglia, thought to have been settled in the early 7th century. There are reasons to believe that the settlers who created the burial mounds there had come from Sweden, perhaps from Götland. The best discussion of this subject is to be found in *The Origins of Beowulf and the Pre-Viking Kingdom of East Anglia* by Sam Newton (cf. Bibliography.)

2651ff. – The items mentioned here have been found at Sutton Hoo.

2679ff. – There is a deliberate echo here in Wiglaf's warning about future kings of the warning Samuel gave the people of Israel (I Samuel 810–18).

2732 – Ranulf is my own creation, but there were Saxon kings of East Anglia in the early seventh century with similar names.

2862ff. – There are several battle descriptions in *Beowulf*; the story of "the Fight at Finnsburh," (lines 1068–1159) is one example. The Early English poem "The Battle of Malden" is also helpful. The Bernard Cornwell novels about the Arthurian legend provides some very careful descriptions of Saxon and British armor and battles.

3079ff. – Wiglaf's death scene is similar in many ways to Beowulf's death scene (*Beowulf*, lines 2715–2722).

3132ff. – The details of the ship burial are based on the descriptions given in *Sutton Hoo, Burial Mound of Kings* by Martin Carver (cf. Bibliography.)

END NOTES FOR YRFA'S TALE

41 – Trolls: cf. *Beyond Beowulf* 1255.

128 ff – Aelric is frequently referred to in *Beyond Beowulf* (hereafter *BB*).

133 – Laefstan: cf. *BB* 1449–1561 and 1608.

174 – calling Wiglaf "king", cf, *BB* 2666ff.

240 – Wederas: another name for the Geats (the tribe of Beowulf and Wiglaf), who are also called the Weder-Geats.

278 – cf. Similar Creation poems are in *Beowulf*, 93ff., and *Beyond Beowulf, 2516ff.*

367 – "that awful day / When Weo wandered off" cf. *BB* 1257ff. for the encounter with the trolls.

517 – "why the same stars shine down from the sky" cf. *BB* 1845ff.

554 – "the day when first the dragon came" cf. *Beowulf* 2312ff.

650 – "Beowulf / Was sitting on a stone" cf. *Beowulf* 2717ff. and *BB* 3085ff.

669 – "we asked ourselves / What fate would now befall us from our foes" cf. *Beowulf* 2910ff., 3000ff., and 3150ff.

835 – cf. *Beowulf* 2602 Actually, Wiglaf was at least partly a Geat also.

850 – "The pact of peace expired because Othere, / The king, was killed" cf. *Beowulf* 2394ff.

1185 – "those dark and dreary days" cf. *BB* 379ff.

1267 – These lines are based on such Old English poems as "The Wanderer" (cf. Kennedy, Charles W., *An Anthology of Old English Poetry*.

1283ff. – This poem also is based on "The Wanderer" (cf. above).

1349 – "Of Hilda, how she helped us in our need" cf. *BB* 2386ff.

1382 – "widow's weeds" is a phrase still used though few realize that "weed" was the Old English word for clothing. Such is the power of alliteration that it preserves even phrases we now longer understand.

1406 – "the lone survivor" cf. *BB* 389ff.

1424 – "that dreadful day we left / Our homes" cf. *BB* 1746ff.

1507 – "the trolls" cf. *BB* 1216.

1742ff. – Riddle poems are a form of Old English poetry preserved in various manuscripts. A selection is provided in translation in both Kennedy and Hamer (*op. cit.*). Some of the riddles here are based on those presented there, others are my own creation.

1927 – "Hrothgar." The visit of Wiglaf and his companions to Hrothgar's kingdom is found in *BB* 869–1134.

1950 – Herbrund's plea for peace: cf. *BB* 623ff.

1963 – "tempest." The story of the storm is told in *BB* 1782–1834.

2394ff. These lines are based on the description of the dragon hoard in *Beowulf* 2757–2771.

2944 – The Abbess Hilda (or Hild) (614–680) founded the monastery at Whitby in 657. It was a double community with both men and women living under Hilda's rule. Her wisdom and reputation were such that not only religious leaders but kings and government officials came to her for advice. At least five men she trained became bishops. Hilda is best known for hosting the synod of Whitby (664) that decided in favor of the Roman pattern of Christian life rather than the Celtic pattern. Hilda died after six years of illness in 680.

3033 – "carved of stone." Most English building of this period was of timber but Benedict Biscop (see note on 2953 below) had seen stone buildings at Rome and was determined to use that material in his buildings.

3040 – "the windows in the walls." Stained glass was unknown in England until Benedict brought continental craftsmen to Wearmouth and Jarrow to create stained glass windows and train native craftsmen. Some of that ancient glass survives and is incorporated in the present parish church in Jarrow.

3049 – "Brother Benedict." Benedict Biscop (628–690) was of royal birth but became an influential monastic and founder of the great monasteries at Jarrow and Wearmouth. He traveled to Rome on a number of occasions and brought back valuable manuscripts and various treasures to enhance the life of his monasteries.

3076 – "Bede." The Venerable Bede was the first historian of the English Church. Given to the monastic life as a child of seven, in his monastery at Jarrow he interviewed visitors to learn about the history of kings and clerics as the basis for his *History of the English Church and People*.

3086 – "sang . . . strangely." Plainsong was one of the new practices that Benedict brought back from Rome.

3091 – "painted pictures." These were also brought from the continent by Benedict.

3105 – Oswy and Ecgfrith. Oswy (or Oswiu) (612–670) was king of Mercia for twenty-eight years and, for a few years, the dominant king in all of England. At the Synod of Whitby he accepted the Roman customs for the English church. Ecgfrith (645–685) succeeded his father Oswy as king of Northumbria after Oswy's death in 670 snd reined until his death in battle in 685.

3137 – Wearmouth Abbey was established by Benedict Biscop in 673. Building began the following year.

3162 – "had died that day." Hilda (or Hild) died on November 17, 680.

3187 – Aelfflaed (654–c. 714) was given to Hilda as an infant in thanksgiving for a battle her father, Oswy, had won and she spent the rest of her life at Whitby. She inherited a joint leadership of the Whitby community after Hilda's death with her mother, Eanflaed, (626–?) and then alone from her mother's death until her own death. Since Ecgfrith was her brother, Aelfflaed was influential in the affairs of the kingdom.

SELECT BIBLIOGRAPHY

TRANSLATIONS OF *BEOWULF*

Alexander, Michael. *Beowulf.* **London: Penguin Books, 1973.**
This edition includes a very interesting introduction and useful notes. The translation itself is in free verse with two stressed alliterations per line.

Chickering, Jr., Howell D. *Beowulf, a Dual Language Edition.* **New York: Anchor Books, Doubleday, 1977.**
This is the fullest edition I know of, complete with the Early English text and extensive notes and commentary. The translation makes no effort to preserve the alliteration.

Heaney, Seamus. *Beowulf, a New Verse Translation.* **New York: Farrar, Straus and Giroux, 2000.**
Includes the Early English text.

Jack, George. *Beowulf, A Student Edition.* **Oxford: Oxford University Press, 1994.**
The original text with introduction, running glossary, and supplemental glossary; no translation.

Porter, John. *Beowulf, Text and Translation.* **Middlesex, England: Anglo-Saxon Books, 1991.**
A useful, fairly literal translation with the Early English text.

Raffel, Burton. *Beowulf,* New York: Penguin Books, Ltd., 1963.

A verse translation that deals freely with the alliteration but does not keep to the divided line of the Early English or provide the original text.

Rebsamen, Frederick. *Beowulf, a Verse Translation.*

A very good translation that preserves the pattern of the Early English poetry.

EDITIONS OF EARLY ENGLISH POETRY

Hamer, Richard. *A Choice of Anglo-Saxon Verse.* **Selected with an introduction and a parallel verse translation, London: Faber and Faber, 1970.**

No particular effort to preserve the alliteration; original text provided.

Kennedy, Charles. W. *An Anthology of Old English Poetry.* **New York: Oxford University Press, 1960.**

An alliterative translation without the original text.

GENERAL BACKGROUND

Bair, Peter Hunter. *The World of Bede.* **Cambridge University Press, Cambridge, 1970.**

This is a comprehensive discussion of the origins and influence of the monasteries in which Bede lived and the society in which they were set.

Whitelock, Dorothy. *The Beginnings of English Society.* **Haermondsworth, Middlesex: Penguin Books, 1952.**

This is a general discussion of the shape of the earliest English society: the role of loyalty, the society from king and court to town and trade, law, church, literature, and art.

SOURCES FOR THE RELATIONSHIP BETWEEN *BEOWULF* AND SUTTON HOO AND EAST ANGLIA

Carver, Martin. *Sutton Hoo: Burial Ground of Kings?*. **British Museum Press, 1998.**

A careful study of the burial mounds at Sutton Hoo and the possible significance of the findings.

Newton, Sam. *The Origins of Beowulf and the Pre-Viking Kingdom of East Anglia*. **Cambridge, England: D.S. Brewer, 1994.**

An analysis of the relationships between Beowulf and East Anglia centered on texts and genealogies.

ABOUT THE AUTHOR

Christopher L. Webber, a graduate of Princeton University and the General Theological Seminary in New York, is the author of a number of books ranging from a guidebook for Vestries to a study of Christian marriage. His most recent books include *Dear Friends: Letters of St. Paul to Christians in America*; *American to the Backbone*, a biography of pre–Civil War abolition leader James W. C. Pennington; *Welcome to the Christian Faith*, an introduction to Christian life and teaching; and *Beyond Beowulf*, the first-ever sequel to the old English saga, *Beowulf*. Webber has given lectures and workshops on his various books across the country. He now lives in San Francisco.

Find a full list of our authors and titles at www.openroadmedia.com

FOLLOW US
@OpenRoadMedia

www.ingramcontent.com/pod-product-compliance
Lightning Source LLC
Chambersburg PA
CBHW030517230426
43665CB00010B/656